Securing
America's Future

Securing America's Future

A Bold Plan to Preserve and Expand Social Security

Max J. Skidmore

ROWMAN & LITTLEFIELD PUBLISHERS, INC.
Lanham • Boulder • New York • Toronto • Plymouth, UK

Published in the United States of America
by Rowman & Littlefield Publishers, Inc.
A wholly owned subsidiary of The Rowman & Littlefield Publishing Group, Inc.
4501 Forbes Boulevard, Suite 200, Lanham, Maryland 20706
www.rowmanlittlefield.com

Estover Road
Plymouth PL6 7PY
United Kingdom

British Library Cataloguing in Publication Information Available

Library of Congress Cataloging-in-Publication Data

Skidmore, Max J., 1933–
   Securing America's future : a bold plan to preserve and expand social security /
Max J. Skidmore.
      p. cm.
   Includes bibliographical references and index.
   ISBN-13: 978-0-7425-6243-1 (cloth : alk. paper)
   ISBN-10: 0-7425-6243-3 (cloth : alk. paper)
   1. Social security—United States. 2. Medical care—United States. I. Title.
   HD7125.S563 2008
   368.4'300973—dc22   2007040180

Printed in the United States of America

∞™ The paper used in this publication meets the minimum requirements of
American National Standard for Information Sciences—Permanence of Paper
for Printed Library Materials, ANSI/NISO Z39.48-1992.

Contents

Foreword

George McGovern

This book by Professor Max J. Skidmore, a longtime authority on Social Security, should be read and pondered by Americans who want to know about health and income security, especially by those who are concerned about the reality of our Social Security system and its prospects. Contrary to the views held by our current president, George W. Bush, and other critics, as Professor Skidmore makes clear, there is no crisis in this most essential and successful program of Franklin Roosevelt's New Deal.

This is not to say that we face no economic troubles. There is a looming crisis in the average person's private savings and investments that are non-existent or even negative, in corporate pensions that are rapidly disappearing, and in America's health-care system that costs too much and often delivers poor care or no care at all. Skidmore goes to the heart of all these issues.

When it comes to health care and income security, our public systems are performing far better than our private ones. For more than seven decades, the Social Security system, our soundly conceived and self-financing public program, has provided security to America's elderly and their dependents and, for about half a century, to those disabled at any age.

These programs are not financed from the U.S. Treasury. From its beginning in the 1930s until today, Social Security has had its own financing mechanism: a modest withholding tax on the worker's pay that is matched by the employer. There is currently a large surplus reserve backed by U.S. government bonds.

In the 1980s, President Ronald Reagan and Congress decided that the Social Security trust funds were getting a little too low, so they worked to correct a cash-flow problem. They were also concerned that some revisions were needed to cover the so-called baby boom generation. A bipartisan commission was named by the president to firm up the reserves. It recommended several things, including a modest increase in the withholding tax. Congress adopted the commission's recommendations, the president signed the bill into law, and, since then, trust funds have been growing. The entire reform process took only a few months.

Even most of Social Security's critics agree that with no changes at all, the system will continue to function well until at least 2041. They admit that the program after that would still be able to pay three-fourths of the benefits now projected, and those would be higher than benefits are today. If the critics are right, it might be necessary to make another small change in the self-financing formula, as was done in 1983, and such a change would be able to deliver the level of benefits now projected.

As Professor Skidmore points out, though, it is very likely that there will not need to be any adjustments at all. He and a number of other authorities in recent years have demonstrated that the projections calling for trouble are almost surely much too pessimistic. If the American economy performs at anywhere near the level that it always has over an extended period, Social Security will need no boost, ever.

Instead of using alarmist language about an imaginary "crisis," this book calmly proposes several rather modest changes for making a good, existing, solvent program even better. For example, the present withholding tax is regressive in that it taxes low-income participants at the same rate as higher-income persons. In fact, it even taxes them at a higher rate than it does those earning much higher incomes of more than $97,500 per year. Earnings above that figure are completely free from Social Security taxes (although not from taxes for Medicare). Professor Skidmore would exempt the first $20,000 of a worker's wages from the withholding tax but would begin taxing all earnings above $97,500 in the same manner as income below that figure. And why not?

Note that this would not reduce workers' Social Security benefits, as the health plan President Bush proposed in his 2007 State of the Union Address would. Workers would still receive full credit for the first $20,000 of earnings each year because the employer would still report the wages and would still pay the match (Social Security benefits are based on wages, not on the amount of tax paid in). Professor Skidmore also calls for a carefully developed plan for incorporating a broader retirement security for all workers.

This book discusses frankly the hostile attitude of the late President Reagan toward Social Security and the encouragement that Reagan's attitude gave to those who oppose the program. It makes clear that the efforts by the current president, George W. Bush, to substitute private investment accounts for Social Security would be a high risk, and almost assuredly a losing deal, for most Americans.

Social Security is the one major component of government activity that is solvent and self-financing. Replacing it with individual gambles with the stock market is too big a risk for nearly all Americans other than the wealthiest. U.S. government bonds are far less risky than rolling the dice or taking a ride on the Wall Street roller coaster.

Do yourself a favor and read this excellent, solidly researched, common-sense book before you go off the deep end and support private accounts. Yes, at times you might get a higher return from the stock market than from Social Security, but you might also lose your shirt. If we don't bankrupt the country in senseless wars or other nonproductive government excursions, Social Security will be just fine. It won't make us rich, but it will put in place for our lives a dependable income floor protected against inflation for the rest of our years, and in the meantime, it will give us disability and survivors' coverage.

Introduction

National security is of grave concern to modern Americans, as well it should be. It is appropriate to be certain that the country has the military strength to protect our interests and efficient police power to secure our borders and protect us at home. Self-serving politicians, though, often act as if military power and effective police forces are all that is required to provide Americans with security. That such a simple-minded view could be accepted at all in the twenty-first century would have astonished a great twentieth-century president, Franklin D. Roosevelt. Nearly three-quarters of a century ago, he warned forcefully that true security required much more than action against those who would use force against the United States. It is time we remembered his warnings and followed his advice.

Almost from the Republic's beginning, Americans have honored the spirit of Thomas Jefferson, the "Apostle of Liberty." We have built our political language upon his notions of limited government and individual freedoms, even when we have acted more in the spirit of Alexander Hamilton and built a mighty empire of corporate industrialism. Partly as a result of this paradoxical heritage, our population has unleashed enormous energy. The private accomplishments of Americans have been legendary. No less impressive are our public accomplishments. Working through government we have—to cite only a few examples—constructed the Panama Canal, won the greatest wars in the history of the planet, built the interstate highway system, created the Internet, and made it possible for human beings actually to depart the earth and step out upon the moon. Everything Americans have done has flowed from the most magnificent political achievement of all history, the U.S. Constitution.

The Constitution sets up a system of divided and strictly limited power, and we maintain it by keeping power limited. Jefferson taught us that skepticism toward government is necessary. If it grows beyond its proper bounds, however, a healthy skepticism becomes decidedly unhealthy. Therein lies the darker side to our Jeffersonian heritage. It has caused many of us to be too skeptical of governmental programs, thus receptive to demagogic appeals to selfishness. Ronald Reagan was certainly reflecting the Jeffersonian spirit when he told Americans in his first inaugural address that government was not the solution to our problem, government was the problem—but he was wrong.

Unfortunately, many Americans accepted President Reagan's generalization as gospel. Many of us came to think in simplistic terms that government cannot provide solutions. We now are reaping the consequences of that rigid ideological view. It is time once again to recognize that in many situations, government is the best solution. Sometimes, it is the only one.

In 1935, Americans recognized that reality. That year, following the lead of President Roosevelt, the United States adopted the Social Security Act. By every measure, Social Security has been a resounding success. It has never missed a payment, and it operates far more efficiently than any private program. Nevertheless, it has been the subject of ferocious attack, not least from the current president of the United States, George W. Bush. Bush has called for privatization and has made reckless charges about the system's stability.

In 1999, I published *Social Security and Its Enemies*, demonstrating the strength and stability of Social Security and exploring the efforts to eliminate the most effective program of income support in America's history.[1] That was before Social Security's attackers had found open support from the White House, before they had enlisted a president of the United States in their campaign to undermine the program that means so much to Americans.

The danger to Social Security has become much greater now than when I wrote because of the forces that control the executive branch of our government and long controlled the legislative branch as well. In addition, the people of America are finding themselves with lower wages, almost no savings, less and less health care, and more and more frequently with no company pensions. If we are to confront the entire economic threat to Americans, it thus is no longer adequate merely to protect Social Security and deal with its enemies. We need an examination of the overall threat to America's economic well-being, a threat that has escalated sharply with Bush's presidency. This book does just that. It brings *Social Security and Its Enemies* up to date, expands it considerably, and demonstrates the need for both health care and retirement security for all. Additionally, it proposes a plan for revising Social Security that would make its financing progressive, just as its benefit structure is progressive.

Among government's purposes is to provide for the general welfare. When we are reluctant to let government do so, we let problems grow and fester. When it ultimately becomes obvious that we must turn to government—and it will ultimately become obvious—we can only hope that it is not too late.

America is rapidly approaching the point at which it must turn to government to salvage its system of health-care delivery. Companies are discovering that they can no longer afford to provide health coverage for their workers or retirees. They must compete with industries in countries that have government health benefits. Their foreign competitors do not have to bear the cost of providing health insurance to their workers. Wise business leaders in foreign countries often were among the strongest advocates of government health insurance as a way to lessen the burden on industry. Government health care worked for them, while our industries struggle to compete, and our workers are called upon increasingly to do without.

Similarly, the time is upon us when Americans must turn to government for a complete retirement system. A mechanism already exists that can be expanded to salvage the wreckage of workers' retirements and compensate for the prevailing lack of savings in the United States. That mechanism is America's system of Social Security. As this book makes plain, Social Security is strong. Far from racing toward disaster, as hostile politicians and commentators allege, it has emerged as the one best hopes for a secure future for the citizens of our great country.

NOTE

1. Max J. Skidmore, *Social Security and Its Enemies: The Case for America's Most Efficient Insurance Program* (Boulder, CO: Westview Press, 1999).

1

The Forgotten Piece of National Security: Franklin D. Roosevelt's Economic Bill of Rights

In 1944, President Franklin D. Roosevelt included in his State of the Union message a ringing call for American national security. This did not mean military protection alone. To have true national security, President Roosevelt pointed out, Americans needed an "Economic Bill of Rights."[1] A year later, in his final State of the Union message, FDR renewed his call for such an expanded bill of rights. Shortly thereafter, the great New Deal president and wartime leader was dead.

Roosevelt's successor, Harry S. Truman, worked valiantly and successfully to preserve the principles of the New Deal. A lesser president would likely have failed, and the results would have been tragic. Reactionary politics typical of immediate postwar years prevailed in the 1946 elections. Such politics brought into power what Truman called the "Republican Do-Nothing, Good-for-Nothing Eightieth Congress."

Facing such a Congress, it is little wonder that the new president was only marginally successful in his attempts to build upon and expand Roosevelt's domestic legacy. Although Truman defied both polls and predictions and won reelection, he was unable to expand his own "Fair Deal" to include the Economic Bill of Rights that FDR had recognized as so important. We are only now beginning to recognize the damage caused by our failure to follow FDR's and Truman's urgings and are seeing just how much we have permitted our national security, in its most basic sense, to erode.

Truman's bold call for health care for all, for example, went nowhere. Despite the notable achievement of Medicare under Lyndon Johnson, America remains isolated among advanced industrial countries in failing to provide health care for every citizen. This lack affects us not only in the obvious way of making individual security precarious but also in putting much of America's industrial enterprise at a disadvantage when competing with firms from countries that have national health coverage. To make matters even worse, the United States spends far more per capita on health care than any other country in the world, including those with complete health coverage. That is the insult. The injury is at least twofold: first, by nearly every measure, America falls far short of other countries in its health-care outcomes (that is, in the overall quality of the health care that its citizens receive); second, the rate of medical errors in the United States is huge.

A look at what FDR meant by an Economic Bill of Rights will demonstrate just how far we have drifted. He pointed out that with its great effort in World War II, America became "an active partner in the world's greatest war against human slavery." He noted that the world had been "gravely threatened with gangster rule" and that we joined with others in defense. Mere survival, however, was not enough. The sacrifices that we and our allies made imposed "upon us all a sacred obligation to see to it" that, out of the war, "we and our children will gain something better than mere survival." Security, he said, was the "one supreme objective for the future," both for "each Nation individually, and for all the United Nations." This meant more than physical security; it meant "economic security, social security, moral security—in a family of Nations."

How sad it is to contrast FDR's broad vision with today's selfish concern that government's greatest obligation is to cut taxes, especially for those most able to pay. Quoting his call to action should lead us all to reexamine our priorities and to recognize that we can do better. FDR said to Congress and to the American people

> We have come to a clear realization of the fact that true individual freedom cannot exist without economic security and independence.
>
> "Necessitous men are not free men." People who are hungry and out of a job are the stuff of which dictatorships are made.
>
> In our day these economic truths have become accepted as self-evident. We have accepted, so to speak, a second Bill of Rights under which a new basis of security and prosperity can be established for all regardless of station, race, or creed.
>
> Among these are:
>
> The right to a useful and remunerative job in the industries or shops or farms or mines of the Nation;
>
> The right to earn enough to provide adequate food and clothing and recreation;
>
> The right of every farmer to raise and sell his products at a return which will give him and his family a decent living;
>
> The right of every businessman, large and small, to trade in an atmosphere of freedom from unfair competition and domination by monopolies at home or abroad;

The right of every family to a decent home;
The right to adequate medical care and the opportunity to achieve and enjoy good health;
The right to adequate protection from the economic fears of old age, sickness, accident, and unemployment;
The right to a good education.
All of these rights spell security. And after this war is won we must be prepared to move forward, in the implementation of these rights, to new goals of human happiness and well-being.
America's own rightful place in the world depends in large part upon how fully these and similar rights have been carried into practice for our citizens. For unless there is security here at home there cannot be lasting peace in the world.

President Roosevelt's words were clear and striking. They suggest that we should ask ourselves a fundamental question. Should our priorities actually be to make the most privileged among us even more comfortable, with little or no regard for the rest? It would be bad enough if this were an unintended side effect of national policy, but it has clearly been the explicit policy goal of George W. Bush's administration. An article in the *Los Angeles Times* shortly after the beginning of his second term appropriately called Bush's policies "Undoing the New Deal."[2]

The result of Bush's presidency has been a staggering growth in the disparity between workers' and executives' earnings. To be fair, this income gap did not begin with him, but his policies have greatly—and deliberately—accelerated this most unhealthy and inexcusable trend. Before long, it will have been three-quarters of a century since FDR died. The fact that our current policies are causing this, the wealthiest country in the history of the world, to retreat farther from such a goal should be a source of national embarrassment.

THE DESTRUCTION OF THE "THREE-LEGGED STOOL"

The worker is not only being left out but ground underfoot. Although FDR died before he could secure his Economic Bill of Rights, he could boast of the greatest economic protection in the history of the Republic: Social Security. That great program, however, was never intended to be a complete system and was not designed to provide a full retirement. With its passage in 1935, Social Security became "one leg of a three-legged stool." That metaphor meant that it would provide one supporting leg for the "stool" of income protection for the retired worker; the other two would be company pensions on the one hand and private savings and investment on the other. With the twenty-first century now well under way, the metaphor is no longer appropriate. There is no longer a secure and stable stool. Despite the attack upon Social Security, it is the only leg left.

The American worker has little or no savings, resulting in the collapse of the second leg. The third leg is crumbling as well, with companies rushing to eliminate pensions for their workers as they shift the entire burden of risk to workers with "defined-contribution" programs instead of time-tested "defined-benefit" plans. This has not prevented the same corporations from providing astronomical pensions and bonus packages for their executives, notoriously often equaling far more than $100,000 for every *day* those executives spend as their employees!

However much conservatives may decry spending habits, the sad truth is that workers' incomes have fallen. They are no longer sufficient to provide a decent standard of living for the typical worker who attempts to set aside enough to ensure a comfortable retirement. After a quarter-century of replacing grants with loans, the middle-class college graduate frequently embarks upon a career shouldering such a huge debt that it will be impossible ever to save. Those who earn minimum wage are at an even greater disadvantage. In a perversion of "family values," that wage is so low as to be insufficient to provide an acceptable standard of living for a single person, let alone for the breadwinner of a family. Even the well-paid worker can be devastated by a medical emergency that wipes out any savings and destroys all economic hope for the future.

It is not only the workers who are disadvantaged by our warped policies. Our corporations are discovering that it is increasingly difficult to compete with companies in other countries that have comprehensive social programs. A flood of news stories has described how American auto manufacturers spend more on health coverage for their workers than they spend to buy steel, how the price of each car made in America is greatly increased by the costs of insuring auto workers, and how American companies face heavier expenses than their counterparts in other countries that have national health coverage. Every person who buys an American car is paying considerably more for that car than would be necessary if the United States followed the example of other advanced countries and provided its citizens with health coverage. Even worse, due to the lack of health coverage for millions of Americans and the spotty nature of the coverage that many others have, an American is far more likely than the resident of any other advanced country to be destroyed financially—completely ruined—by expenses related to health care.

AMERICA'S INADEQUATE HEALTH CARE AND HOW TO IMPROVE IT

It is clear upon thoughtful reflection that this country needs a government health plan, even though our Jeffersonian heritage makes America resist government programs until they become inevitable. That time has come. Immediately, there will be two objections.

First, we will be told that a government program would deny Americans freedom of choice, that a choice of plans is superior to a "one-size-fits-all" scheme. "Choice" always sounds better than "no choice," but the assertion that a choice of plans is always better is either sloppy thinking or pure propaganda. Personal choice in many aspects of life is a function of freedom and should be protected and enhanced. With regard to health insurance, however, "choice" has little, if any, relation to quality. In any case, there is very little true choice in American private medical practice as it exists today.

A situation drawn from real life will illustrate this point dramatically. A university vice president had a lifelong goal of becoming president of a college or university. After progressing through a series of interviews, a college in his home state made him an attractive offer. He thought he had achieved his dream, when he discovered that the college's health plan would cover no preexisting condition, not even for its president. Although he was vigorous, he was also a diabetic who had lost a foot to the disease. He needed regular medical care to survive, and taking a position with no health coverage for his diabetes would have been accepting a sentence of early death. He had to reject the offer.

A national health plan would have enhanced his choice. It would have provided him the freedom to change jobs. As it was, the American system of health-care delivery effectively denied him choice and kept him bound to the position that already supplied him with private health coverage, coverage that would have been available to him nowhere else in the United States.

A program is good for you when it provides you with the health care you need, when you need it, under acceptable conditions, with assurance of quality. Whether you have chosen that plan over another has nothing to do with its adequacy. If two plans each provide everything that is needed, when it is needed, under the same circumstances, there is no need for "choice"; they are the same. If one provides what you are more likely to need, and the other does not, then certainly the other is deficient. Note, though, that "choice" implies that some plans provide things that others do not. What is important is complete coverage, not a choice of plans that provide it. In most instances, people cannot have a good basis for choice among incomplete plans because no one can foretell the future. No one can be certain of all that he or she will need as time passes. Thus, the only completely satisfactory plan is one that provides whatever care might be needed when it is needed. Only government coverage will ever be able to come close to being truly comprehensive for the entire population.

Nevertheless, Americans have such a preference for choice that government coverage should make it possible. It can be accomplished. The plan outlined below does just that.

The second issue that opponents will raise is that of quality. Government health care, they will assert, cannot be quality care. Only private medicine, such as we have in America, can be good. After all, America has the world's finest health care.

Sadly, America does not have the finest health care. Our system is vastly more expensive than any other in the world, but in terms of its outcomes, it falls behind those of almost all other advanced countries. By any measure— be it longevity, infant-mortality rates, general health assessments, medical or hospital errors, or any other—nearly every other country boasts better outcomes from its system of health care than does the United States. Even the British, who have starved their National Health Service so drastically that its quality has sharply declined over the last quarter-century, are far healthier than Americans.[3] America's health-care delivery system is so inefficient and its overall outcomes so poor, despite the huge amounts that we pour into it, that we suffer in comparison not only with other industrial nations. America's economy is the strongest in the history of the world, but as measured by their outcomes, some less-developed countries put us to shame in terms of the quality of their health-care systems.

Private does not always mean better; government does not always mean worse. The best health care in the United States today, in fact, comes not from private medical practitioners. It comes from the health system of the Veterans' Administration (VA). Please note that Walter Reed Hospital, with its shortcomings that became infamous in 2007, is not part of the Veterans' Health Administration (VHA).

At one time, VA hospitals supported the worst fears of those who decry "government medicine." With almost no publicity, however, the situation has changed dramatically. As Phillip Longman writes in a startling article in the *Washington Monthly*, the VHA now provides "the benchmark for quality medicine in the United States."[4] Although policymakers have largely ignored it, this is not recent news. As long ago as 2003, the *New England Journal of Medicine* reported a study that examined eleven measures of quality that VA institutions provided and compared them with those offered by private medicine. In every instance, the study found that the quality of care in the government institutions was "significantly better" than elsewhere.[5]

A leading think tank, the RAND Corporation, reported similar findings in December 2004 in the *Annals of Internal Medicine*.[6] There were four key results of the RAND study. First, VA patients were more likely than patients in the national sample to receive appropriate care. Second, VA patients received care of higher quality than others on all measures except for acute care—and for acute care the quality was similar in both samples. Third, the greatest differences were in those "areas where the VA actively measured performance." Finally, when the VA applied performance measurement in specific areas, there were beneficial effects on other, related care.

Longman details how the VA system improved so dramatically in such a brief period. A few "key players" in the VA itself began examining how the system might be reformed for its patients' benefit. The leader of this group, Kenneth W. Kizer, M.D., became undersecretary for health for the Veterans' Administration in 1994. By 1998, the system had made a major turn-around. Note that those who accomplished this were "government bureaucrats," not private-sector corporate CEOs or "captains of industry."

One major reason for the improvement is the coordination and computerization of all records. A patient's entire record is immediately available to the health professional providing treatment, and the system constantly checks for errors. The same software is also in use in some public health systems in other countries. Longman indicates that it is available free for use here, "yet VA officials say they are unaware of any private health care system in the United States that uses the software. Instead, most systems are still drowning in paper," and there is strong "resistance to information technology among private practice doctors." Furthermore, Longman points out, VA has a lifelong relationship with its patients. They do not constantly shift from one plan to another, which means that in contrast to private providers, "the VHA actually has an incentive to invest in prevention and more effective disease management." It also makes a difference, he says, that VHA physicians are salaried, so they are not "profit maximizers." They have no need, he says, "to be fearful of new technologies or new protocols that keep people well. Nor do they have an incentive to clamor for high-tech devices that don't improve the system's quality or effectiveness of care." The result is that quality is dramatically higher than in private medicine, while costs are sharply lower. The flaws in VA health care, such as waits for care that give rise to veterans' complaints, result not from the system but from the poor funding that the Bush administration makes available to that system.

Longman does not write from an ivory tower or as a disinterested observer. He has been tragically affected by the shortcomings of private health care. Ten months after his wife received a diagnosis of cancer, after tangles of red tape that impressed upon them the failings of America's health-care delivery system, she died.[7]

The VHA is not perfect. Frequent criticisms include long waiting periods (of course, there are often long waiting periods in the private system as well). The VHA's shortcomings, though, nearly always reflect inadequate funding rather than flaws in the system. This should be expected from an administration concerned more about keeping taxes low than providing services.

There are several ways in which government could improve America's health care. At the minimum, it should mandate for private medicine many of the reforms that have been so effective in the system for veterans, such as the coordination of medical records. As for providing coverage, there is a range of possibilities, each better than the current hit-or-miss arrangement. States could arrange for health care, but that would be less than ideal considering the extent to which Americans move from one location to another. Former senator George McGovern has suggested that Medicare should be expanded, first to include expectant mothers and children from birth to age five, then progressively expanded further until it covers the entire population. Alternatively (or, even better, simultaneously) and most radically, the VHA could be expanded to cover more and more of the population, or a similar, parallel agency could be created. This would be the most efficient, and probably the most effective arrangement. Certainly, though, it also would be the most resisted in view of the special interests involved and their skill at influencing American public opinion.

Perhaps the best approach, one that would provide Americans with a choice, would be to make both plans available. This book supports that option: a dual system. One could choose the more traditional Medicare coverage or opt for the VHA-type plan. Coverage would be universal; yet, each American would have a choice of systems. The two systems could in fact compete for enrollees, improving both efficiency and quality.

Increasingly, leaders in American business and health care are coming to recognize the desirability of government health coverage. A recent example appeared in the *Wall Street Journal,* in which Benjamin Brewer, M.D., wrote that it had taken him a while to conclude that a single-payer health system would be the best approach. He said that his "fear had been that government would screw up medicine to the detriment" of his patients and his practice. His attitude changed when he recognized that autonomy in medical practice even now has become "largely an illusion." Medicare and Medicaid already wrote rules for 45 percent of his patients, and the rest were "privately insured under 301 different insurance products," with companies setting fees and imposing nonnegotiable contracts upon doctors. His conclusion was that "if done right, health care in America could be dramatically better with true single-payer coverage," and this meant a simplified system "that would cover all Americans, including those who could afford the best right now." On the whole, he said, such a system would be far more efficient and would afford doctors no less autonomy than the cumbersome one that now exists.[8]

AMERICA'S VANISHING RETIREMENT
SYSTEMS AND HOW TO IMPROVE THEM

Although not yet widely recognized, the dynamics are the same for retirement systems as for health care. With the collapse of two legs of the "three-legged stool," the time is here to expand Social Security into a complete system of income maintenance. This would ensure a secure workforce with complete portability for retirement: workers could change jobs as they chose with no concern that their retirement benefits would suffer. A decade ago, an outstanding economist, the late Robert Eisner, wrote an excellent little booklet with a title that was right on target: *Social Security: More, Not Less.*[9]

Social Security benefits should be increased to two to three times their current levels, thus establishing a complete package of protection. This package would continue to provide benefits for survivors of deceased workers and for the disabled, in addition to retirement and spousal benefits. All benefits would continue to be protected from erosion by inflation, something that private plans do not ensure.

Discarding the notion of a three-legged stool and expanding Social Security would free companies from the expense and complications of administering their own retirement systems; many companies are withdrawing from this responsibility in any case. Workers would gain the security that increasing numbers are lacking, and companies would gain the advantages of a secure and confident workforce. This would also help level the playing field between American firms and their foreign competition.

Among the immediate objections will be that this would require higher taxes. Of course it would, but because of Social Security's unparalleled efficiency, the overall costs to society would be reduced. No private program can match Social Security's low administrative costs, and none duplicates its lack of risk. Both employees and employers should be obligated to pay the Social Security, or Federal Insurance Contributions Act (FICA), tax on the employee's full salary, not merely the first $97,500, which is the amount taxable for 2007. The government should direct other resources, as outlined in chapter 7, to the trust funds to ensure that they will be adequate permanently. Note that one of these revisions already applies to Medicare; that is, for Medicare there is no cap on taxable income.

Despite the propaganda directed at destroying confidence in Social Security, the system is sound. Ideology, not economics, generates the concern for its finances. Here is a key question to ask doubters: when every part of the government of the United States is running at a deficit right now—that is, the Federal Bureau of Investigation, the U.S. Marine Corps, the Department of Labor, the White House Office, the Department of Homeland Security, and all the rest—why is it we are told that Social Security is currently in "crisis" and must be fixed immediately? Social Security, at least for now, continues to generate a huge surplus. It is the one large government program that is not generating a deficit. Much about the economy at the moment should cause all Americans concern, but the economics of Social Security are sound.

The following chapters make this clear and examine the history and financing of America's most efficient insurance mechanism. They also establish the importance of this most valuable program, which has become an essential part of the American way of life.

NOTES

1. The definitive work on FDR's proposals is Cass Sunstein's fine study, *The Second Bill of Rights: FDR's Unfinished Revolution and Why We Need It More Than Ever* (New York: Basic Books, 2004); Sunstein includes FDR's 1944 address in Appendix I.

2. Michael Hiltzik, "Undoing the New Deal," *Los Angeles Times*, June 26, 2005, www.latimes.com/business/investing/la-tm-hiltzik26jun26,1,714492.story; see also Michael Hiltzik, *The Plot against Social Security* (New York: Harper Collins, 2005).

3. See, e.g., James Banks et al., "Disease and Disadvantage in the United States and in England," *Journal of the American Medical Association* 295, no. 17, 2006, 2037–45.

4. Phillip Longman, "The Best Care Anywhere," *Washington Monthly*, January/ February 2005, www.washingtonmonthly.com/features/2005/0501.longman.htlm (accessed April 3, 2005), 2.

5. Longman, "The Best Care Anywhere," 2.

6. Steven M. Asch et al., "Comparison of Quality Care for Patients in the Veterans Health Administration and Patients in a National Sample," *Annals of Internal Medicine* 141, no. 12 (December 21, 2004); for a summary, see RAND Health at www.rand.org.

7. See Phillip Longman, *Best Care Anywhere: Why VHA Health Care Is Better Than Yours* (Sausalito, CA: Polipoint Press, 2007).

8. Benjamin Brewer, "Government-Funded Care Is the Best Health Solution: Multiple Insurers Create Expensive, Draining Hassle," *Wall Street Journal*, April 18, 2006, available at http://online.wsj.com/public/article/SB11452892568292763, retrieved 9 November 2007.

9. Robert Eisner, *Social Security: More, Not Less* (New York: Century Foundation Press, 1998).

2

Misinformation about Social Security: It Ain't What People Don't Know . . .

"What if you up and die on me?" Tammy Whitebread was thirty-one, but Ron Taylor was fifty-five. Her question to Ron brought them to the altar. Most of their associates assumed Tammy and Ron were already married. "Like many couples," said the *Kansas City Star*'s feature on civil weddings, "they chose the courthouse in an attempt to keep the ceremony small, low-key, even a bit of a secret." After ten years as a family, the couple had as their "biggest reason for a quick courthouse connection: 'Social Security,'" Tammy said.[1]

She wanted assurance that she and the children would be fully eligible for benefits if Ron were to die. Fortunately, she was aware of Social Security's value. She might not have had so sound a judgment if she had relied on television, magazine, and newspaper coverage for her information, including the lurid and alarming reports about Social Security that the *Star* itself at the time was publishing regularly. In recent years, the *Star* has developed a more nuanced, perhaps one should say a better-informed, approach to the subject.

WHAT CAN AMERICANS REALLY EXPECT FROM SOCIAL SECURITY?

What is it that Americans can expect from Social Security? Fortunately, the realities are sharply different from what the doomsayers suggest. Propaganda campaigns, often directed especially to the young, have attempted to convince people that Social Security "won't be there" when they need it. Many have come to accept the dire predictions as fact. The fear that it will

15

fail them is the natural result of a coherent and well-financed campaign by Social Security's enemies to kill the system. To understand what is happening, it is necessary to examine the criticisms thoroughly, to study the nature of Social Security, and to brush aside propaganda and look at the real situation.

The late humorist Will Rogers is supposed to have remarked, "It ain't what people don't know that's so dangerous—it's what people know that just ain't so!" That is certainly true about Social Security. Looking at the real situation, as this book makes clear, reveals some unexpected things:

- Despite the projections and the virtually universal assumptions of journalists and television commentators, it is highly unlikely that the trust funds in which the money that runs the system accumulates, will be depleted by 2041, or anytime. For that depletion to happen, the American economy would have to perform much more poorly than it normally does, and it would have to keep up that poor performance over a uniquely long period.
- Despite allegations from opponents, the trust funds do contain real value, not "worthless IOUs." The government bonds that the trust funds hold have value as secure as the dollar bills that every citizen holds—and they are secure for the same reasons.
- Despite criticism of governmental borrowing from the trust funds, those funds could not just sit uninvested. Simply investing them in the private market not only would introduce risk that government bonds do not carry but also, because of their huge amounts, could give government control of private markets. Even if some arrangement, such as an independent body that made investment decisions, could insulate the market from government control, the influx of enormous amounts could cause prices to inflate, while the withdrawal of the amounts that will be needed when the "baby boomers" retire could cause the market to collapse. Moreover, involving the market would introduce risk, while government bonds are secure.

  Many people misunderstand the true nature of the trust funds' use of governmental bonds. The bonds in the trust funds do mature and do pay interest back into the funds. It is important to recognize that the trust funds did not create government borrowing. If they were not available, the government still would have to borrow, but the borrowing would be from private investors and other nations. That would mean that the government would be borrowing vastly more from the countries that in recent years have already come to hold huge amounts of America's debt: China, Japan, and Korea. In the absence of the trust funds, it also would likely be necessary to borrow additional amounts from Arab states. All of this has to be paid back, of course. The amounts borrowed from the trust funds also must be paid back, but these amounts go back to those trust funds, that is, back to ourselves. Amounts borrowed from China, Japan, Korea, and other countries must be paid back to those countries, which increases the amount of money flowing out of America.

- Despite the frightening use of demographic statistics, the number of workers supporting each beneficiary will decline only slightly. At its low point, it still will be greater than it was in the 1960s. How can this be when the workforce is aging? First, about a third of Social Security's checks go to beneficiaries who are under retirement age: disabled workers, dependents, and survivors of dependents. Second, the past decades have brought a huge influx of women into the workforce. Third, although the population is certainly aging, the baby boomers are not immortal; they will pass through the system like a bubble.

- Despite the attempt to convince citizens that Social Security offers poor value, any genuinely objective study demonstrates that it offers exceptionally good value and will continue to do so.

- Despite the arguments of the critics during the 1990s (this argument is heard less often today), it is not wrong or unfair to pay benefits to those who are wealthy and do not "need" them any more than it is wrong or unfair for a company pension plan to do so. Building in "need" as a criterion to qualify for benefits would require the majority of Americans to contribute for a lifetime to a program from which they could draw no benefits. It would also require a person seeking benefits to go through the humiliating process of applying through a welfare office and proving poverty. Social Security's universal coverage is one of its greatest strengths.

- Despite the rosy promises of its advocates, "privatization" (or in the George W. Bush administration's new euphemism, "personal accounts") would not guarantee a better return, a good return, or even any return at all. It offers no guarantee whatsoever, except this one: it guarantees widely varied results. Some people would do much better; most people would do worse; and some would lose everything.

- Despite the glowing propaganda about the success of privatization in other countries, the results of foreign attempts to privatize range from doubtful to catastrophic. For example, the propagandists loudly praised Great Britain's partially privatized system as a model until the *Wall Street Journal* embarrassed them with its page-one report on August 10, 1998, under the headline, "Social Security Switch in U.K. Is Disastrous; a Caution to the U.S.?" Subheadlines read, "Many Britons Suffer Losses on 'Personal Pensions'; Insurers Have to Pay Up, and Tab May Reach $18 billion." Did the "privatizers" admit their error? No. Their response was to become strangely silent about the British system but to continue their campaign—as witnessed by Tom Miller's article "How to Get Real Social Security" in the mass-circulation *Reader's Digest* for December 1998.

Privatizers continued to wax enthusiastic about the system that the former military dictatorship of Augusto Pinochet imposed upon Chile, even though that system increasingly suggested the need for extreme caution with regard to private accounts. José Piñera, who served as minister of labor and social security for the Pinochet government, is now employed as cochairman of the Cato Institute Project on Social Security Choice (until recently, named the Project on Social Security Privatization). On Cato's payroll, he tirelessly extols the Chilean system that he helped design.[2] Although many people, including President Bush, find him persuasive, he is clearly engaged in salesmanship, not analysis.

Piñera presents a rosy picture of the Chilean system, but its performance for Chilean workers has not been rosy at all. Its administrative and managerial costs are huge, between 15 and 20 percent, which wreaks havoc on benefits. Note that America's Social Security system is so efficient that it costs less than 1 percent of its income to administer.

The phrase "pension damage" has become common in Chile. In the system's early years, after Pinochet imposed it in 1981, earnings were quite high, but they have become progressively less; at times, there has been no return at all. In the late 1990s, the Chilean government had to ask workers to postpone their retirements because of the lack of earnings.

Pinochet's regime was notorious for being a brutal military dictatorship in which the army held a privileged and protected position. It is highly significant that the military required Chilean society to adopt privatization, but in the words of Chile's former minister of labor and social security, Ricardo Solari, the army was "careful to preserve its own advantages and exclude fellow soldiers from the system." The military was wise to have stayed in the public system, which pays its retirees pensions far greater than those who were forced into private accounts.[3]

In late 2006, as the *New York Times* reported, the inevitable happened. The Chilean government recognized that the Pinochet plan was a disaster for Chile's workers and "recommended that it be supplanted by a system in which the state would play a much larger role." Workers had been promised some 70 percent of their wages in retirement but were actually receiving pensions "between 30 and 50 percent."[4] It will be interesting to see how the advocates of privatization deal with the failure of the Chilean system they praised so lavishly—or whether they will even acknowledge that plan's collapse. George W. Bush, especially, is in an awkward position since he "proposed using the Chilean model as the basis for a reshaping of Social Security."[5] In view of his fierce resistance to admitting an error, his endorsement of the Pinochet system will likely add to the many actions that will return to haunt his uniquely disastrous presidency.

- Despite the apparent plausibility of the calculations privatizers make to show that workers will be better off under a privatized system, those calculations are in fact based on false assumptions. Increasing numbers of impartial economic studies from universities and elsewhere are concluding that workers would lose substantially if they were to divert money from Social Security into private accounts.

Those who openly support full privatization tend to assume that, without Social Security, each worker would have not only the 6.2 percent Social Security taxes to invest but the employer's 6.2 percent match as well (some have even argued for the full 7.65 percent plus the match, which would include the Medicare tax, making the total 15.3 percent). Why do they maintain that the worker would have the employer's match? Because, they say, it is "part of the salary." Regardless of how economists might argue this as a philosophical question, in the real world employers are more likely to downsize, outsource, and employ part-time workers to minimize fringe benefits. There is no way that they would voluntarily add their match of Social Security, or Federal Insurance Contributions Act (FICA), taxes to the employees' salaries.

Moreover, in the real world, a worker earning, say, $50,000 per year declares only $50,000 to the Internal Revenue Service, not $50,000 plus the employer's 6.2 percent of $3,100. Nor could that worker obtain a mortgage by saying that his or her "real" salary was not $50,000 but rather $53,100. In the real world, the "salary" does not include the employer's match, and it certainly would not do so if the employer were suddenly freed from the need to pay into Social Security.

The privatizers' arguments, therefore, begin with a false premise that the worker would have an amount to invest that is double the FICA paycheck deduction. It would not happen. When they compare the supposed benefits from Social Security with those from private accounts, privatizers also tend to use as their example a single worker with no dependents, one whose average lifetime wage is at or above the maximum for Social Security taxation. Using as an example a worker in the top income groups will always produce a result less favorable to Social Security than using as an example a worker from the middle- or lower-income levels.

Social Security provides a proportionally greater return in relation to their taxes to lower-paid workers than to those who make more. This is deliberate; it is a policy designed to reduce poverty. Also, most workers are not single, and most have dependents. These workers have considerable additional coverage. They can expect a spousal benefit, and they have protection for their survivors. Even the single worker with no dependents has disability coverage. Privatizers do not figure the value of these additional coverages into their skewed comparisons. On the average, to duplicate Social Security's disability and survivors coverage on the private market would require policies in excess of $750,000. Social Security provides this value; under private accounts it would vanish.

Privatizers ignore these values of Social Security and tend to argue as though it were solely a retirement scheme—when it is much more— and as though it were an investment scheme—which it decidedly is not. Social Security provides insurance to help prevent poverty, not investments to make one rich. It is equally misleading when privatizers ignore the inflation protection built into Social Security. Its benefits are indexed to inflation, while private benefits are not. Social Security benefits do not lose value with time; payments from private accounts do. Social Security provides benefits that no beneficiary can outlive. Those who live longer than they had anticipated can discover that they have outlived their private investments.

- Despite the allegations of the critics, Social Security does not involve "intergenerational inequities," a notion that is not only suspect but vague and probably impossible to define. Nor does Social Security involve the unjust enrichment of one economic class at the expense of another. Virtually the entire population is covered, deferring consumption in order to receive not only retirement benefits but also health benefits, coverage against disability, and protections for survivors. Not only are younger workers protecting themselves and their dependents with their Social Security payments, but in most cases they are also ensuring that they do not have to care directly for elderly parents and grandparents, as pre–Social Security generations were required to do.

This list could go on, but these points should be enough to cause some rethinking about the dire predictions relating to Social Security. These are important points that are worth repeating, and so the following discussion will repeat them—without apology.

WHY IS SOCIAL SECURITY STILL SO POPULAR?

Remarkably, in spite of the campaign and the skepticism, studies consistently rate Social Security as highly popular. In fact, it is arguably the most popular program that the United States has ever enacted. There are good reasons for its popularity. Before Social Security, poverty was a common condition for the elderly. Now, the aged are financially much better off. In lifting the elderly as a group from destitution to relative comfort, Social Security has done, and is doing, precisely what the country designed it to do: it is enhancing security by providing benefits.

Does this mean that Social Security is enriching the elderly beyond the rest of the population? Are Americans at the mercy of a bunch of "greedy geezers," as the *New Republic* called them some years ago? Many others have echoed this charge, but it is false. There still is a greater rate of poverty among the elderly than among other adult Americans.[6] In addition, about one-third of all Social Security benefit checks go to people who are younger than retirement age, primarily the disabled and survivors of deceased workers. In fact, Social Security provides more support for American children than "welfare" does.

Thus, it bears repeating that Social Security's benefits are not at all limited to the elderly. They do provide a floor for retirement income, but they also protect Americans against loss of income resulting from disability, and they protect children and their caregivers in the event of a breadwinner's death or disability. As mentioned above, the protections that Social Security provides to those below retirement age would require policies that in the private market would exceed $750,000 in face value. Social Security also protects the younger generation indirectly by making it likely that parents and grandparents will be self-sufficient. The system ultimately helps nearly everyone, and its benefits come without the need to demonstrate poverty.

Americans have earned their benefits; they are not charity. That is the major reason why the system remains so popular. Could it remain popular if the American public reacted in outrage (as its enemies hope will be the case when they now and then raise the issue) at the fact that "millionaires receive Social Security?" Since they, too, have paid in, is there any good reason why millionaires should not receive benefits? Wealthy retirees receive private pensions, even when the companies from which they have retired complain of low profits, as noted above, and no one argues that private pensions should be means-tested.

If Americans ever gave in to the plea that the wealthy should not receive benefits, would the strong incentives not to save (because doing so might make it impossible to collect Social Security later on) damage an economy already suffering from a rate of saving that nearly all economists believe is too low? If it were necessary for everyone to go through the humiliating process of demonstrating poverty in order to receive benefits, could middle-class support for Social Security continue, or would it vanish overnight? If that support vanished, there is no doubt that the system would vanish also.

President Bush's proposal in his 2007 State of the Union address, as many observers noted, was itself an attack on Social Security. Those observers failed to note, however, that his proposal would introduce into the system a principle for some Americans that Cato and other privatizers have been urging all along: some Americans would have the option of claiming a reduction of their FICA taxes, or partially opting out of Social Security, at the expense of lowered Social Security benefits. Bush proposed taxing workers who receive employer-provided health insurance and exempting all workers who purchase health insurance from paying income or FICA taxes on their first $15,000 of wages.

Administration spokesmen in a press briefing shortly before the presidential address said this would not hurt the poor, who depend so heavily upon Social Security, because they could refuse to claim the deduction. They could choose health coverage or higher benefits.[7] What they did not say—and even the most perceptive critics have failed to notice this—is that this would permit these workers to choose whether to participate in the Social Security system, at least for the first $15,000 of their earnings.

We should note that the Bush administration has quietly succeeded in introducing an element of means-testing into Medicare. Since everyone pays a 1.45 percent payroll tax, matched by the employer, for Medicare benefits, and since there is no cap, or limit, as to the amount of wages subject to the Medicare tax, those who are wealthy pay far more for precisely the same hospitalization benefits as do others.

Nevertheless, under Bush, the cost for the voluntary portion of Medicare for which beneficiaries must pay extra—Part B, which covers visits to doctors' offices and the like—now is based on the income of the beneficiary. This is a rare instance in which Bush proposed a policy that did not favor the wealthy, but apparently he was willing to do this in order to plant in the program the seed that might someday grow into fully developed means-testing and thus undermine its universality.

Does this mean that critics from both extremes of the political spectrum have been correct when they have called Social Security a "middle-class program"? It does not. Surely the program helps the middle classes, but it helps the wealthy as well, and it helps the poor most of all. It is far from perfect. The taxes hit the poor harder than the middle class and the middle class harder than the wealthy, but the poor receive considerably more in benefits, in relation to the taxes they pay, than other income groups do. In addition, the earned-income tax credit offsets FICA taxes for many of the working poor. In chapter 7, I suggest a true reform that would relieve the poor of their burden and make the funding of Social Security somewhat progressive.

The public once understood the nature of the Social Security system. Now, attacks and misleading rhetoric from opponents, as well as from some misguided supporters, have obscured this understanding. Social Security is a program not merely for the middle class but for the whole of American society. The public needs once again to understand this fact.

Many figures in prominent political positions today would be delighted to see the entire system, including Medicare, vanish. Of course, generally, they cannot say so because they fear public reaction. They content themselves, therefore, with calling for benefit cuts and privatization, now carefully euphemized as merely "personal accounts," or "personal choice in Social Security." In the 1990s, they called for means testing. In nearly all cases, they maintain piously, and deviously, that they intend, of course, only to "save the system."

Consider the controversy in 1995 and 1996 over whether the Medicare proposals that President Bill Clinton vetoed would have provided "cuts" in the program, as the president said, or merely "reductions in the rate of growth," as supporters of the reductions alleged when they argued that they were attempting to "save the system." The Republicans were correct when they pointed out that their proposals would have resulted in increasing the money spent on Medicare. Thus, they could claim that they proposed merely reductions in the rate of growth, certainly not cuts.

They attempted to hide, however, that inflation and a growing population require growth simply to maintain the same level of benefits. Their proposals would have resulted in benefit reductions. Undoubtedly, the program would have continued to grow in the sense that the total dollars spent would have been greater, but it would have provided considerably less in benefits to each person. Providing less, thereby reducing benefits, is a rather good definition of a "cut," and all parties to the debate were well aware that the proposals would create reduced benefits. In this sense, "cut" was an appropriate description.

Similarly, when President George W. Bush began to speak of private accounts (before, that is, he came to call them "personal accounts" and deny that they were "private"), he argued that they were needed to strengthen Social Security because, he said, the system was in crisis, and the trust funds would soon be unable to provide benefits. When it became clear to anyone who examined the situation that this did not make sense, that if the trust funds would have too little money, taking money away from them to fund private accounts would cause an even greater shortfall, he finally conceded that "personal accounts" would not solve the problem. Thus, he admitted that the radical revision he had argued was necessary to "fix" the system would not do so. This did not change his argument, though, and he continues to argue that it is essential to Social Security to have private accounts. The approach seems to be that only repetition is required, not explanation or analysis.

The Social Security system covers a huge number of Americans. Now, virtually all can look forward to receiving benefits. Remarkably, those benefits are provided at an administrative cost of less than one cent of every tax dollar collected. The trustees' annual reports verify this year after year. This is far more efficient than any private insurance program, so much so that no private program is even in the same league, let alone ballpark.

All private insurance companies, including the most efficient and best managed, take many times what Social Security does out of every dollar paid in. Even a well-managed, profit-making HMO returns in benefits less than ninety cents of every dollar received. This is a novel idea for Americans, and political propaganda makes it even more difficult to believe: government is not only more efficient, but far more efficient, than private industry. In the case of Social Security, though, that clearly is the case. This observation is true not only in the United States but generally around the world.

The hidden—and to Americans, astonishing—truth is that government in general operates to provide benefits much more efficiently than any private plan can. This includes health benefits. Government provides health care, when it does so, at much less cost than private industry can. The private health-care system in the United States costs more for what it delivers than any other health-care system in the world. The Medicare system delivers vastly more for every dollar paid in than the best-managed private health plan can accomplish. Even the much-maligned Medicaid program (which provides care for the poor) does so. The Veterans' Administration (VA) is a sterling example of government's potential to provide care based on quality, not profit. Although the VA was once known for the deplorable nature of the care it provided, the situation has changed radically. Because of reforms signed into law by President Clinton, the Veterans' Health Administration has attracted attention for providing care of far greater quality than is available in American private medicine. Several medical journals have noted this phenomenon in recent years. As Phillip Longman has noted, veterans' hospitals now produce "the highest quality care in the country."[8] Note that this high-quality care is found not in the private sector but in government institutions.

Yet, we hear that government can never do anything right. When we hear this, we are inclined to think, Yeah, that's right! We rarely think in detail. We ignore such things as, for example, constructing the Panama Canal, winning two world wars and a cold war, putting a man on the moon, and setting up the Internet; we even ignore the fact that the Social Security system has never failed to provide its benefit checks when due. The insurance industry certainly cannot say the same for itself. It would come as a shock, perhaps, to many Americans to discover that most retired people do not receive private retirement benefits at all. Something like 92 percent of American retirees receive Social Security, while only about 31 percent receive anything from private pensions.[9]

In response to propaganda favoring privatization, we hear people say, "Social Security's a great idea, but it's going broke, and won't be there long." President Bush says it's facing a crisis, and we gotta do something now. As I have said, Social Security remains popular, but it is obviously true that confidence in the stability and future of the system has declined. Is our declining confidence the result of a true need for privatization that presidents have overlooked until George W. Bush uncovered it, or does it stem entirely, or almost entirely, from exaggerations of the troubles that the system faces?

WHAT HAPPENED TO THE SURPLUS? OR, THE CASE OF THE CURIOUS CALCULATIONS

In the early 1980s, Social Security faced troubles with cash flow in its Old-Age and Survivors Insurance Trust Fund. Gleeful politicians may have been happy to exaggerate, but the troubles were real and led to the creation of the 1982–1983 national Commission on Social Security Reform, chaired by Alan Greenspan (yes, that Alan Greenspan, before he was appointed to head the Federal Reserve Board). The Greenspan Commission's recommendations became the basis for the restructuring of the system in 1983.

Among other things, the revisions led to a gradual increase in the full retirement age from sixty-five to sixty-seven (for those born in 1938, the age increased by two months and rose incrementally until it became sixty-seven for those born in 1960 or later), and they mandated a schedule of FICA tax increases that culminated in 6.2 percent on employees plus the employer match, where it remains today. These changes were calculated to bring the system not only into balance but also slightly into surplus. Any deficit would occur far in the future and would be minor. The changes shifted Social Security from a pay-as-you-go system to one that is partly prefunded. The taxes were raised to build up huge balances in the trust funds in order to accommodate the coming bulge in baby boomer retirement. The trustees' projection then was for an actuarial surplus of 0.02 percent over a seventy-five-year period—that is, indefinitely.

Within a few years, however, concern began to develop about a deficit. Were the 1983 projections too optimistic? Did economic conditions not live up to the 1983 expectations?

On the contrary, the actual experience has been more favorable than the trustees projected in 1983. In other words, conditions in the years to follow— 1995, 2000, and 2005, for example—were better than the 1983 projections anticipated. How, then, could the trustees have begun projecting deficits when they had previously projected surpluses under less favorable conditions than actually developed? Could the trust funds have failed to perform up to expectations? No. The performance of the trust funds has mirrored the performance of the economy in general. They have been and are stronger than the trustees in 1983 anticipated. Where did the surplus go?

Answering this question—solving this mystery—requires a look at the actual projections, which makes the answer quite clear. *Nothing* happened demographically or in the economy to make the projected surplus vanish. All changes have actually been for the better, except for the calculations themselves. Only one thing accounts for the vanishing surplus: the trustees decided to adopt more pessimistic assumptions in making their "intermediate" projections.

A careful reading of the annual reports reveals a fact that the propagandists hide but the trustees themselves admit. Economic conditions did not lead them to project a deficit rather than a surplus. Their projections suddenly became more pessimistic simply because they chose to adopt more pessimistic assumptions upon which to base their calculations!

In the 1991 report, for example, the trustees admitted that "the new test, while more complicated than prior tests, is also more stringent."[10] Not only were the tests more stringent but the trustees reduced the number of optional scenarios they proposed. Whether they intended it or not, this gave the impression of greater precision. "It may be noted," said the report, "that recent annual reports, through the 1990 report, included four alternative sets of assumptions, including the two intermediate alternatives, II-A and II-B. Beginning with this report, a single intermediate set, alternative II, is shown."[11] Among the economic assumptions required to arrive at the projections are "gross national product, labor force, unemployment, average earnings, productivity, inflation, fertility, mortality, net immigration, marriage, divorce, retirement patterns, and disability incidence and termination."[12]

The reporters and policymakers who assume without question that "the trust funds are to be exhausted in 2041" should ask themselves just how accurately these factors can be predicted ten or twenty years into the future, or even one year, let alone seventy-five. Consider, for example, that about a year before the government announced a balanced budget in the late 1990s, America's best economic projections anticipated budget deficits years into the future; consider that no one predicted, or has yet adequately explained, the sharp and steady drop in crime in America since the early 1990s; consider also that the most sophisticated analysis was unable to predict even the dissolution of the Soviet Union, one of only two superpowers on earth.

It might be instructive, also, to consider that no one in the final year of the Clinton administration could have predicted that the new president, George W. Bush, would inherit a large budget surplus, insist on enormous tax reductions, and turn the huge surplus into a huge deficit in a matter of months. Ask also whether projections in 1932 could have anticipated conditions in 2007 (seventy-five-year projection), or even whether you would wish to rely on 1971 projections to draw conclusions about 2007 (a thirty-six-year projection).

If projections of this kind raise doubts, so, too, should projections of trust fund exhaustion in 2041 (another multidecade projection), especially when the calculations have been based on increasingly stringent tests. Although the trustees moved the year of exhaustion one tiny year closer, from 2042 to 2041, in their 2005 annual report, another year closer, from 2041 to 2040, in their report of 2006, and back to 2041 in their 2007 report, the tendency in recent years has been for the "doomsday" year to recede; like the vanishing point in the distance driving along a flat, straight, highway, one never reaches it.

Since the trustees began their pessimistic projections in 1988, the projected year of trust fund exhaustion has never been nearer than thirty-two years in the future. In 1982, because of the cash-flow shortage, depletion truly was imminent. Then, Republican senator Robert Dole and Democratic senator Daniel Patrick Moynihan worked together on the Greenspan Commission to correct the situation, and they corrected it quickly. Now, we are told that a "crisis" is upon us because the trust funds ("they" say) will be depleted decades from now. Therefore, the propagandists say it is urgent to take radical action immediately. To put it bluntly, this is simply nonsense; it makes no sense whatever.

Among the increasingly stringent tests is a requirement that the balance in the trust funds at the end of the projection period be adequate to cover the full costs of a year's benefits. Imagine the difficulties if personal finances were calculated in this manner. To avoid bankruptcy, a household would have to have enough money on December 31 to pay all living expenses for the next year without any further income. Yet, this is the test of solvency applied to Social Security, a test that considers a deficit to exist if there is not "a trust fund level at the end of the period equal to about 100 percent of the following year's expenditures."[13] In the trustees' words, "A targeted ending trust fund level of 1 year's expenditures is considered to be an adequate reserve for unforeseen contingencies; thus, in addition to the total outgo during the projection period, the summarized cost rate includes the cost of reaching and maintaining a target trust fund ratio of 100 percent through the end of the projection period."[14]

The trustees' reports recognize and concede the tentative nature of their projections, even if journalists and propagandists do not. "The resulting estimates should be interpreted with care," warned the 1991 report, for example. "In particular, they are not intended to be exact predictions of the future status of the OASDI [Old-Age, Survivors, and Disability Insurance] program."[15] Yet, that is precisely the way in which Social Security's opponents use them.

Sadly, those opponents now include the president and other officials of his administration. Former secretary of the treasury John Snow, for example, who by virtue of his position was one of the trustees, made the absurd statement in announcing the 2005 report that Social Security is "unsustainable." It is Social Security's actuaries who actually write the trustees' reports. Thus, the reports' language tends to be professional, not propagandistic. The trustees themselves, however, are highly partisan and are dominated by administration officials. They consist of six members, with only two appointed from outside. The other four include, in addition to the secretary of the treasury, the secretary of health and human services, the secretary of labor, and the commissioner of social security. So politicized is this administration that, to some extent, it has even made the Social Security Administration (SSA) an agent of partisan politics. It is unfortunate that the ridiculous "unsustainable" charge now is included on the SSA's own official website. For example, in a question and answer section (http://ssa.gov/qa.htm) SSA poses the question, "How big is the future problem?" and answers, "Social Security is not sustainable over the long term at present benefit and tax rates without large infusions of additional revenue. There will be a massive and growing shortfall over the 75-year period." Among "alternatives for modernization," the website discusses "prefunding future benefits" through "personal savings accounts." Note the air of certainty, and the sly use of the word "modernization," to imply that Social Security is old-fashioned and out of date.

Regarding journalists' tendency to fail to look at the propaganda critically, consider, for example, the comments made about Social Security by Susan Denzer, a cautious writer who was formerly an economics columnist for *U.S. News and World Report* and is currently a correspondent for *The NewsHour with Jim Lehrer*. In a 1998 discussion published by the National Academy of Social Insurance, she warned against "cover stories that crow about how Social Security is irretrievably broken," as well as against what she called the other extreme, which sees all "privatization or partial privatization proposals as simply the result of stealthy machinations of Wall Street." She asserted that the "press should acknowledge the uncertainties and resist unequivocal doom-and-gloom scenarios about the future of Social Security. This will be tough going," she said, "since to date the doom-and-gloom school appears to have thoroughly captured and dominated much of the press and public opinion. A case in point is the many books and treatises written by investment banker Peter Peterson, which have been excerpted time and again in many publications."[16]

She cautioned, quite correctly, that "projections about the potential future underfunding of Social Security are not necessarily wrong," but admitted that "we cannot say with 100 percent certainty that they are right, either. We do not know whether any of the most dire fiscal outcomes that we think might come to pass will in fact come to pass. We cannot say what the future will look like." In fact, she went on to say,

> Few policymakers will admit this publicly, so it is up to journalists to help fill this void. After all, as the National Academy of Social Insurance's own Robert Myers, formerly deputy commissioner of Social Security (and long-time chief actuary of the Social Security Administration), has pointed out in congressional testimony, under the low-cost estimate of Social Security prepared by the system's actuaries, the program is projected to experience no long-term financing problem whatsoever. Yet when was the last time you read in the popular press that under some plausible—if not especially likely—circumstances, Social Security might never be in trouble at all? I confess that not even I have raised this possibility in any of my written work to date on Social Security.[17]

One might reasonably ask, why not? In fact, one might conclude that it is unreasonable to fail to ask that question. To be sure, Denzer deserves credit for her recognition, which at the time was exceedingly rare, that the press had been irresponsible in dealing with Social Security. She also deserves praise for her confession that she herself had been guilty of having failed to report the situation accurately and completely, as well as for her skewering of scaremongers such as Peter Peterson. Her opinion that the more optimistic projections are "not especially likely," though, apparently made it impossible for her to present the full picture to popular audiences. A year after she had written her candid assessment of the state of reporting on Social Security, she wrote an article for the January–February 1999 issue of *Modern Maturity*, the journal of the American Association of Retired Persons, in which she carefully dealt with questions regarding privatization, but she continued to speak of "the system's projected long-term deficit," discussing it in detail as if there were no doubt that it would materialize, as though it were definite. Nowhere did she even hint that there might be no long-term trouble at all. In other words, a year after she wisely warned that reporting on Social Security had been misleading, and after she implicitly apologized for her own misleading reporting on the subject, she continued to treat the intermediate projection as though it were precise and not open to question. That is, she continued to mislead in her own reporting.

Denzer could have refreshed her memory by referring to the trustees' reports themselves, which explicitly warn against treating projections as though they are more than educated guesses. In the 1998 report, for example, which would have been available to her at the time she wrote for *Modern Maturity*, she could have found an extraordinarily pointed warning. The report described "the uncertainty inherent in projections of this type and length. In general," it said, "a greater degree of confidence can be placed in the assumptions and estimates for the earlier years than for the later years." It continued by admitting that "nonetheless, even for the earlier years, the estimates are *only an indication of the expected trend and potential range of future program experience"* (emphasis added).[18]

Those who would dismantle, or radically revise, a superbly functioning program based on such a shaky rationale should look even further into the reports. As the 1998 version made plain, the intermediate projection, which then called for trust fund exhaustion in 2032, assumed a rate of gross domestic product (GDP) growth far below actual experience. From 1999 through 2075, the highest anticipated growth rate was 2.0 percent, and that was to occur only in five of the years.[19] Subsequent annual reports continue this trend. In very few years since 1960 has the rate of growth been 2.0 or below. Nearly all have been above the maximum projected for the future, and usually far above. In other words, the trustees' intermediate projections, the only ones that they or the media publicize, assume that the best years in the future will be far worse than the average years in the past. The projected figures for inflation, similarly, are far more pessimistic than actual experience.

The figures given in all the reports clearly demonstrate that actual experience has been far better than the trustees' projections. Moreover, in report after report, the descriptions of the reasons for changes in the projections are candid. Nearly all result not from experience in the real world but from "assumptions and methods," "changes in economic assumptions," and the like.[20] In the 2005 report, for example, some of the indicators in its "Projections of Future Financial Status" even became more positive. Nevertheless, "changing the valuation period for this measure" brought the projected depletion year slightly closer, from 2042 to 2041, because of its "negative impact" (Section II.D.5). Here, of course, the report itself treats the alternative II, or intermediate, projections as though they were the only ones; alternative I, though, the low-cost projections continue, even in the 2005 and later reports, to project no trouble with the trust funds.

One of the assumptions that the actuaries use as a foundation for the trustees' projections is an ever-increasing life span. It is dubious, if not biologically impossible, that life expectancy will steadily increase forever, but such a notion undergirds the calculations and increases their pessimism. Such an assumption means that each year's projection will contain a more expensive year at the end of the valuation period than that contained in the projection for the previous year. In other words, the projections assume that the simple passage of time will cause costs to increase steadily.

The trustees issue annual projections because the law requires them to do so. Until the opponents of Social Security began to use them in their campaign to undermine the system, the projections rarely attracted attention. Now, thanks to opponents' propaganda, even most of Social Security's supporters accept the intermediate, or alternative II, projections, however questionable, as prophecy rather than qualified possibility. The feeble defense of these supporters tends not to question the projections but rather to protest that the system, after 2041, will still be able to pay three-fourths or so of the promised benefits (they do concede that three-fourths of the benefits at that time, because of indexing, will actually be a higher dollar amount than the system pays currently). Their acceptance of the notion that the future of the trust funds is gloomy is a tribute to the success of the critics, who themselves could hardly damn the system more strongly with praises so faint. To be sure, the intensity of the administration's campaign for privatization has generated a growing number of enlightened analysts who now are beginning to question the pessimism of the trustees' reports. They are welcome additions to the handful of us who all along have pointed out the projections' tenuous nature. Unfortunately, though, those who take an enlightened view remain barely more than a handful.

The few of us who recognize how unrealistic the trustees' projections actually are and how those projections play into the hands of Social Security's greatest enemies sometimes wonder at the motivation behind them. We do not know what those motivations have been; nor is it likely that we ever could know. Even though some of the more conspiratorially minded analysts sense an intent to harm the system or to encourage an accumulation of funds greater than necessary for the program in order to mask government spending, it is better not to fall into that trap and simply to assume the best: that the actuaries' motivation has been to be professional and to err on the side of caution.

If one wishes to uncover evil intent, it is not the actuaries who present the greatest evidence. Remember that the Greenspan Commission recommended that the system become prefunded, and as a result, Congress and the administration of Ronald Reagan raised FICA rates far above what was necessary to pay benefits. This was to accumulate a huge trust fund to accommodate the retirement of the baby boomers. Now that the boomer retirement is imminent, however, the Greenspan who argued in 1982 that workers should pay higher taxes in order to fund their benefits when they retired argues that those same benefits should be cut. Otherwise, he says, it will be necessary to raise taxes to redeem the bonds in the trust funds. One might reasonably ask a pointed question: why if it was acceptable to tax workers heavily to finance their benefits is it now unacceptable to tax the wealthy to redeem the promise the country, in the person of the unquestionable Alan Greenspan, made to those very workers?

Anyone who studies the situation can easily recognize that the last decade and a half or so has seen concerted and consistent attacks upon Social Security by political forces that have always opposed governmental activity in support of the Constitution's charge to "promote the general welfare." Any reader of newspapers can see that these forces were especially emboldened by the reelection of a president obviously suspicious of the principles underlying Social

Security, if not, in fact, dedicated to the complete destruction of the framework of social insurance in this country. There can be no doubt that major political forces are devoted to Social Security's elimination and that the president's role has elevated their strength to such a degree that they mounted a serious political effort, only to be stymied by fierce public reaction at first, then by the massive repudiation of Republicans in the 2006 elections.

All this is not to argue that the Social Security system has no flaws, but in truth, its flaws are minor. In fact, they are so minor that any major attempt to "reform," or to "save" the system is almost guaranteed to have disastrous results. Social Security is a huge program, but it is small in comparison with the total American economy. Even if the projections of increasing costs turned out to be correct—and, as indicated, there are good reasons to believe that the projections are much too pessimistic—the increase between now and 2070 would turn out to be only about 2 percent of GDP. Such a 2 percent increase is "less than the variations in the share of the GDP devoted to defense since the mid 1970s."[21] The economy is capable of handling such fluctuations quite well—and in fact has done so.

Nevertheless, because of the tremendous flood of negative propaganda, restoring full public confidence in the system will likely require more than mere reassurances. Social Security's enemies have skillfully created fears for the future. Reasonable as it may be to point out that the projections are unreliable or to remind the public that a better indication of future performance is the excellent performance of the past, some action may be necessary to convince the public that all is well.

There are, in fact, some incremental changes that could provide absolute assurance for the trust funds without changing the nature of Social Security or damaging the system. These changes include removing the cap on earnings subject to taxation, raising the interest rate on the bonds in the trust funds, earmarking certain portions of the income tax to the trust funds, and devoting trust fund surpluses to loans that pay down the national debt, rather than to loans to the Treasury to finance general expenses. Chapter 7 discusses these beneficial changes in more detail. It also discusses a major change to Social Security that would make its financing, as well as its benefit structure, progressive. The trouble with Social Security as currently constituted is not that the trust funds will be depleted. Rather, it is that its regressive financing forces the poorest Americans to pay FICA taxes beginning with the first dollar of earnings, while it relieves those who earn above $97,500 per year (in 2007) of the obligation of paying FICA taxes on wages beyond that level. Chapter 7 sets forth a plan in which workers will be freed from having to pay FICA taxes on the first $20,000 of their wages.

In the meantime, it is necessary to examine Social Security, to look at the system carefully. Evaluating the fears and criticisms requires an understanding of the nature of social insurance. First, we examine what the system is, how it operates, and how it came to be what it is. Only then are we truly in a position to analyze in depth what the critics are saying and to understand why they are saying it.

HOW SOCIAL SECURITY WORKS AND WHAT IT PROVIDES

Workers become eligible for benefits by accumulating "credits," or "quarters of coverage" (that is, by earning wages of a certain amount in covered employment). For 2007, the minimum amount required is $1,000; a worker may accumulate a credit for each $1,000 up to four credits for a year. Eligibility generally is based on forty credits, or ten years of earnings, although there are exceptions in certain circumstances. For example, the survivors of a very young worker who dies may be eligible for benefits even though the worker had been in the workforce for much less than ten years.

The FICA tax rate is 6.2 percent on the first $97,500 of wages (for 2007); the employer pays another 6.2 percent to match the worker's payment. Additionally, the worker and the employer each pay 1.45 percent for Medicare for a combined total of 7.65 percent. Workers and employers each pay the 1.45 percent for Medicare on all wages, regardless of the amount. Each dollar of the total 7.65 percent tax is allocated to one of three trust funds: seventy cents for old-age and survivors insurance; eleven cents for disability insurance, and nineteen cents for hospital insurance (Medicare). The trust funds pay benefits and administrative costs, and they invest their huge surpluses in the safest investments possible, U.S. government bonds, which regularly pay interest back into the trust funds. Despite fears that the "government has spent all the money," the trust funds are intact. They have no more been "raided" than have the funds of a citizen who invests money in savings bonds.

The benefits available from the Social Security system thus include much more than the familiar retirement benefits for workers and their dependents, but those benefits are still the heart of the program. They are available to workers who retire at the full retirement age (sixty-five for those born before 1938 and progressively older for those born after that year, up to sixty-seven for those born in 1960 or later) or at a reduced level to those who retire as young as sixty-two. Workers who do not retire until after their age for full retirement will have their benefits increased for every year they delay retirement until they are seventy. Spouses of retired workers, similarly, can receive full benefits at their age for full retirement (the amount is normally half the benefit paid to the retired worker), or they also can apply for a reduced benefit as early as age sixty-two. Note that once a beneficiary has opted for early retirement at a reduced benefit, that benefit remains reduced for life.

A person has the option of retiring on his or her own wage record or on that of the spouse, whichever would provide the greater benefit; one cannot, however, receive full benefits on both records. A divorced spouse who is not currently married can receive benefits on a worker's record, just as though he or she were still married, provided that the marriage lasted at least ten years (or regardless of the length of the marriage if the divorced spouse is still caring for the worker's child and that child receives benefits). The requirements are otherwise the same as those for current spouses. An important thing to note is that this provision is in no way a threat to the current spouse: payments to a divorced spouse have no effect upon those paid to a current spouse and do not count against the worker's family maximum.

Also important are Social Security's life insurance elements, which discussions frequently overlook. They are substantial. As long ago as 1993, Social Security provided Americans with some $12.1 trillion in life insurance protection. That exceeded by "$1.3 trillion the combined value of all private life insurance policies of all types in force in the United States."[22] The amounts today, of course, are far greater. Spouses of deceased workers may receive survivor's benefits when they reach the age for full retirement, or they may retire as young as age sixty. If they are disabled, they can also receive benefits beginning at the age of fifty. Children of deceased workers receive Social Security benefits if they are unmarried and under eighteen or until age nineteen if they are still in school. (Previously they could receive benefits until age twenty-one if they were in college, but Congress, at the request of the Reagan administration, eliminated the college benefits in 1981.) Surviving children disabled before reaching the age of twenty-two can receive disability benefits at any age. The spouse of a deceased worker receives benefits as a mother or father if providing care for the worker's children who have not yet reached the age of sixteen. If a deceased worker had dependent parents age sixty-two or older, they can receive benefits.

Disability benefits at one time required "permanent and total disability." Now, however, a worker whose impairment may prevent engaging in any "substantial" work for at least a year may be eligible. The definition of "substantial" would mean, as a rule, that the person is incapable of earning (for the year 2007) $900 or more a month. Additional benefits may be available if the ailment is one from which death may be anticipated. The requirements are quite strict, both medically and in terms of eligibility for coverage. To be covered, a worker who is under the age of twenty-four must have six credits in the three years immediately prior to the onset of the disability. Workers aged twenty-four to thirty-one must have credits for half the time (that is, an average of at least two credits per year) between the attainment of age twenty-one and the onset of the disability. Those thirty-one or older must have a total of credits that increases gradually with age (from twenty at age forty-two, for example, to forty at age sixty-two or above), but there is another strict requirement. The worker must have earned twenty credits in the ten years immediately preceding the onset of the disability.

The health-benefits program, Medicare, comes in two primary segments. Part A is hospital insurance. This coverage provides benefits paid for from the Medicare portion of Social Security taxes. Part B is medical insurance, which provides payments for bills from physicians. The beneficiary pays a monthly premium for Part B coverage and, thus, has the option of rejecting it. Additionally, there are two other segments. Part C is for those who opt to join an HMO under Medicare rather than stay in the traditional program. Part D is the complicated prescription-drug benefit that began in 2006. A covered worker may enroll for Medicare at the age of sixty-five even if he or she delays applying for other Social Security benefits (the age of eligibility for Medicare has not been increased as it has for other Social Security benefits).

Medicare benefits are extensive, but they are limited. Hospital benefits include payment for all covered services for the first sixty days of a stay, except for a deductible. For days sixty-one through ninety, benefits are the same, except the patient must pay a daily coinsurance amount. Hospital benefits end after the ninetieth day and do not resume until the beginning of another "benefit period," which starts after sixty days of no hospitalization. There is an exception to the end of benefits at ninety days. Each beneficiary has a lifetime total of sixty "reserve days," which can be used to extend a ninety-day stay in the hospital.

Under certain circumstances, Medicare will pay for skilled nursing care for up to one hundred days in an approved facility, but only following a hospital stay. The first twenty days of such care are covered in full; the remaining eighty days require payment of a daily coinsurance amount. One should be aware that there is an enormous shortage of nursing home beds available to Medicare patients. There also is no coverage for custodial care. Under certain conditions, however, Medicare does cover the full cost for home health visits from an approved home health agency.

Numerous other items fall outside Medicare's coverage. Nursing home care is excluded, as noted, except after a hospital stay. There is no coverage for routine dental care, dentures, eyeglasses, or hearing aids. There is no coverage for most immunizations or for most routine examinations. Before the start of "Part D" benefits in 2006, no coverage for most prescription drugs existed, and the coverage under Part D is severely limited. Because of this, because the legislation establishing Part D prevents Medicare authorities from negotiating drug prices, and for various other reasons, those who benefit most from Medicare's prescription-drug benefit almost assuredly will not be the patients but the pharmaceutical companies.

For terminally ill patients, Medicare under certain circumstances will pay for hospice care. The patient's physician and the hospice medical director must both certify that the patient has a life expectancy of six months or less, the patient must agree in writing to accept hospice care instead of standard Medicare benefits, and the care must be in a Medicare-approved hospice.

Part B of Medicare, medical insurance, covers bills from physicians and many other items not included under hospital insurance. In general, in any year the patient must first pay a certain amount, the deductible, before benefits begin. Then, Medicare pays 80 percent of the covered charges for the remainder of the year. The Social Security Administration has numerous pamphlets available free of charge. These provide clear explanations of the various benefits, eligibility requirements, and the like.

According to the Social Security Administration, its retirement benefits currently replace about 40.6 percent of preretirement income for the average retired American and 54.7 percent for low-income retirees. High-income workers have 35.6 percent of their preretirement wages replaced, while those who average at the very top of the taxable income scale receive even less.[23] This progressive benefit structure helps offset the system's regressive funding, but Social Security succeeds in "keeping tens of millions of Americans out of poverty."[24] It is responsible for a dramatic drop in the poverty rate among the elderly, but Social Security alone is certainly not sufficient to provide a comfortable living—or even the necessities.[25] Its benefits are modest but vital.

This is consistent with the original purpose of the Social Security Act. Its purpose was to provide retirement benefits, not a complete retirement. One common description was that it was to provide a floor of protection to which other resources could be added. Another common metaphor was that Social Security provided one leg of a "three-legged stool," the other two legs being company pensions and private investments and savings. Other benefits, of course, including those for spouses and dependents, as well as coverages for disability and health needs, have been added through the years. Despite misleading propaganda, however, the program was never intended to be a mere supplement to retirement for those who needed it; "need" has never been a factor in determining eligibility for benefits. Social Security has operated exactly as intended: it has been a major part of the retirement benefits of Americans. It was intended to be permanent, and the people have accepted it as such, so much so that Social Security clearly has become a basic part of the "American way of life."

None of this is to argue that Social Security cannot be improved. Its enemies seek to "improve" it by cutting benefits and privatizing. They would destroy this vital part of the American way of life. What needs improving more than anything else is the regressive nature of the current funding mechanism. Chapter 7 offers a way to keep Social Security, make it unquestionably solvent by nearly anyone's measure, avoid cutting benefits, put more disposable income in the pockets of nearly all workers, and shift a bit of the burden of its funding upward. The benefit structure is already progressive. My proposal in chapter 7 would make Social Security's financing progressive as well, at least mildly so.

Despite the importance of Social Security, its practicality, and its unparalleled efficiency, establishing it in America was not easy. An understanding of the forces against it and what was required to overcome them will help in understanding why Social Security is under attack now. Therefore, in the next chapter I examine in some detail both the program's history and its opposition.

NOTES

1. Eric Adler, "I Do, I Do: Some Days It's Just One Wedding after Another for Courthouse Preacher," *Kansas City Star*, September 30, 1998, F2.

2. See, for example, José Piñera, "Retiring in Chile," *New York Times*, December 1, 2004, Op-ed., A31.

3. See Larry Rohter, "Chile's Retirees Find Shortfall in Private Plan," *New York Times*, January 27, 2005, A1.

4. Larry Rohter, "Chile Proposes to Reform Pension System," *New York Times*, December 26, 2006, A16.

5. Rohter, "Chile Proposes to Reform Pension System," A16.

6. Marilyn Moon, "Are Social Security Benefits Too High or Too Low?" in *Social Security in the 21st Century*, ed. Eric R. Kingson and James H. Schulz (New York: Oxford University Press, 1997), 72.

7. Those speaking for the administration were Julie Goon, special assistant to the president for economic policy, and Katherine Baicker of the Council of Economic Advisors. They held their press briefing on January 22, 2007; see "Press Briefing on the President's State of the Union Health Care Initiative," The White House, www.whitehouse.gov/news/releasesw/2007/01 (accessed January 28, 2007).

8. Phillip Longman, "The Best Care Anywhere," *Washington Monthly*, January/February 2005, 38–48.

9. See Thomas W. Jones, "Social Security: Invaluable, Irreplaceable, and Fixable," *The Participant*, February 1996, 4.

10. 1991 Annual Report of the Board of Trustees of the Federal Old-Age and Survivors Insurance and Disability Insurance Trust Funds, 3. All trustees reports are available at the Social Security Administration's website, ssa.gov.

11. 1991 Annual Report, 38.

12. 1991 Annual Report, 38.

13. 1998 Annual Report of the Board of Trustees of the Federal Old-Age and Survivors Insurance and Disability Insurance Trust Funds, 24, available at ssa.gov.

14. 1998 Annual Report, 92.

15. 1991 Annual Report, 38.

16. Susan Denzer, "The Political Feasibility of Social Security Reform," in *Framing the Social Security Debate: Values, Politics, and Economics*, ed. R. Douglas Arnold, Michael J. Graetz, and Alice H. Munnel (Washington, DC: National Academy of Social Insurance, 1998), 420.

17. Denzer, "The Political Feasibility," 421.

18. 1998 Annual Report, 11.

19. 1998 Annual Report, 57.

20. See, e.g., 1998 Annual Report, 193.

21. Barry Bosworth, "What Economic Role for the Trust Funds?" in *Social Security in the 21st Century*, ed. Eric R. Kingson and James H. Schulz (New York: Oxford University Press, 1997), 175.

22. Robert M. Ball and Thomas N. Bethell, "Bridging the Centuries: The Case for Traditional Social Security," in *Social Security in the 21st Century*, ed. Eric R. Kingson and James H. Schulz (New York: Oxford University Press, 1997), 175.

23. Available at the Social Security Administration's website, www.ssa.gov/OACT/TR02/lr6E11-1.html, www.ssa.gov/OACT/TR/TR04/lr6F11-2.html, www.ssa.gov/OACT/TR05/lr6F10-3.html (accessed April 17, 2005).

24. Jones, "Social Security," 4.

25. Moon, "Are Social Security Benefits Too High or Too Low?" 65–72.

3

The Gospel of Wealth: Amid Acres of Diamonds

More than many, if not all, other societies, America has found it difficult to deal with questions of providing economic well-being for all its citizens. As early as 1795 when he was in France, the most radical of America's founders, Thomas Paine, published a pamphlet, *Agrarian Justice*.[1] In 1797, it became available in English, and Americans were exposed to his economic ideas, ideas that, if implemented, would have provided a social insurance system of sorts. Yet, more than a century later, such American pioneers of social insurance as I. M. Rubinow, Paul Douglas (the future U.S. senator), and Abraham Epstein continued to sound extreme to their fellow citizens.

By the first three decades of the twentieth century, there was ample European precedent for social insurance. Germany, in fact, had put extensive social insurance systems in place in the 1880s under the "Iron Chancellor," Otto von Bismarck. In the Western Hemisphere, Uruguay was an early pioneer. Foreign examples did not, however, seem to impress Americans. The belief was widespread that only individual initiative was required for virtually anyone to succeed in the American scheme of things. At the same time, pride in all things American did not keep Americans from holding their state and its functionaries in low esteem.[2] Such attitudes help explain why the United States has adopted fewer, and less extensive, social programs than other advanced industrial countries. We are virtually alone, for example, among advanced industrial states in failing to provide universal health care. Moreover, antigovernment attitudes recently have risen in response to reckless presidential rhetoric and are certainly worse since the administrations of Ronald Reagan and George W. Bush than they had been previously.

CONDITIONS LEADING TO SOCIAL SECURITY

In the early years of industrialism, with its unsettled conditions that forced many rural people into crowded cities, there were no programs such as Social Security to help relieve economic distress. Vast new fortunes emerged, but so did unprecedented numbers of the very poor. The extremes of wealth and poverty that came to exist as states industrialized brought protest movements in the late nineteenth century. These took many forms, both here and abroad. States dealt harshly with anarchist protest, as one might expect given anarchism's hostility to the idea of the state itself. Socialist movements became strong in some countries, but in America socialist successes were minimal. Even Christian socialism, which preached cooperation and love as opposed to what it viewed as the selfishness of competition, made little headway, except briefly and in a few church groups.

There were few calls for true social programs. Justification for unlimited accumulation of wealth as the prime social value was considerably more widespread than criticism, receiving support from Social Darwinists, who purported to be scientific. Others attempted to provide an ethical basis. The first such efforts were based in religion. Mark Hopkins, president of Williams College, argued that accumulation of property was necessary in order to benefit others. Much more crude was Russell H. Conwell's "Acres of Diamonds" speech, which Conwell, the founder and first president of Temple University, gave to countless numbers of eager listeners.

Religion, he said, did not merely permit that one become rich; it demanded it! Accumulation of wealth was a duty, not a privilege. The poorest person in America could become rich and do so honestly and quickly. There was no excuse for poverty, which resulted only from one's own shortcomings or those of someone else. It was a sin to be poor, or even to sympathize with those who were poor, because poverty was invariably a punishment from God. One can only marvel at the way in which Conwell, a Baptist minister, could consider his ideas regarding the poor to be consistent with the words of Jesus.

Conwell's speech was in great demand. He received a civic award—an award for public service, not for persistence—after he had given it for the five thousandth time. The speech's basis was the tale of a man who sold his land to seek riches. He wandered throughout a disappointing life, only to learn finally that the world's richest diamond mine had been discovered on the land that he had squandered. Riches, Conwell, preached, are in one's own backyard.

Such ideas are cruelly unrealistic, especially in a complex modern world, but they were highly popular as the twentieth century approached. It is tempting to write them off as reflecting the conditions of an unsettled time that had not developed an adequate understanding of the social and economic forces that were bringing radical change. Unfortunately, these and similar ideas have never been completely dismissed, and they reemerged with enormous force in recent years as a cursory review of political speeches and leadership-training courses will demonstrate. In fact, they permeate especially the writings of those who would privatize Social Security.

The "robber barons," as those American capitalists of the late nineteenth century who became wealthy by deliberate exploitation are called, felt no sense of social responsibility, but this lack of understanding of what they owed society did not include all industrialists, or "captains of industry," some of whom did have a sense of obligation. Prominent among them was the steel tycoon Andrew Carnegie. After becoming one of the wealthiest persons in American history, Carnegie became the most articulate spokesman for the "gospel of wealth." In 1900 he wrote a book by that title in which he called upon those of wealth to contribute to society and live without ostentation. He ably defended the system, even while conceding that it was not perfect, and he lived up to his principles by constructing public libraries, establishing educational institutions, founding the Carnegie Endowment for International Peace, and otherwise using his wealth to benefit society. It is worthy of note that he strongly supported an estate tax. He considered it necessary to prevent huge fortunes from being transmitted, unreduced, from generation to generation. Otherwise, such fortunes would increasingly concentrate the bulk of society's wealth in fewer and fewer hands. It is ironic that a century later, political figures frequently work to protect the interests of the wealthy few by whining about the alleged evils of what they cleverly, cynically, and wrongly now call the dreaded "death tax."

Other captains of industry, such as John D. Rockefeller, who created the Rockefeller Foundation and the University of Chicago, followed Carnegie's lead. A contemporary example is the media mogul Ted Turner, who has made huge philanthropic grants. In August 1996, he called upon others with great wealth to do the same and charged that they tended to horde their riches because of preoccupation with—and he was serious—retaining their status on the list of the richest people in the world. He urged them to reject that childish concern and, instead, to compete to see who could do the most good.

Others are joining the call for renewed social responsibility. In 2006 America's second wealthiest person, the investor Warren Buffet, announced that he would join forces with America's wealthiest and would contribute his enormous fortune to the Bill and Melinda Gates Foundation for charitable purposes.

Similarly, former president Bill Clinton has formed the Clinton Global Initiative and is using his vast—and in fact unequalled—prestige throughout the globe to accumulate unparalleled pledges from the world's governments and richest private persons to combat HIV-AIDS, improve education and public health, and otherwise better the lot of humanity. An initial such step came in the 1990s, when former senator and Democratic presidential candidate George McGovern persuaded former senator and Republican presidential candidate Bob Dole to cooperate with him to encourage the U.S. government to inaugurate an international school-lunch program. They succeeded. The program is designed to improve both the nutrition and the education of children in the poorest countries, especially of girls in countries with cultures that otherwise would discourage them from obtaining any schooling whatever.

Thus, even in the harshest political times, there are voices of reason and hope. Moreover, those times are not permanent. We now can see signs that the harshness of recent years is receding from America's political culture. We can only hope that the signs are genuine, as the massive repudiation of conservatives in the 2006 congressional elections suggests they are.

STEPS TOWARD SOCIAL SECURITY IN AMERICA

It was the Great Depression of the 1930s that shook the confidence of many Americans in the ability of their country to provide conditions of abundance without governmental action. It became increasingly evident to them that economic individualism and political liberties were not sufficient by themselves to ensure economic well-being in a complex society; still it required a disastrous collapse of the country's economic structure to bring about such a recognition. The conditions were so extreme that one in every four—perhaps even as many as one in three—workers could find no work at all. Even under such circumstances, the abstract idea of governmental activity continued to raise questions.

The purely ideological (and essentially meaningless) question of how large government should be has often received more attention when considering a policy initiative than the effect of the policy itself. From a practical point of view, the important question regarding a policy should be whether it will make things better or worse, not whether it will affect the size of government. In the 1930s, the emergency was so clearly evident that Americans accepted the New Deal, oriented to action rather than to ideology, which emerged to counter the crisis. The New Deal brought forth the Social Security Act of 1935, which set up the system that may well lay claim to being the most popular government program in American history.

The term "social security" can be defined in various ways and can include many things. Broadly interpreted, it encompasses all social welfare measures. In a stricter sense, it refers to the programs that the Social Security Act itself authorizes. For most Americans, though, it has an even stricter meaning: the contributory social insurance programs (old age, disability, and survivors insurance); it can also include the health-benefits coverage of Medicare.

Despite American discomfort with government action, the Social Security Act did not emerge from a vacuum. The idea of involving the government in ensuring basic economic security for its citizens was not completely new in American history. In January 1909, President Theodore Roosevelt himself chaired a White House Conference on Care of Dependent Children and called for Congress to establish a Children's Bureau (it ultimately did so in 1912). Roosevelt's conference brought attention to the idea of governmental pensions or allowances to widows with dependent children. Subsequently, under the leadership of Gertrude Vaile, Denver, Colorado, saw the first of the mothers' pension plans. Vaile had been active in the Charity Organization Society movement and had studied under one of its most prominent figures, Mary Richmond.

In 1914, writing in Paul Kellogg's magazine of social reform, *The Survey*, Vaile outlined the difficulties facing those who hoped for similar programs. She wrote that apathy was prevalent and that only meager results were likely. A number of states did pass laws, but many of them did no more than authorize localities to establish programs if they chose to do so.

There was, however, ferment in the years following the 1909 White House Conference. Numerous progressive associations and groups were bringing together social workers, such as Jane Addams and Grace and Edith Abbott, with such other influential figures as Eleanor Roosevelt (Theodore Roosevelt's niece and the wife of Theodore's distant cousin and future president, Franklin D. Roosevelt), Newton D. Baker, Louis Brandeis, and the prominent University of Wisconsin economist John R. Commons. These and others lent their prestige to efforts to encourage reform.

One of the most militant of the organizations involved in pressing for reform was Florence Kelley's National Consumers' League. Another, the Women's Trade Union League, fought long and hard against the exploitation of industrial workers. The American Association for Labor Legislation (AALL), headed throughout its existence by John B. Andrews, grew from about two hundred members in 1906 to more than three thousand in 1919. Through writing and lobbying, it helped bring about the adoption of rudimentary workmen's compensation laws in many states. Andrews had studied and collaborated with Commons, and he and his wife, Irene Osgood Andrews, exerted great influence on many other reform groups.[3]

By 1912, the former Republican president Theodore Roosevelt, a great reformer, had become disillusioned with the conservative policies of his successor, President William Howard Taft. Although Roosevelt had strongly supported Taft, his former friend's complacency and relative unwillingness to pursue reform offended him profoundly. Roosevelt therefore attempted to regain the Republican nomination from Taft in 1912. Although TR carried most of the primaries, the Republican leaders found Taft's policies much more congenial than those that the uncontrollable Roosevelt might adopt and renominated the president.

Roosevelt then launched a third-party candidacy as the candidate of the "Bull Moose" Progressives, a new party that included in its platform a call for social insurance. Roosevelt favored not only retirement benefits but also health-care and unemployment coverage. "Progressive" was an apt name for his short-lived party. Its platform was enormously farseeing, especially considering how much remains to be done nearly a century later. Although Roosevelt's second-place finish was uniquely strong for a third-party candidate, his defeat ensured that social insurance was unlikely to be considered seriously for some time.

Shortly thereafter, I. M. Rubinow, a physician turned economist and statistician, set forth the theoretical justification for what came to be called the Social Security Act in his classic work of 1913, *Social Insurance*. He had been with the U.S. Bureau of Labor and was a lecturer on social insurance at the New York School of Philanthropy. He traced the background of social insurance in Europe and described the various programs then in existence.

With the publication of this book, Rubinow became the leading authority on social insurance in the United States. Until his death shortly after passage of the Social Security Act, which owed much to his pioneering and continuing efforts, he remained one of the foremost of a small group of American experts in the field.

Rubinow refuted the prevailing argument that America's high wages eliminated the need for social insurance. Wages, he wrote, were not sufficiently high to yield a continuous surplus. An annual surplus in income, which would be required to make it possible to save anything for retirement or disability, was in fact quite rare among America's workers.[4] It required the crisis of the Great Depression finally to force recognition of Rubinow's point.

During the rise of the Progressive movement, social reformers developed a spirit of cooperation with government officials at all levels. The reformers tended to consider Theodore Roosevelt's 1912 defeat a blow to their cause. Nevertheless, the cooperation continued to some degree under the administration of Woodrow Wilson until World War I destroyed it by redirecting popular concerns and associating many reform measures with "pro-German" sympathies. It was impossible to restore the relationship during the era of "normalcy" after the war. The mood of the 1920s was apathetic and largely unconcerned with social justice. It was hardly conducive to reform measures.[5]

The first brief flurry of activity in support of governmental health insurance in the United States had spanned the war years. In 1912, the AALL formed the country's first Committee on Social Insurance. In 1913, the association sponsored a national conference on social security. The conference led to the drafting of a model social security bill, including health insurance provisions, for introduction into state legislatures. The Committee on Social Insurance appointed a subcommittee in 1914 specifically to prepare the bill, and the subcommittee completed its task in 1915. In the same year, the American Medical Association (AMA) also displayed interest in compulsory government health insurance and formed its own Social Insurance Committee. Three of its members, Alexander Lambert, I. M. Rubinow, and S. S. Goldwater, all physicians, were members of the committee that the AALL had formed earlier. The AMA and the AALL were prepared to cooperate upon the medical issues involved, but the cooperation was brief. By 1918, serious opposition had arisen within the AMA, and many insurance companies and pharmaceutical houses had also begun to work against the program.[6]

The model social insurance bill was introduced into the New York legislature in 1916, 1917, and 1918. During those years, many state legislatures established commissions to investigate the issues involved; the strongest investigations were in New York and California. Rubinow published a new book in 1916, *Standards of Health Insurance*, that furthered the movement. In 1919, the bill providing for health insurance passed the New York Senate, but even with support from Governor Al Smith, it failed in the assembly's Rules Committee. By 1920, health insurance had ceased to be a serious political issue in the United States, and the AMA went on record with a policy of strenuous opposition that lasted for decades.

In August 1921, during the brief postwar depression that had begun in 1920, President Warren G. Harding called the Conference on Unemployment. The conference accomplished little since improving economic conditions had lessened the pressure on the participants. Comments from the chair of the conference's Subcommittee on Public Works, Otto T. Mallery, reflected the general attitude among those in attendance. Reformers had attacked the conference for not considering unemployment insurance, but Mallery retorted that it would have been unrealistic to do so. If the conference had considered such an untried measure that had no public support, he said, it would have jeopardized serious consideration of other issues. This was ironic, if not ridiculous, in view of the fact that Theodore Roosevelt had called for unemployment protection in his great Progressive Bull Moose platform nearly a decade earlier, in 1912.

The postwar depression had occasioned some talk of public works and centralized employment services, but the rapid recovery quickly stifled such notions. Likewise, when Paul H. Douglas, the University of Chicago economist and future U.S. senator, published his *Wages and the Family* in 1925, his suggestion that America attempt a program providing something similar to the family allowances already widely prevalent in Europe aroused little interest.[7] In many instances, proposals for social security legislation of any sort brought expressions of horror. A Massachusetts study branded ideas for old-age pensions as a "counsel of despair" and said that "if such a scheme be defensible or excusable in this country, then the whole economic and social system is a failure."[8]

Regardless of the prevailing apathy, a few faint sparks of sentiment favoring social reform remained, even in the 1920s. The Fraternal Order of Eagles and the AALL jointly proposed that states adopt old-age pension plans, and they drafted a model bill for state legislatures to consider.[9] Paul Douglas wrote that there were "certain undercurrents of public opinion which were beginning to change on the subject of old-age pensions" even before the Great Depression. He noted that eight states—Colorado, Kentucky, Maryland, Montana, Minnesota, Nevada, Utah, and Wisconsin—had passed acts enabling counties to set programs and that Wisconsin and Minnesota even provided aid to those counties that did so. In 1929, California and Wisconsin became the first states to adopt mandatory acts. New York and Massachusetts followed in 1930. Colorado (replacing the previous act), Delaware, Idaho, New Jersey, and New Hampshire followed in 1931, to be joined in 1933 by Arizona, Indiana, Maine, Michigan, Nebraska, North Dakota, Ohio, Oregon, Pennsylvania, and Washington. By the middle of 1934, twenty-eight states, plus the territories of Alaska and Hawaii, had passed old-age pension acts, all but five of them mandatory.[10] These acts had passed despite continued distaste for governmental activity because the situation had become so grave that the legislatures recognized the reality of the need and concluded that something had to be done.

Although there were no national statistics, and few local governments maintained accurate or adequate information, danger signals existed in the 1920s. Some observers recognized them. Settlement workers especially were likely to sense something amiss. Residents at the Chicago Commons, for example, in 1928 began to report increasing unemployment. Similar reports came from other settlements. Rubinow noted in 1926 that, despite rising wages, there was a rising social service caseload occasioned by increasing unemployment. He called for social workers to turn from their preoccupation with "bad physical heredity, inadequate personality, lack of initiative, psychoses and neuroses, and constitutional inferiority . . . and take up the cause of social insurance." Few paid heed.[11]

One who did was Abraham Epstein, the research director for the Pennsylvania Old-Age Pension Commission.[12] In 1927, he was instrumental in forming a new organization, the American Association for Old-Age Security. Through his lobbying activities and publications, Epstein soon joined Douglas and Rubinow as the most prominent advocates of social insurance in the United States. In 1928, the same year that *Harper's Magazine* rejected one of his articles because the editors sensed in it a "Bolshevik air," Epstein began to notice somewhat more enthusiasm. Not only were more counties adopting pension programs, but his audiences were beginning to increase. In 1931, at the height of the misery of the Great Depression, his organization was suddenly influential.[13] In 1933, he changed its name to the American Association for Social Security to reflect the group's broadened interest.

Early in the 1930s, three books added considerable impetus to the social insurance movement: Paul Douglas's *The Problem of Unemployment* (1931), Epstein's *Insecurity: A Challenge to America* (1933; revised 1936), and Rubinow's *The Quest for Security* (1934). Epstein writes of social insurance as carrying the principle of private insurance "to its logical limit."[14] Rubinow's *Quest* extends his 1913 work, *Social Insurance*, the first comprehensive treatment of the subject in the United States. *Quest* deals with what Rubinow saw as the confused, illogical state of mind of most Americans on the subject of "relief" (now we can substitute the word "welfare"). He asks why accepting assistance should be considered a disgrace when no one minds taking advantage of free concerts, regardless of whether some patron of the arts finances them or the city—which is government.

He writes that social workers who administered relief occasionally saw clients who possessed such pride that they refused material assistance. In such situations, he notes, the social workers used strong arguments to break down the client's "dignity" (for example, why should your family suffer because of your pride?) but secretly admired it. He cites studies showing that a "respectable non-pauperized family" typically endured from six to eight months of unemployment before applying for relief of any sort.[15]

Despite complaints in recent years about a "welfare culture," much of this sentiment remains among the needy. Many potential welfare recipients have refused to apply for benefits from means-tested programs. This point shows clearly through Martha Derthick's cautious language, for example, when she writes that analyses of Supplemental Security Income (SSI), a means-tested program for the poor, "in operation have consistently estimated the rate of participation among the elderly at 50–60 percent of those who are eligible. It seems possible that many of the aged, at least, continue to be deterred by the stigma attached to means-tested assistance."[16]

Fortunately, there is no stigma attached to Social Security because the public perceives its benefits as earned. It also reduces the need for other forms of assistance. The Social Security system was a response to the need for government action in a society that remained suspicious of government, and its designers crafted it to preserve individual dignity.

No such concern for individual dignity motivated President Bush's suggestion that benefits be curtailed for all but the poor. Converting Social Security into the equivalent of a welfare program would destroy it. This quite likely was Bush's intention.

The story of this chapter culminates in the legislation that brought forth the Social Security program that we all know. In the next chapter, we turn to that legislation, the Social Security Act of 1935.

NOTES

1. Available at the Social Security Administration's website, www.ssa.gov/history/paine4.html (accessed April 17, 2005).

2. See Karl Mannheim, preface to *Diagnosis of Our Time* (New York: Oxford University Press, 1944), vii; for a more nuanced approach, see Theda Skocpol, *Protecting Soldiers and Mothers* (Boston: Belknap Press, 1995).

3. See Clarke Chambers, *Seedtime of Reform* (Minneapolis: University of Minnesota Press, 1963), 3–11.

4. I. M. Rubinow, *Social Insurance* (New York: Henry Holt, 1913), 6.

5. Chambers, *Seedtime of Reform*, 89.

6. See Odin W. Anderson, "Compulsory Medical Care Insurance, 1910–1950," *Annals of the American Academy of Political and Social Science* 273 (January 1951), 106–13.

7. Chambers, *Seedtime of Reform*, 158.

8. John D. Hicks, *Republican Ascendancy* (New York: Harper and Row, 1960), 73.

9. Irving Bernstein, *The Lean Years: A History of the American Worker, 1920–1933* (Boston: Houghton Mifflin, 1960), 237.

10. Paul Douglas, *Social Security in the United States* (New York: McGraw-Hill, 1939), 5–7.

11. For an extensive discussion of the danger signals apparent in the 1920s, see Chambers, *Seedtime of Reform*, 93–180.

12. See Pierre Epstein, *Abraham Epstein: The Forgotten Father of Social Security* (Columbia: University of Missouri Press, 2006).

13. Bernstein, *The Lean Years*, 475.

14. Abraham Epstein, *Insecurity: A Challenge to America*, rev. ed. (New York: Harrison Smith and Robert Haas, 1936), 22–23.

15. I. M. Rubinow, *The Quest for Security* (New York: Henry Holt, 1934), 520–21.

16. Martha Derthick, *Agency under Stress* (Washington, DC: Brookings Institution, 1990), 212n4.

4

Franklin D. Roosevelt's Plan and Its Enemies Emerge

All hesitation about social insurance ended when Franklin D. Roosevelt became president in March 1933. FDR, a distant cousin of Theodore Roosevelt, had always looked up to his predecessor. Although TR was a Republican and FDR a Democrat, much in FDR's New Deal built on the groundwork TR laid down during the Progressive Era, both during his time as president and subsequently. The platform of TR's Bull Moose campaign of 1912, when he attempted unsuccessfully to regain the presidency, proposed a comprehensive system of social insurance (see chapter 3).

Franklin Roosevelt came into office promising the American people a "New Deal." Two of his New Deal's most influential federal officials in attempting to provide social security were federal emergency relief administrator Harry Hopkins and Secretary of Labor Frances Perkins, the first woman ever to hold a position in the cabinet. Both had long experience in social-reform movements, the settlement houses, and the field of social work. Perkins had been with Jane Addams at Hull-House and had studied economics under Simon Patton (the progressive economist at the University of Pennsylvania known as an advocate of government economic planning). She had been executive secretary of the Consumers' League in New York and had long been within the inner circle of the social work profession.[1] She had also traveled to England in 1931 at Roosevelt's request when he was governor of New York to study the British system of unemployment insurance.[2] Hopkins had worked at Christodora House, a settlement in New York, and was a past president of the American Association of Social Workers.[3]

On June 29, 1934, the president issued Executive Order 6757 creating the Committee on Economic Security; its members were the secretary of the treasury, the attorney general, the secretary of agriculture, and the federal emergency relief administrator. In addition, the secretary of labor served as chair. The previous day, the attorney general had ruled that the National Industrial Recovery Act had empowered the president to create such a committee. The committee's report, dated January 15, 1935, contained the outline of what was to become the Social Security system. The report incorporated some of the principles of private insurance, or an "insurance-company model," into the provisions for old-age benefits.

Representatives David J. Lewis (D-MD) and Robert L. Doughton (D-NC) introduced the committee's recommendations into the House; Senator Robert F. Wagner (D-NY) introduced them into the Senate. Although Representative Doughton, who chaired the powerful Ways and Means Committee, had not previously been noted for support of social insurance, his own bill (HR 4120) took precedence in the House. At that stage, it was called the Economic Security Bill.

The Ways and Means Committee, however, rewrote it extensively and substituted its own bill (HR 7260). Thereafter, the measure was referred to as the Social Security Bill. It was this bill that the House passed and sent to the Senate. There, it went to the Finance Committee, which reported it, and not the Wagner bill, to the full Senate for passage.[4]

The example of the private insurance company was certainly not the only argument that the proponents of the Social Security Bill used to garner support, and that argument applied to only one of the bill's benefits. Even so, it was among the supporters' most forceful arguments and seemed to have the greatest appeal to the public. The idea of incorporating the principles of private insurance, such as "premiums," certain provisions of individual equity, and the like, into a social insurance system was not unique to the United States, but these principles were so in keeping with American experience and preferences that apparently no one even seriously proposed an alternative to the insurance-company model.

That model, of course, applied only to the general program, the one for old-age benefits. The notion of insurance did not apply to benefits limited to special categories (such as aid to the blind or aid to dependent children) or to those that involved means tests. A program applicable to the general population, however, seemed to require rationalization: "old age" in this sense is not a special category since, in general, the entire population can anticipate becoming elderly.

Members of Congress seemed to be even more insistent upon the insurance-company model for this program than were the original planners. Both the administration and the Congress were anxious to avoid contributions to old-age benefits from general revenues, as the original draft had contemplated. Accordingly, the tax rates that they finally approved to finance the program were higher than those recommended in the report of the Committee on Economic Security.[5]

Many prominent members of both parties supported the Social Security Act or similar programs, but the Republicans as a group tended to be more reluctant to support such an innovative measure. The final vote in the House was 372 in favor (288 Democrats, 77 Republicans, 6 Progressives, and 1 Farmer-Laborite) to 33 opposed (13 Democrats, 18 Republicans, and 2 Farmer-Laborites). In the Senate, the final vote was 77 in favor (60 Democrats, 15 Republicans, 1 Progressive, and 1 Farmer-Laborite) to 6 opposed (1 Democrat and 5 Republicans), but the Republicans just prior to the final tally voted 12 to 8 to eliminate old-age insurance.[6]

President Franklin D. Roosevelt signed the act into law on August 14, 1935. Payroll taxes began in 1937. That same year, the Supreme Court approved the Social Security Act and declared it to be constitutional.

The act originally provided for administration by a Social Security Board, which began operation in 1936. Later, during the administration of Harry S. Truman, the Social Security Administration (SSA) replaced the board and became part of a newly created Federal Security Agency (FSA). During the subsequent administration of Dwight D. Eisenhower, the FSA achieved cabinet status, becoming the new Department of Health, Education, and Welfare (DHEW). Under President Jimmy Carter, that huge department split into two separate cabinet agencies; with the creation of the Department of Education, the old DHEW became the Department of Health and Human Services (which included the SSA). Because of its enormous size, in August 1994 under President Bill Clinton, the SSA came full circle and once again became an independent agency, reporting directly to the president.

The contributory program of old-age insurance was purely federal, and it has remained so. The original act also established other kinds of protections besides old-age insurance; these generally involve federal-state cooperation. Among its innovations were unemployment benefits and various other federal-state programs to aid specific groups.

Under the original act, for example, the old-age assistance provision made possible pensions for the elderly poor. This provision has been expanded into Supplemental Security Income (SSI), a means-tested program. Assistance to poor children took the form of Aid to Dependent Children, also means-tested, which became Aid to Families with Dependent Children. This program was vastly curtailed under the Clinton administration, becoming Temporary Assistance to Needy Families. Critics argue that it has been virtually eliminated. Responding to public outrage regarding "welfare," President Clinton worked closely with a Republican Congress to tighten requirements for benefits and to make them available only for a restricted period to any person during that person's entire lifetime.

Other sections of the Social Security Act set up grants to the states to assist in providing services for the blind or disabled, for vocational rehabilitation, and for public health services. The tendency of the public, of course, is to think only of old-age insurance, the contributory federal program, when thinking of "Social Security." The better informed may also include survivors and disability insurance, along with Medicare (all these were later additions to the original act, all are contributory, and all are purely federal). "Social Security," at least in popular usage, never includes a means-tested program (such as SSI) or one that is not contributory social insurance.

THE REACTION: POLITICS, PARTIES, AND THE PUBLIC

The results of the 1936 elections returning Franklin D. Roosevelt to power were devastating to the Republican Party. FDR remains one of only four presidents in U.S. history to attain 60 percent of the popular vote. Warren G. Harding in 1920, Lyndon B. Johnson in 1964, and Richard M. Nixon in 1972 were the others (Johnson is the only president ever to achieve 61 percent). That a total of 60 percent or less constitutes a huge landslide in presidential politics is an indication of how broad the split in American political opinion is. To be sure, there tends to be an American consensus on many fundamentals of the political system—one probably as great as in any Western democracy. Nevertheless, there is sharp disagreement on ways in which to implement those fundamentals, as the continuing debate over Social Security illustrates. Even when a major party goes down to a crushing defeat, as the Republicans did in 1936, it remains a large minority and one that commands a considerable following.

The party platforms for that year are illuminating. As was to have been expected, the Social Security Act was a major subject of debate in the campaign. Various minor parities called for additional programs to assist those in need.

The Prohibition Party claimed in its platform that it had been the first party to endorse the idea of old-age pensions, and it called for additional governmental aid to the elderly and the disabled.[7] Father Charles Coughlin, a Roman Catholic priest and early radio demagogue noted for his anti-Semitic diatribes, had established his Union Party, which also called for security for the aged. His platform said that they had been "victimized and exploited by an unjust economic system which has so concentrated wealth in the hands of a few that it has impoverished great masses of our people." The Socialist Party called for immediate appropriation of $6 billion—at the time, an almost unheard of amount—for relief to the unemployed for the coming year. To this, they added a call for unemployment insurance, old-age pensions for all over sixty (to be financed through income and inheritance taxes as in the Frazier-Lundeen Bill), and health care for all to be provided "as a social duty, not as a private or public charity." The platform of the Communist Party contained an entire section entitled "Provide Unemployment Insurance, Old Age Pensions, and Social Security for All." The Communists defined social security in a broad sense, advocating the addition of health and maternity benefits. The Democrats, of course, boasted of the Social Security Act. They described in glowing terms the measures that it provided and pledged to use it as a base to erect a "structure of economic security" for everyone.

The official platform of the Republican Party, on the other hand, declared that real security would be possible only when the country's productive capacity was sufficient to provide it. To attain that goal, it said, Republicans looked "to the energy, self-reliance and character" of the people and to the system of free enterprise. Following this, however, their platform proposed a system for old-age security based upon four parts: first, a pay-as-you-go system requiring each generation to support the aged and to determine "what is just and adequate"; second, a supplementary payment sufficient to provide income large enough to protect all American citizens over sixty-five from want; third, graduated payments to states and territories for cooperative financing of security programs that have met "simple and general minimum standards"; and fourth, "a direct tax widely distributed" to finance the federal part of the program. They would require contributions from all since all would be benefited. The Republicans said the system under the Social Security Act would be too complicated to administer and charged that the tax burden would be too great. Moreover, they said, the program would benefit too few people.[8] Many supporters of social insurance who had hoped for something more extensive than the Social Security Act greeted the Republican proposals warmly. An editorial in *The Nation* of June 24, 1936, for example, said that although "a direct tax widely distributed" sounded suspiciously as if it meant a sales tax, the social security plank of the Republican platform was better than the plans of the Democrats because it called for revenue to support the program to be derived from general taxation. (It is ironic to contrast the Republican position then with that of today, which assumes that everything necessary for whatever purpose can be accomplished with no tax increase, or even by reducing taxes!)

Evelyn M. Burns, then a prominent economist at Columbia University and vice president of the American Association for Social Welfare, replied with a letter to the editor that cut through the misunderstandings and fuzzy conclusions that so often mark comments on Social Security. She was "very surprised" when she read the editorial, her letter of July 11 said, because the Republican platform did not provide at all for social insurance as the phrase was generally understood. She pointed out that the platform did not mention benefits as a matter of right, only on the basis of need.

Much rhetoric on Social Security since around 1980 is phrased subtly to give the impression that it supports the system but nevertheless remains based on the same idea that Burns criticizes in her letter. The proposals by

Peter Peterson and the Concord Coalition are the most widely publicized examples. They would "strengthen" Social Security by what Peterson calls "affluence testing," which would deny benefits to all but the needy while still requiring all workers to pay into the system. Even more pernicious because of their source are the suggestions in 2005 by President George W. Bush, who would index the benefit formula in a way that would convert what now is a social insurance system into one limiting any significant benefit payment to those who "need" it, thus converting the program into a welfare system solely for the poor.

Burns agreed that means-tested programs had a place in a broad social security scheme but believed that they were "complementary." Such provisions had already been established by the Social Security Act as old-age assistance. She added that the Social Security plan, regardless of the merits of its financing, at least gave something in return to the contributor. The Republican plan, she said, would tax everyone but pay benefits only to those who subjected themselves to a means test. Further, as a cooperative program with the states, it would provide no benefits at all in states that did not elect to participate.

The editors retreated hastily. They had not meant to contrast the "illiberal Republican plank with the Social Security Act," they said, "but with the party's complete silence on the subject in 1932." They agreed with Burns's statements, they said, and had written their editorial "largely because of the reactionary nature of the platform as a whole." As is often the case, the liberal tendency to attempt to be "objective" and to be fair to the opposition led them to undermine their own case. Their explanation was not only lame but inaccurate. Moreover, they could as easily have contrasted the 1936 Democratic platform with that of 1932, which had also remained silent on the subject. The only parties that had specifically advocated social insurance in their 1932 platforms had been the Socialist and Farmer-Labor parties. Each had supported social insurance for many years, the Farmer-Labor Party since 1920 and the Socialists in every presidential election since 1900.

The closest the idea had come to acceptance by a major party before Franklin D. Roosevelt was the inclusion mentioned above in Theodore Roosevelt's 1912 Bull Moose campaign. Neither Republicans nor Democrats had dealt with it in their platforms until 1936, a year after passage of the Social Security Act. The only earlier mention of a related subject by the Democrats appears to have been in their platform of 1916, which supported a law providing for "the retirement of superannuated and disabled civil servants" so that a "higher standard of efficiency may be maintained."

The Republicans' record was similar. Their only mention of a related subject before 1936 seems to have been in their 1924 platform, which called for the creation of a cabinet post of education and relief to coordinate the various departments administering the federal government's "numerous and important" welfare activities. This proposal is ironic in view of the calls by Ronald Reagan—and many other Republicans for a time after his presidency—to eliminate the Department of Education.

There was nothing ambivalent about the public reaction, which was enthusiastic about the program. So great was the public enthusiasm that it invested Social Security with an effective shield against most criticism from elected officials. That shield made certain that Republicans as well as Democrats would officially accept Social Security's general principle that the welfare of the people was a legitimate concern of government and that government had an obligation to assist in ensuring that welfare. Official Republican criticism of the Social Security Act did not extend to criticism of the principles of Social Security.

Their 1936 presidential candidate, Governor Alf Landon of Kansas, remarked in a radio address on May 7, "I'm for it. Every big industrial nation has had to move in that direction. In America we could once handle the problem pretty well by depending on individual thrift, family aid, local taxation and private contributions. These still have their place and a vital place it is." He also mentioned the pension systems of some of the more progressive business concerns but said it then had become necessary for the government "to take a hand." Reversing cause and effect, he maintained that while the administration's program did increase public attention to the problem (as though the public had not known of the problems people were facing), it was "complicated legislation the Administration rushed through in characteristic fashion."[9]

The recognition of Social Security's popularity dampened criticism from politicians, but it did not completely protect the system from attack. The first concerted effort came in the form of notices that many employers nationwide included in their employees' pay envelopes. During the 1936 campaign, workers throughout the country discovered printed notices with their pay charging that Social Security was nothing but a scheme to raise taxes. The notices typically failed to mention that the program involved benefits or that the employer was to pay half the tax. Joseph P. Kennedy, who then headed the Securities and Exchange Commission—and who was certainly anything but a radical—said that the pay-envelope campaign was grossly unfair and false and that it attempted to "create the impression that giving old age insurance at half-price to the worker is an unfair tax on the worker."[10]

President Roosevelt gave an address in Madison Square Garden on October 31 in which he attacked employers engaging in the pay-envelope campaign, calling them deceitful for neglecting to tell the complete story. He charged that they were attempting to mislead their workers into voting against him. Social Security provided two "policies," he said, unemployment insurance to be paid for by the employer and the old-age program

paid for jointly by the employer and the employee. On the second of November, an editorial in the *New York Herald Tribune* called the president's
speech "bitter and defiant."

Sociologists who at the time were studying Muncie, Indiana, found that
"Landon and higher wages" was the theme of the attack there.[11] Pay envelopes from Muncie factories included stuffers critical of New Deal programs. They emphasized the deductions from workers' pay and charged
that Social Security would make raises impossible. They did not mention
benefits but did charge that the system would soon collapse.

Some of the most strident criticism of Roosevelt and the New Deal came
from the Hearst newspapers. Discussing Landon's views on social insurance, for example, an editorial in late May said,

> He is careful to imply that it . . . must be along AMERICAN lines, and not be a
> detail in a general scheme such as this Administration has put forth, to reduce
> millions of Americans to the condition of STATE PARASITES. In fact, one great
> fault of Mr. Roosevelt is that he has, by his extreme and extravagant methods,
> discredited all progressive ideas. Governor Landon, however, indicates that no
> social security legislation based on COLLECTIVIST DELUSIONS or that is
> plainly UNCONSTITUTIONAL will receive his assent.[12]

In a speech in Syracuse, New York, in September 1936, the president defended the Social Security Act against such attacks and denied that it was
"radical and alien."[13] All the while, Governor Landon was working to bring
his state under the provisions of the act. He called the Kansas legislature
into a special session on July 7, 1936, to begin work on an amendment to
the state's constitution that would permit it to participate.

The most severe criticisms came from groups with special interests. Henry
Ford issued a statement during the campaign that was typical of much of
this criticism: "Under some social security systems abroad a man cannot
quit his job, or apply for another, or leave town and go to another even to
get a better job because that would break the 'economic plan.' Such a re-
striction of liberty will be almost a necessity in this country too if the present Social Security Act works to its natural conclusions."[14] At the same time,
the U.S. Chamber of Commerce took a somewhat more moderate view-
point and expressed it in a "Statement of Principles" said to represent the
opinions of its fourteen hundred member organizations, including some
seven hundred thousand individual members. Of Social Security, the chamber said,

> Business would ignore its gravest responsibility if it failed to provide the great-
> est possible degree of economic security to the individual. The attainment of
> this end so necessary to the furtherance of American ideals will require not
> only the maintenance of high wages but likewise a constructive solution to the

complex problem of security to the individual when he or she has outlived capacity to earn a comfortable living. Here again interference by government in attempts to reduce the whole complex problem to one of legislative formulae can only postpone the final solution by making it more difficult for business to assume its own obligations in the matter.[15]

Some three years after FDR's landslide victory, Professor Raymond Pearl of Johns Hopkins University, then president of the American Statistical Association, made some remarks that should still give us food for thought. They illustrate that the opposition had not been extinguished, but more important they reveal just how extreme was some of the criticism. Pearl, who was himself sixty years of age at the time, suggested that, by their advocacy of old-age pension "nostrums," the aged might be proving themselves too foolish to be allowed the privilege of voting. He said that the elderly, together with the young, "are ganging up on the half of the population that does the work." The demands of the young had decreased somewhat, he conceded, but the increase in the proportion of persons who have "finished whatever biological justification there ever was for existence" constituted a social problem of the first magnitude.[16]

Most comments of this kind since then have employed somewhat more tactful phrasing, but it would be a grave mistake to conclude that such attitudes no longer exist. More than hints of them appear in the comments of some of the more candid opponents of social welfare when they discuss the baby boomers and issue their dire forecasts for Social Security, especially if the discussions are off the record. Such expression since the turn of the century, in fact, again has become brazen, as a rather brief exposure to AM talk radio will verify.

Several commentators in the early years did praise the purposes of the Social Security Act, even while criticizing its provisions. An editorial in *Collier's* said that "few have quarreled with the broad purposes underlying the Social Security Act. On the other hand, many of the most experienced and sincere advocates of social insurance are aghast at some of the provisions."[17] *Collier's* neither identified these "experienced and sincere advocates" nor specified which of the act's provisions so perturbed its editor. The chairman of the board of Chase National Bank, Winthrop W. Aldrich, echoed the sentiments in *Collier's*. Many people were sympathetic to Social Security's intent, he said, but its form created a "grave menace to the future security of the very people it is designed to protect."[18]

Opposition was not limited to words: there were lawsuits as well. For example, a stockholder in the Union Elastic Company of Easthampton, New York, Dean A. Fales, filed a suit asking the court to declare the Social Security Act void. He believed that it would reduce the value of his shares and constituted an illegal seizure of property.[19]

The pervasive criticism died quickly because of its futility; the public obviously supported Social Security strongly. Public-opinion polling was in its infancy, but early polls were unanimous in identifying powerful public support for the program. Paul Douglas marveled at the abrupt change. Before the Great Depression, he wrote, public opinion held overwhelmingly that "American citizens could in the main provide for their old age by individual savings."[20] In a series of Gallup polls taken from December 1935 to November 1939, the American Institute of Public Opinion revealed that no fewer than 89 percent of those interviewed said that they were in favor of "government old age pensions for needy persons," and 91 percent indicated approval in the July 1941 poll that even deleted the phrase "for needy persons."[21]

One of the gravest concerns that those fearing the effects of Social Security expressed had to do with the assignment of identification numbers. The Social Security Act emerged when the threat of totalitarian systems was concrete and immediate, not merely potential. Some critics were terrified that the Social Security number would become the identifier that permitted government to keep track of each citizen and delve deeply into his or her private life. In response, Social Security officials assured the public that they would maintain vigilance against the misuse of the numbers. For the most part, they restricted their use completely to the purposes of the Social Security system. Even after President Roosevelt's Executive Order 9397 in 1943 ordered all agencies of the federal government to use the Social Security number when creating new identification systems for people, Social Security's administrators continued to work diligently to demonstrate that the early fears had been groundless.

In the 1950s, whenever other government agencies sought to use Social Security records for law-enforcement purposes—perhaps to trace someone—the Social Security Administration adamantly refused. It continued to hold its files confidential. SSA folklore had it that occasionally the agency would discover and discharge an infiltrator, a government agent perhaps from the Federal Bureau of Investigation, who had gained employment undercover to work in its files. A breach occurred in 1975 when legislation permitted the use of Social Security records to help locate absent fathers who were not paying child support as ordered to children who were receiving welfare payments. The justification was that such use of the records was for Social Security purposes because payments to dependent children and their families came under a program that the Social Security Act created.

The barrier had already begun to crumble in 1961, when the Civil Service Commission adopted the Social Security number as the official federal employee identifier, and legislation required each taxpayer to report his or her number on tax returns. The Internal Revenue Service the following year converted it into a federal identification number to be used on tax returns and other records. In 1967, the Department of Defense substituted the Social

Security number for the former service numbers as personal identifiers of military personnel. In 1970, legislation required banks and other financial institutions to obtain the Social Security numbers of all customers and to report by the number any transaction exceeding $10,000.

Now, the use of the number is virtually universal and ties together a vast array of information having nothing to do with Social Security. Tax returns, records regarding health, banking, driver's licenses, military records, pilot's licenses, and almost every conceivable kind of data—public and private, local, state, and national—that can be recorded can now be uncovered through the use of what was previously the sacrosanct Social Security number. All the while, legislation continues to proclaim that there is to be no "universal identification number" in the United States.

Perhaps not, but the early critics were at least close to correct in their predictions that the numbers would become all-purpose identifiers, despite the assurances of supporters that this would not happen. Happily, though, the critics' worst fears have not been realized. For a variety of reasons, including some protective legislation, the data-driven police state that they assumed would follow has not materialized—at least not yet. Pressures since 9-11 are making it more difficult to maintain a realm of privacy free from government intrusion, and the pressures have greatly increased the government's powers. Vigilance will be necessary to retain freedom at home while the president asserts that America is spreading freedom abroad.

There is little controversy regarding the Social Security number any longer. The world is so dominated by records and files that we have come to accept as necessary some form of identifier, and that number is as good as any other for the purpose. The enormous good that Social Security accomplishes overshadows concerns about its records, as does the fact that other agencies now hold far more extensive records on us all.

Far from engendering the intergenerational conflict that some of its opponents allege, Social Security is one program that binds Americans together, regardless of generation. It benefits all. It also ensures that all contribute to their country's well-being.

The next chapter examines how Social Security has expanded over the years, how the emphasis of the program has shifted, and how, despite fierce opposition, Medicare came to be.

NOTES

1. Arthur M. Schlesinger Jr., *The Age of Roosevelt: The Coming of the New Deal* (Boston: Houghton Mifflin, 1959), 298.

2. Irving Bernstein, *The Lean Years: A History of the American Worker, 1920–1933* (Boston: Houghton Mifflin, 1960), 475.

3. Ralph E. Pumphrey and Muriel W. Pumphrey, eds., *The Heritage of American Social Work* (New York: Columbia University Press, 1961), 439n.

4. For an excellent history of the Social Security Act, see Paul Douglas, *Social Security in the United States* (New York: McGraw-Hill, 1939), ch. 4.

5. Committee on Economic Security, *Social Security in America: The Background of the Social Security Act as Summarized from Staff Reports to the Committee on Economic Security* (Washington, DC: Government Printing Office, 1937), 212–13.

6. Max J. Skidmore, *Medicare and the American Rhetoric of Reconciliation* (Tuscaloosa: University of Alabama Press, 1970), 60 (now available online from Questia Media); voting figures are from *Congressional Record*, 74th Cong., 1st sess., 9648–50 and 6069–70.

7. The next few paragraphs rely heavily on Skidmore, *Medicare*, 52–64.

8. For complete party platforms for 1936 and for the following two decades, see Kirk Porter and Donald Johnson, *National Party Platforms, 1840–1956* (Urbana: University of Illinois Press, 1956); the American Presidency Project has made Democratic and Republican Party platforms from the mid-nineteenth century through 2004 available at www.presidency.ucsb.edu/platforms.php. This site contains some minor party platforms as well.

9. "New Deal Blocking Jobs, Says Landon," *New York Times*, May 8, 1936.

10. "Scores Republicans on Security Attacks," *New York Times*, November 1, 1936.

11. Robert Lynd and Helen Lynd, *Middletown in Transition* (New York: Harcourt, Brace, and World, 1937), 361.

12. *Washington Herald*, May 28, 1936.

13. *New York Herald Tribune*, September 29, 1936.

14. Henry Ford, *New York Herald Tribune*, November 2, 1936.

15. "Issues, Principles, to Guide Business," *New York Times*, August 30, 1936.

16. See Laurence E. Davies, "Burden on Earner Held Lower Now," *New York Times*, December 30, 1939.

17. Editorial, *Collier's*, November 28, 1936, 66.

18. See "Aldrich Assails Profit Tax Bill," *New York Times*, May 8, 1936.

19. Asks Security Act to Be Voided by Court, Stockholder in Boston Suit Says It and State Jobless Law 'Seize Property,'" *New York Times*, May 8, 1936.

20. Douglas, *Social Security in the United States*, 1.

21. Hadley Cantril, ed., *Public Opinion, 1935–1946* (Princeton, NJ: Princeton University Press, 1951), 541.

5

From Miss Fuller's First Check

The original Social Security Act of 1935 provided for a rebate to those who had paid taxes but did not qualify for benefits. The act did not provide for initial benefits to begin until January 1, 1942, but amendments in 1939 revised the benefit formula and changed the date of first benefit payments to January 31, 1940. The first check was for $22.54, and it went to a retired legal secretary from Vermont, Ida Mae Fuller. She never married and lived for another thirty-five years, dying at the age of one hundred.

The original provisions, designed for strict individual equity, were never in force for beneficiaries. The 1939 amendments added benefits for the wives and minor children of retired workers, as well as for the widows and surviving children of those who were deceased. They thus incorporated an emphasis upon the family. (As a result of the 1977 *Califano v. Goldfarb* decision, husbands and widowers became eligible for benefits on the same basis as wives and widows.) This family emphasis, coupled with the elimination of the rebate, greatly weakened the principle of individual equity. From that point on, married workers, especially those with children, have received much more for their contributions than have childless or unmarried workers. The 1939 amendments also added an advantage for low-income and short-term workers.

The legislation was a striking departure from tradition for Americans, but it provided considerably less than many programs elsewhere. Germany, for example, the country that had pioneered social insurance in the 1880s, had expanded its system to cover the disabled some two decades before America's Social Security Act. Although the American program has grown steadily both in terms of the number of people covered and the range of benefits offered, it continues to lag behind those in most other industrial countries, all of which also include universal comprehensive health coverage.

The first expansion following the great revisions of 1939 came with the 1950 amendments, which added coverage for the self-employed (farmers and certain professionals, such as ministers and physicians, remained uncovered). Domestic and farm workers also came under coverage. The amendments also raised the tax rate to 1.5 percent and increased the taxable wage base to $3,600. Amendments in 1952 brought self-employed farmers under coverage and provided voluntary coverage to ministers and certain other professionals.

In 1956, during the administration of Dwight D. Eisenhower, Congress added a huge benefit, coverage for disability. The legislation also made provisions for women to retire early, at sixty-two, if they chose to do so with reduced benefits. The same amendments brought coverage to self-employed dentists, lawyers, optometrists, osteopathic physicians, and veterinarians. In 1958, Congress again increased benefits, raising the taxable wage base to $4,800, and included benefits for eligible dependents of disability beneficiaries. As of 1959, the tax rate went up to 2.5 percent. Originally, disability benefits were available only to those aged fifty or older. In 1960, amendments removed the age restriction. In 1961, men became eligible to retire early at sixty-two, along with women. Beginning in 1962, the tax again increased, this time to 3.125 percent.

The largest addition of benefits came during the administration of Lyndon B. Johnson in 1965 with the addition of Medicare. It was a long and difficult battle. Congress approved the program only after years of acrimonious controversy, with the American Medical Association (AMA) being the most vigorous and bitter opponent. Branding Medicare with the completely inaccurate label of "socialized medicine," the AMA succeeded in delaying the program for decades. The long postponement led increasing numbers of the elderly to go without necessary care, to obtain care only by sacrificing self-respect and seeking charity, or to fall victim to crushing bills that they could not pay.

As early as 1920, the governing body of the American Medical Association, its House of Delegates, met to solidify its strenuous opposition to government assistance in meeting citizens' health expenses. The following resolution was the result of this New Orleans meeting: "*Resolved,* that the American Medical Association declares its opposition to the institution of any plan embodying the system of compulsory contributory insurance against illness, or any other plan of compulsory insurance which provides for medical service to be rendered contributors or their dependents, provided, controlled or regulated by any state or the federal government." The AMA's official history, published in 1947, declared that this resolution was the official policy of the association and had remained so since 1920.[1] Although the association's opposition was strong and consistent and had begun early, the issue in fact lay dormant for another decade after 1920; it did not awaken until the Committee on the Costs of Medical Care released its majority report in 1932. Then, the subject again emerged as a serious political issue, and discussions of social insurance included the possibility that it might be incorporated as part of the system. President Franklin D. Roosevelt decided against proposing health care as a part of Social Security because he feared that organized medicine's powerful opposition might defeat the entire program.

In 1939, Senator Robert F. Wagner of New York introduced a proposal to establish a national health program providing grants to the states, which were to develop health plans conforming to federal standards. There had been several related bills previously, but this was the first to receive serious attention. The subcommittee examining the bill issued a favorable interim report, the AMA produced twenty-two arguments against it, and there was no further action at the time.[2]

The year 1943 saw the introduction of the first of a series of Wagner-Murray-Dingell bills that would have established a national system of hospitals and medical benefits, financed by a payroll tax on employees and employers. It would have provided the patient with free choice of participating physicians and authorized the surgeon general of the Public Health Service to set fee schedules and regulate the number of patients each physician would treat. The reaction from organized medicine was immediate, hostile, and predictable. The National Physicians Committee (NPC) charged that "the processes proposed and the mechanisms indicated are designed to act as the catalyst in transforming a rapidly expanding Federal bureaucracy into an all powerful totalitarian state control. Human rights as opposed to slavery is the issue."[3] The bill died in committee.

A similar fate lay in store for the second Wagner-Murray-Dingell bill in 1945, even though it had strong support from the administration of Harry S. Truman. The Republican Eightieth Congress considered a revised Wagner-Murray-Dingell bill in 1947. Both this and the 1945 version provided for state administration of a federal program. Both failed.

The last major Truman administration health bill was that of 1949. This bill, similar to the Wagner-Murray-Dingell Bill of 1947, was based upon the Federal Security Agency's report to the president, *The Nation's Health: A Ten-Year Program*, by Oscar Ewing. During the 1948 campaign, the president had strongly urged the adoption of the principles of the Ewing report. Truman's election victory heightened anxiety for many members of the AMA. There had also been Republican alternatives to the Wagner-Murray-Dingell proposals. Senator Robert A. Taft of Ohio had sponsored a series of bills in 1946, 1947, and 1949 calling for state-operated programs of aid to those unable to pay for health care. The AMA did not attack Taft's proposals but failed to support them because of concerns about lay administrators at local levels.[4]

When the AMA did employ its propaganda machinery, it did so vigorously. Its advertising tended to link policies it opposed with socialism and communism. It even tried to tie such policies specifically to the Soviet Union. During the 1940s, the association developed a consistent, coherent pattern of strategic attack. From 1939 to 1948, it expressed its opposition through NPC for the Extension of Medical Service, which it apparently brought into existence as a direct response to the Wagner-Murray-Dingell Bill of 1939. Although the AMA denied any connection with the NPC, AMA members headed it, and AMA fund-raising mechanisms supported it. Both the profession and the public considered the NPC to be the official voice of the AMA. Presumably, the rationale for the arrangement was fear that the AMA's charter as a nonprofit organization would prevent it from any extensive, direct lobbying. If AMA activities during subsequent years are any indication, such fears lessened sharply as the years passed. For many of those years, the AMA was among the most active of all lobbying groups and was at or near the top in the amount of spending to influence legislation. During the NPC's existence, however, the association confined its "official" activities of opposition to speeches, editorials, legislative testimony, and resolutions by its House of Delegates.

The NPC worked through physicians' offices to distribute a huge number of pamphlets and other printed material concerning governmental health insurance. By 1948, however, owing to a growing reaction against some of its propaganda tactics and a public distaste for some of the right-wing extremist groups with which it had become associated, the NPC's influence had waned.[5] Even before then, the AMA had taken some steps to cleanse its reputation. In 1946, it hired a special public relations counsel for the purpose. Then, in 1949, Dr. Morris Fishbein, who had been intimately involved in the association's opposition to government health insurance, specifically with much of the extreme language that had characterized the AMA's political activities since the 1930s, retired as editor of the *Journal of the American Medical Association* (*JAMA*). He had received considerable criticism from within the profession as having been largely responsible for much of the tarnish on organized medicine's professional image. Although his successors generally adopted less vitriolic language, any observers who might have hoped for more moderate policies were certainly disappointed.

With Truman's 1948 victory, the AMA began extensive efforts to launch strong and positive programs of opposition to governmental health insurance and to appeal to the citizenry for support. With great haste, the House of Delegates levied an assessment of $25 (then a significant amount) on each member to build a $3.5 million (then an enormous amount) "political war chest to fight socialized medicine." It planned its National Education Campaign, consisting of a barrage of advertisements, to "educate" the American people, and it employed the public relations firm of Whitaker and Baxter to direct the project.

Initially, there was opposition within the association to the assessment, but the National Education Campaign successfully sold the idea to the membership. Virtually all members displayed posters and distributed pamphlets to patients. Physicians and their wives (women physicians were rare in those days) distributed some twenty million pamphlets in the first year. Instructions to wives called for them to "tuck pamphlets into all . . . personal correspondence—even invitations to dinner parties," but to avoid debates (the men in charge no doubt feared that women would be unable to hold their own in a political give-and-take).

Additionally, AMA members decided to take advantage of the doctor-patient relationship. The personal physicians of members of Congress urged their powerfully placed patients to support AMA views. Cooperating with the physicians were (among others) insurance agents and companies, dentists, and pharmacists.

The 1949 campaign, Whitaker and Baxter reported, resulted in the distribution of fifty-five million pieces of literature reaching approximately one hundred million people. Coupled with the attack on governmental programs was a successful effort to promote the sale of commercial health insurance policies under the slogan "The Voluntary Way is the American Way."[6] The success of this effort was a major cause of the inefficiency, waste, and horrendous expense that has come to make America's health-care delivery system unique in the world.

Unquestionably, the techniques of this campaign were new, skillfully applied, and thorough. The major arguments in this and subsequent efforts, though, were not new; they differed little from those that Morris Fishbein had used extensively and elaborated fully during the 1930s. Madison Avenue added the public relations techniques, but the medical profession itself had already refined the arguments.

The 1950 campaign made use of the same techniques that had proven so effective in 1949. In addition, physicians formed political committees in many congressional districts. In Wisconsin, for example, Physicians for Freedom helped defeat Democrat Andrew Biemiller in his bid for reelection to the U.S. House of Representatives. Tactics included posters, advertisements, and campaign literature included with monthly bills to patients. Biemiller was an outspoken advocate of health-care legislation. Similarly, Senator Claude Pepper (D-FL) lost his seat in the U.S. Senate partly as a result of organized medicine's opposition. The actions of a Tallahassee hospital were representative of the campaign: patients there found cards reading "This is the season for canning Pepper" on their food trays.[7] The hospital and the AMA thus reached voters when they were most vulnerable.

In 1952, an organization calling itself the National Professional Committee for Eisenhower and Nixon mailed its political literature from the address of the former National Education Campaign. Although the AMA was officially neutral in the election, the National Professional Committee used letterheads listing former AMA president Elmer L. Henderson as chair and former presidents John Wesley Cline and Ernest F. Irons as vice chairs; it also included the name of the firm of Whitaker and Baxter. A similar organization called Physicians for Stevenson had no AMA officials as sponsors or any other evidence of AMA support.[8] With the election of a Republican administration avowedly hostile to governmental health insurance, which it agreed would have been "socialized medicine," the intensity of the AMA's formal public relations, or propaganda, campaign rapidly dwindled.

The AMA placed its members on the alert again, however, in 1957. Representative Aime Forand, a Rhode Island Democrat, introduced his first Forand bill (HR 9467). Forand's bill would have paid for certain hospital and surgical services for patients who were receiving Social Security benefits, but it made little headway. He reintroduced his bill in 1959 in the Eighty-sixth Congress (HR 4700). The Ways and Means Committee held hearings on Forand bills in 1957, 1958, and 1959 but took no action. On March 31, 1960, the committee finally rejected the plan by a vote of 17 to 8—ironically, the same vote by which it was to approve the Medicare proposal five years later.

In the same year, Democratic senator John F. Kennedy of Massachusetts introduced a bill similar to those that Forand had introduced. After his presidential nomination, Kennedy made his support of the measure a major campaign issue. His bill failed in the Senate by a vote of 55 to 41, defeated by a coalition of Republicans and Southern Democrats. In 1961, the Ways and Means Committee again held hearings in the House and, again, took no action.

AMA opposition to Medicare during the Kennedy administration reached a peak in 1961 in response to the Anderson-King Bill, sponsored by Representative Cecil King from California and Senator Clinton Anderson of New Mexico, both Democrats. This bill would have provided direct payments to hospitals for services rendered to Social Security beneficiaries aged sixty-five and older. Supporters finally succeeded in attaching a modified version of the bill, the Anderson-Javits Amendment (cosponsored by Republican senator Jacob Javits of New York) to a House-approved public welfare bill. Opponents defeated the attempt by tabling the amendment in July 1962. This was the climax of the controversy over Medicare prior to its actual passage three years later in the Eighty-ninth Congress.

The battle had been intense and bitter. Each side took its case to the people by means of virtually every medium of mass communication—newspapers, magazines, radio, and television—and each side sent prominent spokespeople into debate. The AMA found its champion in the person of the chair of its speakers' bureau, Edward Annis, MD. Almost single-handedly, Annis bore the burden of his association's speech making throughout the country. He debated frequently with such proponents of the legislation as union leader Walter Reuther and Minnesota senator Hubert Humphrey, who in 1965 was to become vice president, then in 1968, the Democratic presidential candidate.

Annis also became editor at large of *Medical Economics*, a magazine devoted largely to the business side of medical practice, distributed free of charge to all physicians. In recognition of his service, the AMA elected Annis its president. He was the first in more than forty years who had not previously been a member of the House of Delegates, served on the Board of Trustees, or served on any of the AMA's councils and committees.[9]

He proved to be a clever leader, and the AMA continued to make effective use of public relations specialists. On May 20, 1962, President Kennedy appeared as speaker at a televised rally in Madison Square Garden on behalf of the Anderson-King Bill. His administration scheduled this as one of forty-two meetings across the country to generate support. The AMA thereupon dispatched half of its "task force on the Anderson-King Bill," headed by AMA director of communication Jim Reed, to New York to obtain paid radio-television time for a rebuttal and to handle relations with the press. The other half remained at AMA headquarters in Chicago to keep in touch with the association's executive director and its other key officials.[10]

The night following Kennedy's address, Annis also spoke at Madison Square Garden. This time, though, the Garden was vacant. Recognizing that the AMA could not hope to match the drawing power of the president or generate the same enthusiasm among a crowd, AMA strategists chose the empty seats deliberately as a contrast with the wildly cheering audiences that Kennedy addressed. They presented the AMA as "the little guys."[11] NBC stations throughout the country carried the Annis speech, except for the station in Boston. The Boston channel refused, saying that its policy was to refuse to sell time to organizations to present one side on controversial questions. The AMA immediately accused the station, which had carried Kennedy's speech, of blacking out one side of a controversy in the president's hometown. Both sides thus had been accused of similar practices. The AMA had long had the reputation of refusing to include in its own publications any opinion from a physician that diverged from AMA positions.

Tom Hendricks, assistant to the AMA's executive director, was candid when interviewed about the extent of the publicity campaign against Medicare. He included as a part of that campaign a forthcoming *Reader's Digest* article by Representative Thomas B. Curtis (R-MO), a member of the House Committee on Ways and Means. Curtis strenuously opposed Medicare but denied that he was speaking on behalf of any special interest. Nevertheless, he had coordinated his article in advance with AMA officials.[12]

Major organizations supporting Medicare were Aime Forand's National Council of Senior Citizens for Health Care through Social Security, the American Nurses Association (ANA), the National Association of Social Workers, the American Public Welfare Association, and a number of other social welfare and public health organizations.[13] The ANA reported considerable pressure from physicians to change its stand and charged that many nurses had been forced by their physician employers to resign from the association. The ANA's Washington, D.C., representative, Julia Thompson, testified during the Ways and Means Committee's hearings on the bill that medical societies in no fewer than thirty-five states had sought to pressure nurses' associations in those states to disavow the pro-Anderson-King stance of the national organization.[14]

Among the major organizations opposing the bill were the AMA, almost all insurance companies (with the notable exception of Nationwide Insurance Company, which endorsed the bill strongly), the National Association of Manufacturers, the U.S. Chamber of Commerce, the National Association of Retail Druggists, and most other professional dental and medical organizations. Although officially opposing the bill, the Blue Cross Association and the American Hospital Association were more willing than most opponents to compromise, and they worked rather closely with the administration in preliminary planning for the organization and administration of any proposal that might materialize. Both organizations spent many hours in meeting with federal representatives, who were also permitted to make numerous visits to hospitals and to the administrative headquarters of several local Blue Cross plans.[15]

Much of the controversy revolved around charges designed to arouse emotions that the Anderson-King Bill would create "socialized medicine." A typical example of an AMA leaflet that physicians distributed to their patients was entitled "An Important Message from Your Doctor." It emphasized compulsion and government control and argued that the program would "place a third party—Washington bureaucrats—between the patient and the physician. It would place politics at the bedside of the ill." Not only would the patient's "free choice of hospital and physician" be limited, it warned, but the proposed program "would eliminate the privacy of the patient-physician relationship . . . making it possible for government clerks to examine the most intimate personal health records—records that are now a private matter between patient and physician."

Even in those days, the idea of confidentiality between physician and patient could hardly be taken seriously. There may not have been "government clerks" inserted into the relationship, but there were certainly hospital clerks, insurance-company clerks, physicians' aides, and others. Nevertheless, the leaflet was perhaps more moderate than many. Instead of charging that the Anderson-King Bill would provide socialized medicine, it said merely that it would be "the first step toward socialized medicine in this country . . . a system that has resulted in the deterioration of medical care wherever it has been tried." It described the need to work together to preserve America's high quality of medical care, and it concluded with the words "Let's keep politics out of medicine."

A leaflet entitled "It's *Your* Decision" assured readers that organized medicine did favor "a *voluntary* program." It advocated "voluntary health insurance" and a program to help the elderly poor who could not afford to purchase it. It warned darkly of "socialized medicine" and said, "We are not crying 'wolf' when we apply that term to the Anderson-King Bill," which "would mean socialized health care . . . immediately for all those over 65 eligible for Social Security and eventually for every man, woman, and child in America." It urged patients to write to Congress to oppose the bill.

In New Mexico, the Chaves County Medical Society placed an advertisement in the *Roswell Daily Record* (May 27, 1962), endorsed by the District No. 5 Association of Registered Nurses, the Chaves County Pharmaceutical Association, and the Roswell Dental Society. It asked, "Can governments doctor? President Kennedy and his associates say YES. We, your physicians, say NO. BUT, this is more than a medical issue. It is an issue affecting not only the health of our people, but the economic and political freedom of our country." The ad even cited the statement in the Declaration of Independence that it is the right and duty of the people to throw off a government when that government "evinces a design to reduce them under absolute despotism." There was more than a hint here of right-wing extremism, that adoption of Medicare should cause the people to overthrow the government!

The Roswell advertisement was somewhat more extreme than most, but similar expressions were published widely throughout the United States. These were precursors of the extreme right-wing views that are so much more in evidence today. Some of the material for the ads was purely local, but much built upon models that the AMA supplied. All of the attacks praised American health care as the best in the world, and many of them contrasted it with the "failed socialized health care" elsewhere. There were numerous declarations from local associations and individual practitioners then and after Medicare's passage that they would refuse to treat Medicare patients. Some members even attempted to persuade the AMA to make such a refusal binding upon its membership. The attempts failed, but the AMA did seriously consider the idea.

One of the most interesting features of the campaign for and against the Anderson-King Bill was a phonograph recording, "Ronald Reagan Speaks Out Against Socialized Medicine" (see appendix A). Reagan, then in the fading stages of an acting career prior to his own bid for office, prepared it for the AMA. The record was at the heart of the AMA's "Operation Coffeecup," a brilliant effort to encourage opponents of the Anderson-King Bill to write to senators and representatives urging them to vote against the proposal. The record itself was in the popular format of the time, a 33⅓ rpm disk with graphics of professional quality on the jacket, as though it were a commercial offering.

The letter accompanying the record was dated April 15, 1961. It was addressed to members of "women's auxiliaries of the AMA," that is, to the wives of physicians. There was an AMA auxiliary in every county in the country that had a county medical association.

The letter instructed the auxiliary members to invite friends and neighbors who agreed with them politically to their homes to listen to Reagan argue why the Anderson-King Bill would be socialized—and bad—medicine. They were to "put on the coffeepot," serve coffee, play the record, provide pen and paper for the guests to write individual letters, collect and mail the letters (three from each person, one to her representative and one each to her two senators), and report back to the AMA how many letters she had mailed.

Reagan's attack on Medicare was interesting, but his attack on Social Security itself—perhaps less dramatic, but no less forceful—was equally important. This is especially so in view of his 1980 race for the presidency. As chapter 8 makes clear, Reagan's attitude toward Social Security was openly hostile until he embarked on his successful bid for national office. During that campaign, he not only professed support for Social Security, but also specifically denied (in his debate with President Jimmy Carter) that he had opposed the principles of Medicare.

The "Operation Coffeecup" campaign was to be kept as secret as possible. It resulted in an enormous flood of letters to Congress, and each letter was individually worded and handwritten. It was an ingenious tactic, contributing to the defeat of the Anderson-King Bill and the later Anderson-Javits Amendment. It certainly helped hold off the adoption of Medicare, and the secrecy was also largely effective. Although there were some public reports of "Operation Coffeecup," most people were completely unaware of its existence, and members of Congress tended to believe that the outpouring of letters following the campaign was simply a spontaneous mass expression of public opinion.

Because of the secrecy, few people today are aware of Reagan's role in delaying Medicare's adoption. Nor are they aware that if he had had his way, the country would never have had a program of health care for the aged— or for anyone else.

For many years, it appeared as though there were no copies of the record still in existence. The AMA library reported that it had lost its copy. Even the Reagan Collection in the Hoover Institution at Stanford University failed to locate one, although I did finally locate the text of Reagan's speech there. I published it in 1989, along with images of some of the materials that accompanied the recording. Even then, the remarks of the unnamed announcer that followed Reagan's comments remained missing.[16]

After nearly two decades of searching, a copy of the record itself surfaced. The full text appears in appendix A, including both Reagan's speech and the announcer's remarks. With the growth of the Internet, it now has become possible to locate an occasional copy of "Operation Coffeecup," but this book and its earlier version, *Social Security and Its Enemies*, remain the only published sources that include the record's entire text.

Reagan's speech indicates clearly (and strangely) that he was suspicious of medical programs in general as possible tools of oppression. Their humanitarian aspects were "disguises." He did grudgingly approve a program to provide support "for people who need it," as did the AMA to head off a general program. The benefits of the Kerr-Mills scheme, which he mentioned as an existing, better alternative, ranged from poor to virtually worthless. In Kentucky, for example, it offered as few as six days of hospitalization, and those only for the destitute and only for an acute and life-endangering illness.

As for Social Security, Reagan conceded that there should be "some form of saving" to provide for times of need. He carefully avoided conceding that the government should be involved. In fact, his clear assumption was that Social Security was improperly supplanting "private saving, private insurance, pensions, programs of unions and industries." Rather than charging Social Security with being bankrupt as he did in other talks (all versions of "the Speech," his standard refrain), Reagan seemed in "Ronald Reagan Speaks Out Against Socialized Medicine," his presentation for "Operation Coffeecup," to imply that it was too effective.

In September 1964, the Senate finally adopted an amendment to the Social Security Act similar to the Anderson-Javits Amendment. That was the first time that either house of Congress had managed to pass such legislation, but its destiny was death in conference committee. Discussion of this amendment had not been accompanied by the intensive public controversy that had surrounded the Anderson-King and Anderson-Javits proposals, probably because the opponents had become sure of themselves. They had not counted on the legislative skills of Lyndon Johnson, who had assumed the presidency.

The only other favorable action on even a slightly related health-care program before the Eighty-ninth Congress came in 1960 with the adoption of the Kerr-Mills Act, the one that Reagan had praised in "Operation Coffeecup." This was actually an amendment to the Social Security Act, becoming Title XVI, "Medical Aid to the Aged." Under Kerr-Mills, states received grants to assist in the health needs of the indigent and the "medically indigent" aged.

The AMA had supported Kerr-Mills as a way of averting action on the Forand Bill or some other program of broader scope. The AMA support did, however, indicate a small crack in the solid front put forth by organized medicine against government involvement in health care or its economics. The crack ultimately widened to permit proposing the Eldercare program, which also called for federal support.

The AMA announced its proposal for Eldercare on January 17, 1962. It would have been a national insurance program for the aged under the auspices of Blue Shield plans. Blue Shield pays physicians' bills, not hospital costs. Shortly before the AMA's announcement, on January 3 the American Hospital Association and the Blue Cross Association proposed a similar plan for hospital benefits, which the AMA rejected. Eldercare would have required the approval of each of the sixty-nine separate Blue Shield plans, and it aroused markedly little enthusiasm among them. The AMA said that Eldercare was its reaction to proposals to "socialize" medicine.

Secretary of Health, Education, and Welfare Abraham Ribicoff attacked the AMA's proposal vigorously. It would not have prevented physicians from charging patients more than the plan would pay, and it had no provision whatever for the greatest cost: hospital charges. Organized medicine was not deterred and, as a last-ditch effort, threw its resources into a massive publicity campaign. Much of this campaign was under the control of medicine's political action committee, the American Medical Political Action Committee (AMPAC).

The AMPAC pursued its task with gusto. Its zeal was so great that when it was hardly a year old, it caused the AMA one of the greatest embarrassments in the history of that venerable organization. Perhaps worse, it brought the AMA face to face with a $400,000 suit for damages resulting from alleged fraud and libel (that amount would be in the millions of dollars today). In November 1963, Paul Normile, director of Western Pennsylvania District 16 of the United Steelworkers of America, filed the suit against the AMA in the U.S. District Court for Washington, D.C.[17]

The suit stemmed from a phonograph recording that the AMA produced in quantity and distributed by the thousands throughout the country (it seemed at that time almost as though the AMA were ready to bring out its own record label). The recording purported to be of a speech by Normile at a political-education meeting of a group of steelworkers in western Pennsylvania. The recorded voice made tough threats in gangsterlike fashion, as though extorting contributions from assembled union members to support the battle for Medicare by threatening those who did not "come across" with the "graveyard shift" and other unpleasantness. The voice sounded rough, and the comments, illiterate.

The president of the American Federation of Labor–Congress of Industrial Organization (AFL-CIO), George Meany, asserted that the recording was an "absolute fraud." Normile denied that the voice was his or that he had made any such speech. Meany denied that there had been any such speech by anyone. The record jacket, entitled "The Voice of COPE" (the AFL-CIO's Committee on Political Education), contained a printed text of the recording and information to the effect that AMPAC had obtained it from a union member "who opposes, as many members of the labor movement do, the high-pressure methods which C.O.P.E. resorts to in its efforts to dominate government at every level within the United States." That anyone could take such a statement seriously then is an indication of how much power organized labor has lost in the last few decades.

The record jacket contained a message over the signature of Donald E. Woodlake, MD, chairman of the board of directors of the AMPAC. Woodlake recommended that all physicians listen to the recording to make them aware that membership in the AMPAC was essential for them to be able to continue to practice medicine freely.

AMA president Edward Annis called the charges in the lawsuit "ridiculous." They were, he said, merely an effort to divert attention from the issues. Nevertheless, the AMA decided to withhold official comment on the suit until it was aware of the full details.

The following January, the judge rejected the union's plea that the AMA be ordered to apologize in the pages of its official publication, the *Journal of the American Medical Association,* for having distributed the recording. He ruled that such a stipulation would be to require an admission of guilt. The court proceedings revealed that the record was allegedly purchased for $20 on a dark street late at night from an unknown middleman. The AMA represented the suit as a dispute between organized medicine and organized labor regarding pending legislation. For a time, its spokesman maintained that the proceedings were merely an effort to discredit the association and said that AMA officials had not entirely eliminated the possibility that the recorded voice actually did belong to Normile, even though a speech expert that Normile employed as an expert witness asserted that this was impossible.

AMA executives admitted that they did not know whose voice really was on the record, but they claimed that they had thought it to be authentic when they purchased it. They argued that they had a right to distribute the record, regardless, because it dealt with pending legislation of great importance; therefore, the AMA should not be held liable for damages. The judge listened to a transcript of the recording that the attorney for Normile and the union read, but he refused to permit the actual record to be played in court.

After a long delay and much bargaining and hesitation, the AMA announced on March 11, 1966, that it had arrived at a settlement out of court with Normile. The organization issued a statement and published it in the following issue of *JAMA*. It also appeared on the front page of the *AFL-CIO NEWS* for March 12:

In March 1963 the American Medical Association was sent a tape recording of what purported to be a political fund raising speech made in Pennsylvania by a Pittsburgh labor leader, Mr. Paul Normile, director of District 16, United Steelworkers of America. Believing in good faith that the tape recording was authentic, the AMA reproduced it and the American Medical Political Action Committee produced and distributed a booklet entitled, "The Voice of COPE," containing the text of the speech and a phonograph record made from the tape as evidence of the tactics which they believed labor used in support of its objectives.

Mr. Normile thereafter filed a lawsuit alleging that he never made the speech in question. Distribution of the tapes and records was immediately voluntarily discontinued pending full investigation of his contention. As a result of its exhaustive investigation, the AMA is now satisfied that Mr. Normile did not make the speech in question. In fairness to him, the statement that he did so is retracted. Furthermore, all copies of the tape recording and the AMPAC booklet and record in the possession of the AMA or AMPAC have been destroyed. To prevent further playing of the recording, it is urged that any person having a copy of either the tape or the record take similar action. The AMA sincerely regrets its error.

The embarrassment that caused the professional association to wait two and a half years before admitting its error is understandable. Moreover, the delay possibly permitted any effect the record might be having to continue for a while. By the time of the apology, the issue was moot.

In 1965, not only was the acknowledged legislative genius Lyndon B. Johnson president of the United States, but he had been elected in his own right; in fact, he had received the largest percentage of the popular vote in American history. He employed a burst of activity to make Medicare a top priority, and the program finally materialized.

Ironically, despite the fierce opposition from organized medicine, the Medicare program quickly catapulted American physicians into even greater affluence than previously. Their elderly patients, many of whom had been destitute and received charity care before Medicare, became able to pay their bills. Even more ironically, the relative income of physicians in recent years has tended to fall sharply, not because of government's involvement, which the AMA had feared so greatly, but because of the private business interests that have come to dominate the distribution of medical and hospital services. The terror that government involvement had struck into the hearts of AMA stalwarts had proved to be based on a fantasy; government involvement had actually improved their income. The attack on their income and on their freedom to practice medicine ultimately did come, but not from government. Rather, it came from the very free market forces that they had embraced as their protector. HMOs and managed-care organizations have restricted medical practice and income with the same force that AMA officials had mistakenly thought only government could exert.

The same amendments to the Social Security Act that added Medicare benefits raised the tax rate to 4.2 percent as of 1966 and increased the taxable wage base to $6,600. It also brought self-employed physicians under coverage, adding them to doctors of osteopathy, the group of physicians already covered. Physicians had fought strongly, and for a long time successfully, to resist inclusion. This resistance by one group but not the other demonstrated the purely political nature of the issue, inasmuch as their practices were and are identical.

Benefit increases came in 1968, 1971, and 1972, with the wage base increasing to $7,800 in 1968 and $9,000 in 1972. In 1973, the wage base went to $10,800, and the tax, to 5.85 percent. Significantly, the 1972 amendments also added automatic cost-of-living adjustments to benefits, tying them to the Consumer Price Index. The adjustments were to begin in January 1975.

For the first time, however, a cloud appeared on Social Security's horizon. The next chapter examines the end of expansion, the beginning of retrenchment, and the explosion of politics that, for the first time, overtly attacked the Social Security system itself.

Although Social Security and Medicare had emerged and expanded to meet an obvious need, the same ideology that had opposed social insurance in the beginning surfaced once again. That ideology held all government action promoting the general welfare to be unacceptable. Social Security's popularity with the people had been its shield against the selfish and the ideologues. It would need that shield as the battle intensified. Recognizing this, its enemies began to strike directly at public understanding. They sought to generate misunderstanding and to cause fear that Social Security cannot be sustained without "reforms." The reforms that they have in mind are designed, cynically and hypocritically, not to preserve Social Security but to eliminate it.

NOTES

1. Morris Fishbein, *A History of the American Medical Association* (Philadelphia: W. B. Saunders, 1947), 318–21.

2. "The American Medical Association: Power, Purpose and Politics in Organized Medicine," *Yale Law Journal* 63 (May 1954): 1008; my discussion of the AMA's anti-Medicare propaganda activities through 1953 relies heavily on this invaluable study. For excellent summaries of proposed federal health-insurance legislation into the 1950s, see especially pp. 1007–18; see also Agnes W. Brewster, *Health Insurance and Related Proposals for Financing Personal Health Services* (Washington, DC: U.S. Department of Health, Education, and Welfare, Social Security Administration, 1958).

3. "American Medical Association: Power, Purpose and Politics," 1009, especially n. 602.

4. "American Medical Association: Power, Purpose and Politics," 1009.

5. "American Medical Association: Power, Purpose and Politics," 1009.

6. "American Medical Association: Power, Purpose and Politics," 1011–14.

7. "American Medical Association: Power, Purpose and Politics," 1016.

8. "American Medical Association: Power, Purpose and Politics," 1017; see n. 676.

9. *Journal of the American Medical Association* 181 (July 21, 1962), 265.

10. *PR Reporter* (May 28, 1962), 1–2; this publication described itself as "a working newsletter for public relations professionals."

11. *PR Reporter*, 1–2.

12. *PR Reporter*, 1–2.

13. See *We Support Health Benefits for the Aged through Social Security* (New York: National Association of Social Workers, 1961) for a list of organizations and prominent persons supporting the Anderson-King Bill.

14. U.S. Congress, *Health Services for the Aged under the Social Security Insurance System*, hearings before the Ways and Means Committee (Washington, DC: U.S. Government Printing Office, 1961), 701–2.

15. Blue Shield plans are generally the creations of medical societies; the national Blue Shield Plan was separate from the Blue Cross Association and was closely allied with the AMA.

16. See Max J. Skidmore, "Operation Coffeecup: A Hidden Episode in American Political History," *Journal of American Culture* 12 (fall 1989): 89–96.

17. This discussion of Paul Normile's lawsuit is taken from Max J. Skidmore, *Medicare and the American Rhetoric of Reconciliation* (Tuscaloosa: University of Alabama Press, 1970), 135–38.

6

Frightening Facts
or Persistent Politics?

The first period of retrenchment in Social Security's history came not long after the 1972 amendments. Fears of a cash-flow shortage caused the administration of Richard M. Nixon to delay the automatic benefit adjustments half a year, until June 1975. Despite this delay, the feared shortage did develop in 1977. It was no crisis, but something did need to be done; and it was done. Nevertheless, long exposure to rhetoric such as Ronald Reagan's (magnified by skilled propaganda on the part of antisocial insurance zealots) had conditioned many members of the public to react with unjustified nervousness.

With the support of the administration of Gerald Ford, Congress had raised the tax to 6.13 percent as of 1979 and put into effect the increased tax rates and wage-base amounts that previously had been scheduled for later years. Carter's 1977 changes also prevented the practice of "double-dipping" for civil servants who qualified for Social Security as a result of earlier employment; they could no longer receive full civil service retirement benefits and full Social Security benefits simultaneously.

This change affected not only civil servants but also all who had qualified for pensions that resulted from employment exempt from Social Security. It reflected the concern that tended to motivate conservatives, many of whom disliked government benefits in any case, who saw the system's most important function as preventing anyone from receiving a benefit greater than they, the conservatives, considered justified; this was in contrast to the views of others who believed that the system's top priority should be to see to it that all who qualified for benefits did, indeed, receive them. The result of this provision has been to deprive many of their full Social Security benefits, especially teachers and their spouses in those states with public school systems that have never been brought under Social Security coverage.

During the 1980s, another cash-flow problem suggested that the 1977 changes had been insufficient to ensure fiscal soundness. Again, regardless of the hysterical recollections of a few of those involved, it was not a "crisis"; still, as had been the case previously, some sort of action was necessary. President Reagan appointed a commission under the leadership of Alan Greenspan (it included prominent Democratic and Republican officials, such as Senator Daniel Patrick Moynihan and Senator Robert Dole, respectively), and Congress incorporated the commission's recommendations in its 1983 amendments.

It is noteworthy that the trouble then was imminent, not projected decades in the future, and that in a few short months it was possible to deal effectively with the issue. This should give pause to citizens who hear that a "crisis" will occur in 2041 (or sometime) and that it is therefore urgent that we deal with it immediately.

Congress responded to the situation in 1983, radically revising the scheme that had evolved through the years, which had come to function largely in a pay-as-you-go manner. Discarding pay-as-you-go, Congress opted for full financing and provided for the accumulation of enormous trust funds in anticipation of the pressure that would develop years later when the baby boom generation retired.

Remember that the 1983 changes, with Greenspan's blessing, took the system away from pay-as-you-go and opted instead to accumulate a surplus to tide it over the baby boomers' retirement. In other words, for generations workers would be taxed more than necessary to pay current benefits. For safety, the surplus would be invested in government bonds. Having taxed workers more than the system needed during their working years, a generation later officials of the administration of George W. Bush, including that same Alan Greenspan who had taken over as chairman of the Federal Reserve, began to argue that it would be necessary to reduce benefits to avoid raising taxes. Workers had already paid the taxes and that was fine, but paying off the bonds might require higher taxes on the wealthy, which was unacceptable.

These same officials, including Bush himself, have argued that the trust funds do not exist, that they contain nothing but "worthless government I.O.U.s." No American president, not even Mr. Bush, would dare go to Chinese, Korean, and Japanese industrialists and their governments and say that the massive amounts of American treasury bonds they hold are worthless. The world financial system would crumble if he were to do so. Yet, that is what Bush has told Americans.

Social Security's enemies argue that the trust funds will be inadequate to pay full benefits beyond 2041. Therefore, there must be benefit reductions. At the same time, they argue that there are no trust funds, that the system continues to be pay-as-you-go. If this is true, it is unnecessary to be concerned about the trust funds since they do not exist anyway. It does not matter at all if they are large, as they are today, or if they will someday be exhausted. If, on the other hand, we do need to be concerned about the trust funds, then clearly they do exist, and the bonds they contain represent real value.

It should be clear to anyone who examines the arguments of the doomsayers—one would think it would be clear even to Mr. Bush—that they simply make no sense; they contradict one another. If the system is pay-as-you-go, it is necessary only to adjust taxes and benefits as you go to keep them in balance (or to operate at a deficit, as the rest of the government is doing under Bush). There is never a need to anticipate a "crisis" decades in the future. If the trust funds are meaningful, again it is necessary to keep only taxes and benefits in balance (or to operate at a deficit, as the rest of the government does under Bush). Either way, there is no "crisis," and because Social Security is a program of the U.S. government, it is impossible for it ever to become "bankrupt."

The inescapable conclusion is that the Bush administration believes several things. Private investments should replace Social Security. It is acceptable to reduce benefits, even though for decades workers have paid the taxes in advance to finance those benefits. It is unnecessary and undesirable to levy taxes to pay fully for government programs, except for programs that provide benefits to workers. Only benefits to workers need to be fully funded. Principles that contradict one another are acceptable justifications for the programs that they do accept. Finally, the truth is irrelevant; assertion and repetition have become a preferable substitute.

Anyone who thinks it too harsh to conclude that Bush's administration sees the truth as irrelevant should pay careful attention to an article on Bush's faith by writer Ron Suskind in the *New York Times Magazine* in October 2004.[1] Suskind's comments were widely reported—if not widely heeded. He quoted a former Reagan aide, Bruce Bartlett, as asserting that Bush truly believed he was God's agent and that, as such, Bush had an absolute faith that overwhelmed any need for analysis, any need for facts or evidence. An administration aide (almost universally assumed to be Karl Rove) gave credence to this by jeering at Suskind as belonging to the "reality-based community." It was out of date, this aide sneered, to draw conclusions from "judicious study of discernible reality." The Bush administration had risen above all that. It created its own reality. Just so.

The 1983 amendments did several other things in addition to requiring workers to pay taxes higher than needed to pay current benefits. They subjected Social Security benefits, for the first time, to income tax. Those beneficiaries whose income exceeded a set amount were required to include 50 percent of their benefits as income when calculating their tax. In 1993, the amount that was subject to tax rose to 85 percent; in other words, for the more affluent taxpayers, only 15 percent of their benefits remained free from income tax.

As a result of the 1983 amendments, states could no longer change their policies and opt out of the system once they brought their employees under Social Security coverage. Finally, in the hope that it would remove any doubt about the ability of income to balance outgo permanently, Congress provided for a gradual increase in the age for full retirement from sixty-five to sixty-seven, delayed the impending cost-of-living adjustment, and accelerated the schedule of tax-rate increases. Under the 1983 law, the normal retirement age begins to increase for those born in 1938, progressively rising, until it becomes sixty-seven for those born in 1960 or later. As noted in chapter 2, projections then were that these changes would bring the system permanently into balance. Although there is no real reason to believe that those projections were too optimistic—in fact, conditions have consistently been better than anticipated—almost everyone now proclaims that Social Security is once again in trouble.

The major concern is fueled by demographics, or rather by an enormous and well-financed propaganda campaign to convince both policymakers and the public that demographics portend disaster. No informed observer who remains relatively free from ideological blinders can deny that Social Security has been an enormously successful government program. It has ensured the welfare of countless numbers of Americans. Many observers now believe, however, that population shifts and increasing life expectancies have changed the situation and are creating clear dangers.

The typical argument goes as follows: As baby boomers retire, the number of people receiving retirement benefits will escalate, while the number of workers paying into the system will shrink. Thus, progressively fewer workers, who must make payments to progressively more beneficiaries, will be supporting the system. Considering retirees as the only beneficiaries, though, presents an inaccurate picture. Nearly one-third of all benefit checks go to persons younger than retirement age, such as the disabled or the children of deceased workers. The number of checks going to the disabled, or to survivors of deceased workers, will be proportionally fewer. Additionally, the percentage of Americans in the workforce will decline very little as the population ages, primarily because of the increasing number of women who work. As chapter 2 makes clear, the actuaries anticipated these changes and planned for them. In fact, the dependency ratio, the proportion of the population in the workforce as compared to all others, is projected never to be as unfavorable as it was in 1965; it will be far better when the baby boomers retire than it was at that low point.

Much of the concern results from publicity given to the reports of the trustees of the trust funds. The trustees make annual reports on the state of the trust funds, including projections far into the future (seventy-five years). As chapter 2 points out, they do so because the law requires them to. They rely on information that the Social Security Administration's actuaries generate, but they are in a position to influence that information. In 2005, for example, the trustees gratuitously issued a projection carried out to infinity, an exercise that is absurd in practical terms but perhaps shrewd in a political sense.

Note that the trustees are far from impartial analysts. The group of six consists of four administration officials, the secretaries of the treasury, labor, and health and human services, and the commissioner of Social Security. The former three are members of the president's cabinet, and all report directly to the president. Additionally, there are two "public" members who also are presidential appointees. Note, too, that the Bush administration, in contrast to past practice, has overtly politicized the Social Security Administration (SSA) and uses the SSA website to propagandize on behalf of the president's Social Security proposals. Under Bush, even the annual statements that citizens receive regarding their Social Security status and future benefits contain the propaganda. Thus, it would be unwise to accept the reports of the trustees as though they had no political position to support.

Even so, the reports have consistently relayed the actuaries' warnings that long-term projections are inherently unreliable. The longer the period forecasted, the less the validity. Projections for thirty years in the future at best would be highly unreliable. Projections for seventy-five years are hardly (if at all) more than fantasy. All lengthy projections on complicated subjects are simply educated guesses, no more. As mentioned in chapter 2, the best analysts in the United States failed to anticipate the dissolution of the Soviet Union right up to its collapse. In the late 1990s, the best economists were projecting the continuation of huge budget deficits; yet, in early 1999, the budget featured a surplus that all projections had failed to foresee a mere six months previously.

Because of the unreliability of long-term projections, the trustees' reports received hardly any attention until the early 1990s. By then, they had begun to use a different and more pessimistic set of assumptions in making their calculations. At the time of the 1983 amendments, the projections had shown favorable fund balances far into the future. When the trustees' assumptions changed, however, so did their projections. This should have been no cause for concern. The intention was never to maintain enormous trust funds forever but to draw them down considerably to pay for the baby boomers' retirements.

Nevertheless, Social Security's enemies seized on the new projections. They began a propaganda blitz that blanketed the news media with pessimistic and startling allegations that the system faced bankruptcy. Their goal was to frighten the public. To a considerable extent, they succeeded.

Most of the news media—one may be charitable and say they were merely lazy or naive—treated press releases from special-interest groups hostile to Social Security as legitimate news items. They published them as genuine news, inundating the public with scare propaganda designed to weaken their confidence in Social Security, even though they might continue to support the system.

The trustees' "alternative II," or intermediate (as opposed to high-cost—more pessimistic—and low-cost—more optimistic), projections for several years in the 1990s, up to and including those for 1997, predicted that the Old-Age, Survivors, and Disability Insurance trust funds would receive sufficient income to cover all benefits until 2013. Then, the increasing benefit outgo would begin to exceed income and would cut into the accumulated assets, which by that time would be somewhere around $1.3 trillion. By 2029, the trust funds would be gone. Only the income would remain, and that would be able to pay only some three-fourths of the benefits projected for that year.

Hidden beneath the propaganda was the fact that the trustees also issued optimistic, or "alternative I," projections. Based on more optimistic assumptions, these projections removed any dangers to the far distant future or, in fact, eliminated them altogether. (There were, of course, also the "high-cost," or "alternative III," projections, but these were so wildly and unrealistically pessimistic that, except in rare instances, even Social Security's enemies have ignored them as too unbelievable to be effective in their propaganda. The alternative II projections are sufficiently pessimistic for their purposes in any case, and using them enables the critics to claim that their approach is "reasonable.")

The optimistic alternative I projections received no publicity and continue to receive none, despite the fact that they are included in every trustees' report. Moreover, comparing economic conditions as they have developed with those projected in earlier trustees' reports reveals that, in every instance, the intermediate alternative II projections are far more pessimistic than actual developments bear out and that the alternative I projections have been consistently closer to real conditions; in fact, they often have been astonishingly accurate. These are the projections that indicate financial stability for Social Security—and no news outlet mentions them.

The public, misled by the drumbeat of opposition, failed to notice that the economy between 1993 and 1997 was exceeding all expectations, yet the publicized projections (alternative II) were remaining constant. If the trustees then were aware of the healthy economy, they were refusing to permit it to influence their "intermediate" projections, and that was before the Bush administration began its overt politicization of the Social Security Administration!

The 1998 projections finally began to take note of America's powerful economy. The trustees' report for 1998 moved the dreaded "depletion year" from 2029 to 2032. In one year's time, the great threat jumped three years into the future. The optimistic projections, of course, continued to anticipate no difficulty.

As chapter 2 explains, there are many reasons to be skeptical of even the 1998 and subsequent reports. The reports themselves caution against using their projections as though they are precise portrayals of what will happen. They also admit that all economic factors have been more favorable than projected in 1983, a time when the trustees' reports projected that the system would have a permanent surplus. It is significant that the reports admit that later projections of deficits result solely from the more pessimistic methods of calculation.

David Langer, a respected actuary, has said that the projections are so unduly pessimistic that the current alternative I should be made the "intermediate" projection, replacing alternative II. He provides ample documentation demonstrating that the current intermediate projection is so pessimistic that it should be downgraded to replace the "high-cost" alternative III projection. His recommendation is that a new "low-cost" projection be formulated to replace what now is alternative I.[2]

If there are good reasons to be skeptical of the trustees' pessimism, there are even better reasons to reject completely the arguments of those who would "reform" the system. In nearly all cases—and this most definitely includes President Bush's proposals—their reforms are steps, however disguised, toward killing Social Security.

Consider, for example, the critics' (not the reports') use of demographics. At best, it is simpleminded; at worst, it is deceitful. There is no doubt that the population is aging. The number of elderly retirees will certainly increase in relation to the number of workers paying into the system. There is more to the story than this, however, as this book already has made clear, although there are great efforts to prevent the public—and policymakers—from recognizing it.

- First, the baby boomers will not draw upon the system forever. They will pass through the system like a bubble.
- Second, the increasing life span has been misrepresented. Much of it results from the declining rate of infant mortality. On average, the population lives much longer because fewer infants die, but the life expectancy of a sixty-five-year-old today is only a little longer than it was in 1940 when Social Security benefits began. According to a table available from the Social Security Administration's website, life expectancy at the age of sixty-five was 12.7 years in 1940 for a man and 14.7 years

for a woman. In 1990, the figures were 15.3 and 19.6, respectively. The new retirement age of sixty-seven offsets two years of that gain, leaving an average increase during the half-century of less than two years.[3]

- Third, as the number of retirees increases, the relative number of those drawing benefits before retirement age, primarily survivors and disability beneficiaries, will decline as a proportion of the whole. This decline will serve as a partial offset to the increasing number of retirees.
- Fourth, the relevant figure is not the number of elderly as compared to the young but rather the number of beneficiaries compared to the number of people in the workforce. "Today, 46 percent of Americans are in the labor force; when the boomers are all retired in about 2030, that number will decline slightly to 44 percent. In 1964, when the baby boomer population peaked, however, only 37 percent of Americans were in the labor force—a ratio considerably 'worse' than can be expected in the 21st century."[4] As a matter of fact, projections of population growth, which in contrast to economic projections tend to be reasonably accurate, call for the dependency ratio never again to be as unfavorable as it was in 1965.

How can the workforce be a greater proportion of the population than previously when there are additional numbers of the elderly? The answer is simple: in 1965, it was rare for a woman to work. Because of the massive influx of women into the workforce since then, it has become, and will likely remain, common for a woman to do so.

There are also other reasons. Immigrants help the system. Legal immigrants pay into Social Security and often retire back to their homelands, never drawing benefits (those who retire in the United States, of course, draw their benefits the same as citizens do). It seems counterintuitive, but illegal immigrants help the most. One cannot legally work in the United States without a Social Security account, and illegal immigrants cannot obtain valid Social Security numbers. Thus, they obtain fake Social Security cards. They then pay taxes to Social Security but into nonexistent accounts. They receive no benefits. Such taxes, as the *New York Times* reported in the spring of 2005, amount to billions of dollars each year; in fact, they account for some 10 percent annually of the trust funds' surpluses.[5]

In any event, if the economy performs in the years to come with anywhere near the strength of the past, the robust economic activity will handle the baby boom retirements with little strain—or, even more likely, with none at all. Planners never intended for the trust funds to maintain enormous balances indefinitely. That would be neither necessary nor desirable. Rather, they provided for a large backlog only in order to handle the baby boom retirements. Their intention was that with the passing of the boomer generation, the funds would shrink to relatively small reserve amounts sufficient to meet unexpected expenses. They anticipated that future tax rates would be adjusted upward or downward as required to maintain the funds at the required level.

Those who advocate drastically changing Social Security for economic reasons are ignoring many important facts. No doubt this results from the fevered publicity. It is most important to put things in perspective. Even if the pessimists should turn out to be correct, what would the magnitude of the financial troubles facing Social Security be?

Certainly, Social Security is a large part of the national budget, but it is only a tiny part of the enormous American economy. The amount needed to correct the shortfall that the trustees project when they use their most pessimistic assumptions would be a smaller portion of the gross domestic product than increases in military expenditures were during the Cold War years. The American economy undoubtedly is powerful enough to absorb any possible Social Security needs with no major disruptions. George W. Bush implicitly acknowledged this when he spent countless billions of dollars on an unanticipated war and at the same time reduced taxes!

What led to such concern about the system? Even the trustees' reports have said that a small tax increase of less than 1.1 percent on the worker (2.19 percent shared equally between worker and employer) would ensure solvency at least through 2070—even for the "intermediate" alternative II projections. That is hardly a frightful prospect. All the baby boomers and nearly all adults living today would be dead by then. Moreover, as I have made clear, the "troublesome" demographic shifts are considerably less fearsome than the critics have portrayed them. What, then, is the origin of the conventional wisdom that Social Security is unsustainable without reform?

Much of the popular view (shared by virtually all reporters until recently, when a few began to look beneath the surface of press releases from special interest groups) originated as a result of tireless actions by an investment banker, Peter G. Peterson, who was secretary of commerce under President Nixon. Peterson, along with former senators Paul Tsongas and Warren Rudman, founded a powerful special-interest lobby portraying itself as nonpartisan and "objective." His Concord Coalition is devoted to supporting balanced budgets and reducing, if not eliminating, "entitlements." Social Security, of course, is the foremost "entitlement."

In May 1996, Peterson brought together the figures that bombard citizens from all media outlets and from every variety of political discussion. Peterson has been highly successful in convincing much of the public that his organization seeks only "good government," or "sound economics," rather than the explicitly conservative ideology that it espouses. Examining his account should help clarify the real situation.

In a strongly worded article predicting catastrophe unless there are drastic changes to Social Security, Peterson wrote, "In 1960 there were 5.1 taxpaying workers to support each Social Security beneficiary. Today there are 3.3. By 2040 there will be no more than 2.0—and perhaps as few as 1.6."[6] The late Robert Eisner, a former president of the American Economics Association and professor emeritus at Northwestern University, responded to Peterson's article by demonstrating that these dreaded figures overlook some important factors, making them, to be candid, complete nonsense.

"We are told," he wrote, "that there are now almost five people of working age—20 to 64—for every potential dependent aged 65 or over, and that by 2030 that ratio will fall to less than 3 to 1." What these figures overlook, he noted, is that "the relevant numbers . . . relate to all potential dependents, those below as well as above working age. Currently, for every 1,000 people of working age there are 709 young and old potential dependents. The intermediate projection puts the number in 2030 at 788. That means that each 1,000 people of working age would have to support 1,788 people—themselves and their dependents—instead of 1,709, only a 4.62 percent increase in their burden."[7] This is hardly the catastrophe that the critics predict.

It is unwise, and certainly "unconservative," to make radical shifts in policy based on projections over decades (all of which, inevitably, are highly questionable). Long-term economic forecasting is about as reliable as long-term weather forecasting. The strength of the economy has been far better than the 1983 projections assumed it would be. The trustees' more optimistic (alternative I) projections through the years have been far closer to actual developments than the intermediate projections have been. Therefore, the intermediate (alternative II) projections have consistently been unduly—and, thus far, demonstrably—pessimistic. Moreover, as I have demonstrated, even those overly pessimistic projections do not indicate that there will be a catastrophe, as the doomsayers allege.

Nevertheless, the intermediate projections make the headlines, and much of the media treatment for the past decade or so has been lurid. Consider this example from 1996: "Social Security is going bankrupt—again," began a *New York Times* article purporting to describe troubles in the system. "In 1983, the Social Security cupboard was nearly bare. This time around, the economic and political crisis is coming in slow motion: the system's income from payroll taxes is expected to exceed pension outlays until 2013." Then, the "relentless growth of pensioners will eat into Social Security's accumulated claims against the Treasury, forcing Washington to raise taxes or slash spending on other programs. And, for the first time in the 60-year history of Social Security, some of its friends are asking for fundamental change before the system cracks."[8]

It is the latter point, that Social Security's friends had been misled by distorted propaganda, that is truly the cause for concern, not the economics of the system. The persistent drumbeat of criticism indeed caused many strong supporters of Social Security to assume that basic changes were necessary. Such a sentiment had become so pervasive that it gave George W. Bush cover to embark upon his plans to secure approval from Congress for a privatization scheme.

He and Social Security's other enemies, of course, go far beyond the supporters in suggesting change. The supporters have hoped to tweak the system to provide stability, while Bush, his henchmen, and assorted free-market zealots push for changes that would destroy social insurance.

Peter G. Peterson takes such a position. His approach is destructive and reveals a thinly veiled hostility to the very idea of social insurance. He would phase in his suggestions, but even introduced gradually, they would eliminate Social Security as it currently exists. Some of his recommendations merely extend recent changes, such as increasing the age for full retirement still further to seventy. The more extreme provisions of his program call for government-mandated, individual retirement investment accounts along lines that Bush later picked up and made part of his own program. These initially would "supplement Social Security," but Peterson has said candidly that over time they "might increasingly substitute for it." His plan would require that "all workers (in some combination with employers) should be required to contribute four to six percent of their pay— which, added to FICA, would come to a total contribution of 16–18 percent of pay." Why not simply increase taxes?[9]

As is common (although unstated) with privatization proposals, Peterson's scheme would ultimately eliminate spousal and survivors benefits. They similarly would work toward the elimination of disability protection and Medicare as well.

The rationale for private investment is that historically the stock market has appreciated more than the interest paid on Social Security's investment in governmental securities. If this supposed advantage is indeed a problem, the solution to it is clear: simply increase the interest on the government securities so that Social Security's investments bring a return equal to returns from the stock market. The stock market always has a potential for loss, however careful private investments may be. Aggregate increases in the stock market do not guarantee that individual investments are free from risk. In fact, the stock market offers no guarantees whatever. President Bill Clinton had planned to devote a portion of the developing surplus to the trust funds. That would have been another way to make the trust funds grow faster and would have carried none of the risk of private investing. Of course, that no longer is possible: because of Bush's policies, there is no more surplus. His administration and its supporters in Congress have sacrificed it to tax cuts for the wealthy. They have returned to the enormous deficits that President Reagan and the first President Bush created.

In Peterson's mind, private accounts would be more virtuous than Social Security because they would make "tomorrow's retirees more self-sufficient." He gives no indication that he has thought through just how this would be so. He seems to believe that mere assertion is sufficient.

Yet, examining his idea immediately raises questions. His program, like Social Security, would be mandatory, not voluntary. In neither case would the retiree have an option of withdrawing funds upon retirement. The only difference would be that the return would not be fixed. Wise (or lucky) investing could bring a high rate of return; unwise (or unlucky) investing would bring poverty. Peterson, in addition, would means-test all federal benefits (or as he puts it, "affluence-test" them). At the most basic level, the notion that reliance upon a government program creates dependence, while reliance upon private investments creates independence, is simply silly. Private investors rely upon brokerage firms, the stock market, and a host of institutions summed up in the term "Wall Street." Reliance upon Wall Street certainly brings no more independence—no more "self-sufficiency"—than reliance upon Social Security. In fact, Wall Street's inevitable element of risk could well be seen as providing far less independence than the risk-free programs of Social Security.

Peterson has noted that while "some have said that an affluence test would constitute a tax on savings, and thus would discourage thrift," "there is no evidence to support this hypothesis." It hardly seems hypothetical that a worker would see saving as counterproductive if saving, thereby postponing consumption until retirement, would eliminate benefits that otherwise would be paid.

Worse, he recognizes that "it has also been said that an affluence test would undermine public support for Social Security and other universal social-insurance programs. The theory seems to be that we must bribe the affluent in order to ensure political support for benefits for the needy. This is dead wrong." To justify his opinion, he points to a Concord Coalition poll that he alleges reflected public support for "reductions in Social Security benefits to higher-income households."[10] Certainly, the wording of the question here would make a dramatic difference, and he did not provide the wording. His use of the phrase "bribe the affluent" is no doubt indicative.

Regardless of how the question is worded, though, it is irrelevant to the basic issue, which is public support for the Social Security system. A universal system receives support because people perceive benefits as their right. Increasing numbers would refuse to subject themselves to the humiliation of proving their poverty to welfare workers if it were necessary in order to obtain benefits. If the public began to see benefits as denied them because of their affluence (significantly, the Bush administration for this purpose considers the "affluent" to be everyone other than the bottom 30 percent!), clearly public support would dwindle. An obvious example here is the reduced level of support for public schools when large numbers of people in a jurisdiction opt out of the system and either have no children, have only children past the age of schooling, or send their children to private schools.

Despite the seriously negative implications of Peterson's suggestions, he is far from the most overtly hostile opponent of Social Security. Because of his stubborn insistence on proposals that would dismantle the program and because of the key position that he occupies, President Bush must assuredly occupy that slot. Others, though, continue to work vigorously to undermine Social Security. Some purely ideological opponents simply resist the idea of government involvement. Financial writer James K. Glassman is an example. "Polls show Americans know benefits have to be cut," he has asserted. "The system must be abandoned."[11] We can find similar sentiments on all sides.

A case in point is a letter to the editor of *USA Today* written a decade or so ago. In this case, the writer was clearly an ideologue, but other letters in various publications since then have been similar in tone if not in detail, even when the writers have been more thoughtful and less ideological. This author identified himself as a professor of economics at Auburn University. He asserted (without giving any reason why) that "the answer clearly does not rest with politicians, more government management, or higher taxes. Privatizing Social Security is the logical solution." He did not explain how that could be done without action by politicians.

He did, however, suggest that a plan advanced by Harry Browne, a former Libertarian candidate for president, should be the model. What would that involve? Simply "sell the federal lands and capital assets, including dams, pipelines, airports, unnecessary military bases and office buildings to American entrepreneurs!" He argued, "It would be more efficient to put these assets in the private sector." How did he demonstrate that efficiency? With a non sequitur: "I have always favored the notion of having a pension rather than being on Social Security." So much for logic.

As I have demonstrated earlier, Social Security operates far more efficiently than any private program. Beyond that, though, what would be the implications for "efficiency," let alone for national security, if all America's infrastructure were to be put into the hands of "American entrepreneurs" who then sold them to Chinese, Korean, and Arab investors and governments—or to wealthy parties who wished the country ill, such as surrogates for Al Qaeda?

An overly ideological approach often leads one to advocate nonsense. The late economist Robert Eisner is one of the few participants in the controversy surrounding Social Security who was able to see through the verbiage, look beyond ideology, and concentrate on realities. In 1996, he wrote that we hear that we must "do something now," and "most frequently that something turns out to be an open or disguised cut in benefits to the elderly. Other, less painful solutions entail some form of privatization to enable retirees to realize the higher returns associated with stock market investments. The facts are that there is no crisis in Social Security now and there is none looming in the future."[12] In fact, he noted that a mere 1 percent increase per year in productivity per worker, which, as he pointed out, is "well within experience," would "easily accommodate the increased number of people the working population will have to support. Indeed, it would be sufficient for a one-third increase in output and income per capita, ample to improve vastly the lot of all—the elderly, the young and those in their working primes." Over the past twenty years, productivity growth has exceeded what Eisner calculated to be necessary.

Privatization may or may not have merits, he said, but in any event, it is unnecessary. Even under the intermediate projections of the trustees, as I have noted above, whatever problem might exist is minor, and the more optimistic projections are much more likely to be the more accurate ones. Yet, no less important a figure than Federal Reserve Board Chairman Alan Greenspan made headlines in January 1999 by announcing that for Social Security to survive, it would soon require either tax increases or benefit cuts. The same Greenspan later supported Bush's sharp cuts in income taxes. Later still, he favored Bush's privatization plan. Remember that in 1983, Greenspan supported the plan to tax workers to cover their future benefits. Since then, workers have paid into Social Security more than would have been required to pay current benefits. When those workers come near to their retirements, however, after having paid those increased taxes for years, Greenspan says that their benefits must be reduced in order to preserve Bush's tax cuts for the wealthy! Is it any wonder than many citizens have become cynical?

Such duplicitous pronouncements have so severely shaken public confidence that, as I have written in chapter 2, restoring full confidence will probably require more than mere reassurances. Social Security has one great shortcoming, but it is not that it is unsound; rather, it is the system's regressive financing. In the next chapter, I outline a plan to make its funding mildly progressive and to improve it greatly for the huge majority of workers.

NOTES

1. Ron Suskind, "Without a Doubt: Faith, Certainty, and the Presidency of George W. Bush," *New York Times Magazine*, October 17, 2004, 44ff.
2. David Langer, "Scrapping Social Security's Intermediate Cost Projections" (letter to the editor), *Society of Actuaries* (March 2004), www.davidlanger.com/article_c67a.html (accessed January 28, 2007).

3. Numerous charts showing life expectancy are available at http://search.ssa
.gov/search?q=life+expectancy+chart&btnG=GO&output=xml_no_dtd&sort=date%
3AD%3AL%3Ad1&ie=UTF-8&client=default_frontend&oe=UTF-8&proxystyle
sheet=default_frontend&proxyreload=1.

4. Richard C. Leone, "Stick with Public Pensions," *Foreign Affairs* 76 (July/August 1997), 41.

5. Eduardo Porter, "Illegal Immigrants Are Bolstering Social Security with Billions, *New York Times*, April 5, 2005.

6. Peter G. Peterson, "Will America Grow Up Before It Grows Old?" *Atlantic Monthly* 277, May 1996, 57.

7. Robert Eisner, "What Social Security Crisis?" *Wall Street Journal*, August 30, 1966.

8. Peter Passell, "Can Retirees' Safety Net Be Saved?" *New York Times*, February 18, 1996, sec. 3, 1.

9. Peterson, "Will America Grow Up?" 55–86.

10. Peterson, "Will America Grow Up?" 75–82.

11. James K. Glassman, "The Only Workable Solution for Social Security Is to Make It Private," *Kansas City Star*, September 10, 1995, J5.

12. Eisner, "What Social Security Crisis?"; see also Robert Eisner, *Social Security: More, Not Less* (New York: Century Foundation Press, 1998).

7

A New Plan that Truly Would Improve Social Security

Suggestions for incremental changes to Social Security generally have taken the form of gradual tax increases, benefit reductions, or a combination of the two. Contemporary politicians, worshipping at the alter of tax cuts as the solution to all problems of government, almost universally rule out tax increases (overwhelmingly in recent years, they have preferred deficit spending—in every area, of course, except Social Security and Medicare), and many have urged benefit reductions. Despite this, there certainly should be no benefit reductions. A huge number of beneficiaries rely on Social Security as their sole source of income, and as many as two-thirds of all beneficiaries rely upon it as the major source. For this group, benefits are already too modest. As I argue in chapter 1, with the collapse of the "three-legged stool," Social Security's benefits should be considerably increased in order to compensate for the lack of personal savings and rapid disappearance of corporate pension plans. The increase should be between two and three times current levels.

One frequent suggestion for "reform" is to raise the age for full retirement to seventy; this would be nothing other than a benefit reduction. It would save money in one way only: by causing any beneficiary to receive benefits for fewer years over a lifetime. Thus, raising the retirement age also should be ruled out.

Diverting a portion of a worker's Social Security taxes to private investments would also lead to a benefit reduction: obviously, it would reduce the amount available to pay Social Security benefits. The amount that would accrue from the private investments would vary. Certainly, some would do better than under Social Security alone, but even more certainly, others would do worse, and some would do far worse. Such a diversion would add risk to Social Security; varied rates of return would be destructive to the principle of social insurance. "Carve-out" private accounts should be rejected.

On the other hand, there are some major revisions that would preserve the fundamental principles of Social Security and considerably improve the system. Former senator George McGovern and I recently provided the outlines of such a plan in a preliminary article.[1] This plan discards the various suggestions for "reform" and attacks the system's one weakness: its regressive funding.

PART ONE: LOWER FICA TAXES ON
THE VAST MAJORITY OF WORKERS

The most important of these revisions would be to exempt the first $20,000 of earnings from Federal Insurance Contributions Act (FICA) taxes for the employee (but not for the employer). This would be an enormous improvement. No longer would the first dollar of earnings be taxed. In fact, workers with very low wages would continue to have Social Security coverage. Their employers would continue to pay the FICA tax as they now do, but the worker would have no deduction for FICA.

Freeing the first few thousand dollars of earnings would reverse the current regressive taxation. It also would boost the economy. Nearly every worker would have additional take-home pay amounting to $1,240 to spend however desired. Many families have two earners. In such an instance, with each partner earning $20,000, the family would have an additional $2,480 to spend per year. This would certainly be the broadest tax cut in American history, and it would probably be the largest. It would result in workers having additional take-home pay for school expenses for their children, for prescription drugs, for health-care costs, or for any other expense. Note that workers could even open savings accounts, as with George W. Bush's plan. The difference would be that workers would have complete control over their own accounts. The economy would benefit from this tax reduction far more than from tax cuts for the wealthy. The rich are much less likely than the rest of us to spend their additional income immediately, and if they do spend the additional funds, they are far more likely than others to use them to purchase luxury goods from Asia or Europe or to travel abroad.

Under this proposal, all workers in America who earn up to $117,500 per year would receive a tax cut. The amount will rise with each increase in wages subject to FICA taxes; the $117,500 figure is based on the 2007 amount for total taxable wages of $97,500. Those receiving the greatest cut on a percentage basis would be those with the lowest earnings. Each of these workers would have an increase in disposable income, that is, in take-home pay. FICA deductions would continue to be made as they are now in order to avoid having checks reduced in amount at the end of the year. Workers would receive a credit on their income tax representing the amount of FICA tax on the first $20,000. They could make adjustments in their rates of withholding to raise their take-home pay throughout the year. Thus, there would be no extra accounting burden upon employers, and workers with more than one low-paying job would have no special adjustments to make.

Most American workers would pay no additional tax, and nor would employers, except for those who employ workers earning more than $97,500 per year (for 2007). The additional take-home pay for low-income workers would help to compensate for America's inexcusably low minimum wage.

Would there be a cost? Of course. The trust funds would receive less income if the initial $20,000 of earnings were freed from FICA taxes on the worker, but the reduction would be similar to that from Bush's own proposal. He has supported permitting each worker annually to divert $1,000 of FICA taxes into private accounts, and he has offered no way to restore that income to the trust funds. His proposal would drastically lower benefits, convert the system into a welfare program subject to means-testing, and require borrowing literally trillions of dollars.

PART TWO: INCREASE INCOME TO THE TRUST FUNDS

The proposal presented here compensates for the reduction of income to the trust funds within the existing framework of social insurance. Moreover, it also compensates for the shortfalls that the trustees' pessimistic projections envision. The precise figures will have to be worked out, but without doubt, this proposal would protect the trust funds, while the Bush plan would damage them severely.

This plan involves several features: removing the cap on earnings subject to FICA taxation, devoting an estate or inheritance tax to the trust funds, and diverting other resources to the trust funds. A detailed discussion of each of these follows.

First, removing the cap on earnings subject to FICA taxation ensures that all do their full share to support Social Security. If a clerk earning $15,000 per year or a teacher earning $50,000 per year can afford to have 6.2 percent of the full salary deducted for FICA, it is not asking too much of the account executive earning $190,000 to pay 6.2 percent of his or her full salary as well. Those of low and moderate income now support the system fully; those of upper income do not. Requiring that all support the system fully by paying FICA taxes on all their income above $20,000 annually would make the system's financing mildly progressive, rather than regressive as it currently is.

This reform would be very popular. Studies indicate that most Americans think that if they pay FICA tax on their full salary, others should do so as well. Higher-income workers and employers with large numbers of higher-income workers would have little to protest because, under the Bush administration, they already have received exceptionally large tax reductions.

Traditionally, there have been objections to removing the cap. One is that paying full benefits on huge salaries could result in some benefits being too large to be acceptable in a democratic society. Avoiding this would be simple. As wages rise, the percentage of lifetime income that benefits replace lowers (Social Security replaces roughly 42 percent of the average retired worker's former paycheck; for lower-income retirees, it replaces about 56 percent and drops to around 27 percent of covered wages for those of higher income). The increase in benefits would shrink to nothing at a certain point; they would be capped.

There is precedent for removing the limitation on taxable earnings. There no longer is a cap on earnings taxed for Medicare benefits. The wealthy pay far more for the same benefits than do those of lower income. They have accepted the additional tax that does not bring additional benefits.

Second, dedicating an estate tax to the trust funds not only strengthens the funds but has other social benefits as well. Several authorities—David Obey, U.S. representative from Wisconsin, and Robert M. Ball, former commissioner of Social Security, among others—have argued in favor of devoting the proceeds of an estate tax to Social Security. Estate taxes are important to society in that they lessen the increasing concentration of huge fortunes among fewer owners as generations pass. Democracy and creativity both suffer when too few people control too much of society's resources. Many firm capitalists, such as Bill Gates Sr. and Warren Buffet, recognize this fact, as did that "captain of industry" Andrew Carnegie as far back as the late nineteenth century.

The tax would apply only to large estates. Proposals generally suggest levying them only on estates of $3.5 million or so. Even if the tax exempted as much as $5 or $6 million, it would achieve its purpose. That is, it would enhance the trust funds, it would curtail the passage of huge fortunes from one generation to another, and it would affect only the very wealthy. Of course, there would be misleading propaganda. There would be thundering denunciations of the "death tax," saying that it would damage small businesses and family farms. This is untrue. The American Farm Bureau campaigned against the estate tax in 2001, and its representatives said such taxes made it impossible for children to keep a farm in the family upon the death of the farmer. When pressed on the issue, the bureau "could not cite a single instance of a family farm lost because of the estate tax."[2] This is not just sloppy preparation on the part of Farm Bureau representatives; rather, it is reliance on popular beliefs that simply are not correct.

The opposition to an estate tax is based almost entirely upon misinformation. Well-financed groups fight fiercely to eliminate the tax for purely selfish reasons. It will be important to explain to the public just what it is and what it is not. What it is not is a "death tax." What it is, is a tax that would affect no one except the extremely wealthy. It will be necessary to dispel absurd arguments that it represents "double taxation." First, much of the amount it taxes is accumulated value (of stocks, securities, expensive items such as jewelry, and the like) that has in fact not been taxed. Regardless, nearly all money is taxed over and over. That's the way the system works. You pay income tax on your salary. When you spend that salary, you are likely to pay sales taxes. Your employer has paid tax on the money before you get it. The person from whom you make the purchase also pays tax on the amount that you pay. And so it goes. The charge of "double taxation" is thus ridiculous and calculated to make it appear as though there is injustice involved.

It will be important to reveal the nature of the well-financed special-interest groups that fiercely oppose any such tax, of course. One group, for example, calls itself Americans Against Unfair Family Taxation. Does it represent families and small business? Hardly. It speaks for the interests of such "small" concerns as the National Beer Wholesalers Association, the U.S. Chamber of Commerce, United States Telecom, and the National Association of Manufacturers.

John Kenneth Galbraith said years ago that one of the most effective ways to counter misleading propaganda is to greet it with great choruses of jeers and raucous laughter. That is excellent advice. Progressives have been far too polite, while reactionaries know no restraint.

Third, this proposal would direct additional resources to the trust funds. In order to lay to rest any allegation that someday the funds might be exhausted, it would be wise to adopt several new policies. An outstanding economist, the late Robert Eisner, who once was president of the American Economics Association, suggested two mechanisms to redirect government resources to the trust funds. One is quite simple: simply increase the interest that the government pays on the bonds that the trust funds hold. Another is to dedicate the portion of the personal income tax that is a "tax on a tax" to the funds. Currently, Social Security taxes are not deductible from federal income tax. In declaring income for tax, for example, the taxable amount includes the amount already paid for FICA. Eisner suggested dedicating the tax on that amount to the trust funds.

These financial mechanisms should lay to rest any concern about the viability of the funds. No longer would Social Security's enemies be able to get away with improperly using the word "bankruptcy" and issuing dire forecasts about Social Security's future. If they try, once again the remedy is Galbraithian jeering and raucous laughter.

PART THREE: USE TRUST FUND SURPLUSES TO PAY DOWN THE NATIONAL DEBT

The current practice is to borrow from the funds for general expenses. If the fund surplus were restricted to paying down the national debt until it reached a manageable level, our horrendous interest payments on that debt would be brought under control. This may seem like double counting, but it is not. Now the government is obligated to pay its debt to Social Security plus paying interest on the national debt. If the government borrowed from the trust funds only to pay down the national debt, it still would be obligated to repay the amount borrowed from the trust funds, but the national debt would be lowered by the same amount, thus reducing interest payments on that debt.

BENEFITS OF THE PLAN

These are commonsense solutions that would ensure Social Security's stability. They would retain the essential nature of Social Security and maintain its social purpose, which benefits the entire society. Additionally, they would provide special benefits to those with low earnings and help to counter the enormous financial disparity that exists so shamefully in today's extremely wealthy American society.

Implementation of this plan would help to clear up many of the common misconceptions regarding Social Security. Throughout the 1990s and well into the administration of the second George Bush, nearly all discussion on the subject accepted that the system was "in crisis." Even mainstream journalistic sources, those that the right has convinced itself are "liberal," accepted the crisis mentality. Witness an article in the *New York Times* that claimed, "Social Security is going bankrupt—again."[3] Neither this article nor other sources revealed the extraordinary extent to which a distorted atmosphere had conditioned perceptions. The distortions resulted from a consistent, coherent, and coordinated attack upon the whole notion of social insurance.

Only a full understanding of that attack can provide an answer to a puzzling question. That question is this: how, since the problems facing Social Security are minor or even nonexistent, did the campaign against the system succeed so well in convincing both the public and policymakers that a crisis existed? I have already given some account of this attack and the history behind it. It is now time to look at it in detail.

NOTES

1. George McGovern and Max J. Skidmore, "Real Reforms to Enhance, Not Curtail, Social Security," *Montana Professor* 18, no. 1 (fall 2007), 13–17; see also George McGovern, *Social Security and the Golden Age* (Golden, CO: Fulcrum Publishing, Speaker's Corner Books, 2005).

2. See David Clay Johnston, "Talk of Lost Farms Reflects Muddle of Estate Tax Debate," *New York Times*, April 8, 2001; quoted in Gary C. Jacobson, *A Divider, Not a Uniter: George W. Bush and the American People, the 2006 Election and Beyond* (New York: Pearson-Longman, 2007), 244n10.

3. Peter Passell, "Can Retirees' Safety Net Be Saved?" *New York Times*, February 18, 1996, sec. 3, 1 and 4.

8

The Enemies Regroup:
Rallying 'Round Reagan

The intense and open opposition that burst into flame after Social Security's passage was especially fierce during the presidential election of 1936, but it did not last long. Public support for the system was so obviously strong that politicians immediately halted their criticism. Attacking Social Security became politically perilous. From then until the 1970s, there were few overt attacks. Of the few that did materialize, most came from elements recognized as being right-wing extremists. They tended not to be taken seriously.

One exception came from the ranks of professionals and generally was not well publicized. The American Medical Association (AMA), of course, was primarily concerned with preventing any government program that provided or paid for health care, but it appeared also to have a broader concern. There was at least some evidence of hostility toward the entire Social Security system. Perhaps it resulted from the theoretical relationship of governmental health care to social insurance in general and to Social Security in particular.

As mentioned in chapter 5, in 1920 the American Medical Association had adopted a resolution expressing its opposition to any government involvement in providing health care or paying health expenses. Morris Fishbein affirmed in the AMA's 1947 official history that the policy had not changed. It was recognition of that policy, as well as fear of organized medicine's political power, that led Franklin D. Roosevelt in 1935 to omit health care from the original Social Security Act. He believed, with considerable justification, that to include health coverage would have energized the AMA to direct its wrath against the entire social insurance program.

Despite FDR's caution, the AMA's opposition did come to expand beyond health issues to include Social Security itself. The December 1939 issue of the *Journal of the American Medical Association* included an editorial saying, "Indeed, all forms of security, compulsory security, even against old age and unemployment, represent a beginning invasion by the state into the personal life of the individual, represent a taking away of individual responsibility, a weakening of national caliber, a definite step toward either communism or totalitarianism." This statement alone would not be sufficient evidence. The association's position is that official policy statements come only from resolutions by its House of Delegates, not from statements by its president or editorials in its official journal. Moreover, it is in fact true that the AMA avoided taking a position for or against passage of the Social Security Act when its representatives testified before Congress in 1935 during consideration of the bill.

Nevertheless, in 1949 the AMA's House of Delegates itself did make the official position on Social Security rather plain. That year it adopted a formal resolution declaring, "So-called 'Social Security' is in fact a compulsory socialistic tax which has not provided satisfactory insurance protection for individuals where it has been tried but, instead, has served as the entering wedge for establishment of a socialistic form of government control over the lives and fortunes of the people."[1] Despite this resolution, the AMA consistently tried to defend itself against charges that it opposed Social Security merely by repeating that it did not take a position on Social Security legislation.

The resolution, itself, it must be said, was total nonsense. There is no instance on record of dictatorial government resulting from social welfare legislation; history simply does not support the lurid allegation that has long been a staple among conservatives. This is not to say that government, even American government, presents no threat. The threat to individual freedom, however, comes not from social programs such as Social Security; rather, it comes from the effects of programs that many conservatives support, from legislation intended to combat drugs and such acts empowering the government to make Americans more secure at the expense of their liberties, such as the ill-named Patriot Act.

Because of Social Security's popularity, in those days overt opposition such as that from the AMA rarely entered into the discourse of formal politics. But there was a small cloud on the horizon that over the years grew into a hurricane of hostility to the social insurance program that had become as American as apple pie. As early as 1954, one spokesman began to gain prominence, around whom gradually coalesced those elements that had long opposed Social Security but had been relatively quiet since the days of the New Deal. That spokesman was former film actor Ronald Reagan, who then hosted *G. E. Theater* on television.

RONALD REAGAN AND "THE SPEECH"

As part of the public relations program of the General Electric Company, Reagan developed what he came to call simply "the Speech." He delivered this address at hundreds of meetings around the country. It was in fact an adaptation of "the Speech" that Reagan used on behalf of the AMA's "Operation Coffeecup" in 1961, altering it to make it primarily an attack on the idea of Medicare with only a glancing blow at Social Security.

Kurt Ritter produced a careful study of "the Speech" in 1968.[2] He found that it varied somewhat according to the audience, but the variations were confined essentially to emphases and the order of topics. "The Speech" always included such themes as the evils of "big government," the dangers of communism, the threat from centralization, and the insufferable burden of high taxes. Reagan warned emotionally of the peril from governmental paternalism and pointed to the "failure" of Social Security (note that this was decades ago).

Such overt attacks on Social Security had become rare since the early days when critics discovered how popular the program was with the public. Officeholders were especially careful in most instances to give the impression that they were strong supporters. Republicans as well as Democrats had endorsed Social Security through the years. Both parties had presided over expanded coverage and benefit increases. Reagan, though, was a private figure. Since he did not hold public office, he was under few, if any, constraints that would cause him to hide his views.

By the early 1960s, he had spoken countless times in virtually every section of the country. The more he spoke, the more strongly he stressed his opposition to Social Security. He began to give that opposition a headline role in his presentations. For example, he gave "the Speech" to the Phoenix Chamber of Commerce on March 30, 1961, and again that year on July 28 to the Orange County Press Club in California.[3] At both presentations, Reagan said that proposals for health care were traditionally "one of the easiest first steps to impose statism on a people" because such proposals could be "disguised" as humanitarianism. In each speech, he went on to say that the Social Security system was an intrusion on liberty. Moreover, he thundered, it was bankrupt!

This, you will note, was nearly a half-century ago. Think of all the checks the system has faithfully and without fail issued in the many decades since Reagan charged that the system was "bankrupt." Those who wish to see for themselves what he actually said in full can find many of these addresses printed in his collected papers or in the relevant volumes of *Vital Speeches*. Even easier, simply turn to appendix A to read "Ronald Reagan Speaks Out Against Socialized Medicine." This is the text of his recording, which was at the heart of the American Medical Association's anti-Medicare propaganda campaign, "Operation Coffeecup."

Reagan's skillful presentation of "the Speech" brought him to the attention of the most conservative officials of the Republican Party and their supporters. He impressed them, despite (or perhaps because of) the unanimous opinion of his mainline critics that he was simplistic and a political extremist. Seeking to harness his admirable and unquestioned powers of persuasion, these conservatives invited Reagan in 1964 to present a thirty-minute nationwide television broadcast defending Senator Barry Goldwater's doomed presidential campaign.

He did so, presenting "the Speech" on Senator Goldwater's behalf on October 27. It was electrifying. Although Goldwater lost, Reagan won. His forceful talk began the political journey that carried him to two terms as governor of California and, ultimately, to election and reelection as president of the United States.

However scornful Reagan was of Social Security in his years as spokesman for General Electric, and however much that scorn had increased by the time of John F. Kennedy's administration, his opinion became even harder as time passed. In giving "the Speech" to the National Association of Manufacturers on December 8, 1972, he told his audience to consider Social Security. "I have to say," he loftily told the group, "that if you couldn't come up with a better idea than that, you wouldn't still be in business."[4]

Although he became adept at shifting emphases in "the Speech" according to his audience, Reagan consistently adhered to his fundamental—or fundamentalist—beliefs from his days as a corporate spokesman until his assumption of high political office. He was too skillful as a politician, though, to be unaware of the need to project a nonthreatening image to the general public. The harder-edged attacks he reserved for talks to private groups or for otherwise less well-publicized addresses. When speaking to general audiences, he was careful to stress, as Ritter put it so well, his "eagerness to solve the problems of age, health, poverty, and housing 'without compulsion and without fiscal irresponsibility.'"

On television, he attempted to portray himself as reasonable, if nothing else. His radio addresses, however, were another matter. They tended to reach only the true believers and received little, if any, general publicity. In speaking to the more restricted body of listeners, he discarded many of his television-induced inhibitions.

There is no easily available source for the contents of his radio broadcasts, and their texts are difficult to find. Some of them are available in the Reagan Collection at the Hoover Institution at Stanford University. Early in Reagan's presidency, the journalist Ronnie Dugger managed to locate several more. These he published in 1983 in an excellent and quite critical study, *On Reagan: The Man and His Presidency.*

It is instructive to examine what Reagan said in his less-guarded moments. In 1975, he emphasized Social Security in many of his radio broadcasts and devoted three programs specifically to the subject. The Hoover Institution has written transcripts of the texts, but they are undated except for the penciled notation "[1975]." Dugger identified the dates as September 24, 25, and 29. In the first program, Reagan said flatly that Social Security "reduces your chances of ever being able to enjoy a comfortable retirement income." In the second broadcast, he described Social Security as "a sure loser" and supplemented that judgment with what he put forth as absolute statistical precision. His numbers, however, bore no relation whatever to reality—giving meaningless numbers was a practice for which Reagan became notorious. "If there were no Social Security," he said, "wages would be 15% higher and interest rates 28% lower." Social Security taxes should be eliminated, he said in the third program, with the employer's share of the tax added to workers' salaries. Workers could then choose to invest in a private pension plan that the government would insure or could choose to purchase a series of "new U.S. Retirement Bonds with annuity payoff."[5] How government bonds would be better than Social Security he did not say.

This was an early shot, however feeble it may have seemed at the time, in a battle that since has escalated into a full-scale war designed to privatize—a euphemism for "eliminate"—Social Security. Early in his presidency, Reagan moved against Social Security. His actions brought a political firestorm, and he agreed never again to attack the program. To his credit, he honored his promise. His actions, though, paved the way for far more overt attacks almost twenty years later by another Republican president, the second George Bush.

Note that Reagan's early proposals contained the basic elements still present in so many efforts that purport to "reform" the massive system. Clearly, such efforts are thinly disguised attempts to eliminate, or at least to narrow, social insurance. They tend to describe Social Security as though it were nothing but a pension program and allege that workers would benefit if they replaced Social Security with private investment. That is dubious—in fact, for a large majority of workers, it is clearly untrue—and it certainly would no longer be social insurance. It would introduce risk, guarantee wide variations in benefit levels for people with similar wage records, and fail to provide for the full population. That failure would dramatically increase the social ills of the country.

It is doubtful that Reagan recognized all of this, but if he did, he disregarded it, as have other critics who have followed his lead, including, most dangerously, George W. Bush. Moreover, it completely, and no doubt deliberately, ignores another shortcoming of privatization. Even if a given worker were to be lucky in his or her investments, and even if employers were to continue to provide their share of what currently are FICA taxes so that workers could invest them (and even assuming that the workers would indeed invest and not spend them), the workers would lose disability protection, survivors

protection, inflation protection for their benefits, spousal benefits, and probably Medicare.

The loss of these protections would be substantial. To replace Social Security's disability coverage and survivors protection on the private market
would require policies for the average worker amounting to some three-
quarters of a million dollars. Even disregarding the loss of Medicare and inflation protection for retirement and other benefits, that would be an enormous price to pay to satisfy the ideological prejudices of those who are
firmly convinced that government cannot function well—even when it
does.

The ideological approach of Social Security's enemies from Reagan to the
younger Bush is anything but conservative. The essence of conservatism is
caution regarding change and skepticism regarding suggestions for social en-
gineering. To be sure, those who call for drastic changes to Social Security
portray themselves as most conservative, yet their calls are explicitly radical—
they would have major and far-reaching consequences.

The modern enemies of Social Security were fortunate that their first and
most influential spokesman had a soothing manner and a genius for dis-
guising the extremism of his views. On October 28 during the 1980 presidential campaign, former governor Reagan was approaching the pinnacle of
his career. He faced President Jimmy Carter on television.

The president was well prepared and had his facts in order. He charged
that Reagan had begun his political career campaigning against Medicare.
Reagan had been well coached and clearly was prepared to deal with the issue. In rejoinder, he charmed the audience, received friendly laughter, threw
President Carter off his stride, and seized control of the situation. "There
you go again," he said. He proceeded to comment that he opposed the program that became Medicare merely because he favored a better program. He
assured the rapt audience that he had never opposed "the principle of providing care" for America's elderly. There is no evidence that President Carter
harbors any bitterness about the exchange, but it would be understandable
if he did.

Carter had been referring to the recording "Ronald Reagan Speaks Out
Against Socialized Medicine" (see chapter 5 and appendix A). As the record's
text indicates, there can be absolutely no question that Reagan in 1961 had
served as the heart of the AMA's "Operation Coffeecup," the purpose of
which was to combat not only the Medicare proposal but also "the principle
of providing care"—or even paying for care—by government action. Even if
we ignore his other speeches, Reagan's words on the AMA's recording establish beyond any doubt the truth of Carter's charge that Reagan opposed, and
opposed most strenuously, any form of social insurance or any governmental involvement in providing health coverage to America's elderly—or, for
that matter, to anyone. Reagan triumphed that year in part by denying his

clearly documented and often-expressed hostility to Social Security and Medicare.

The 1980 election not only resulted in the defeat of Jimmy Carter but for the first time since the beginning of Social Security brought to the presidency a long and determined foe of social insurance. Ronald Reagan in the campaign had professed to support the system and had promised to preserve and protect it. A few months after he took office, however, his administration proposed sweeping reductions in benefits for future beneficiaries, elimination of the minimum benefit (even for those already receiving it), and other restrictions. A huge public outcry caused the president to promise never again to touch Social Security. Reagan's attack, however, was not a complete failure. His actions emboldened critics, who embarked upon a long campaign to convince the public that something was wrong with Social Security, that it needed "reform." That campaign culminated in George W. Bush's efforts at privatization. In this respect—and in many other ways as well—it was Reagan who made the presidency of the younger Bush possible.

There were immediate effects as well. Although Reagan backed down, he did succeed in eliminating some benefits. No longer would there be payments to college students who were children of deceased workers, and no longer would there be a minimum benefit. After initially taking it away, Congress did restore the minimum benefit to those already receiving it, but only to them. The administration was forced to apologize, saying that when it struck those beneficiaries from the benefit rolls, it had not meant them any harm!

Shortly after the beginning of Reagan's first term as president, journalist Ronnie Dugger called him a "dedicated foe of Social Security." Reagan, he wrote, "regards it as welfare, which he detests." Dugger noted that Reagan had agreed in 1964 with Goldwater that Social Security should be made voluntary, in 1975 had "in effect proposed to abolish the whole system," and in 1978 had declared the system to be in effect bankrupt. "From the White House he has led a war on the Social Security system," Dugger wrote.[6] The bankruptcy charge, as we have seen, was not a new theme; Reagan had made the same charge since the 1950s. It was untrue every time Reagan repeated it, and it remains untrue today as Bush echoes Reagan's errors.

Laurence Barrett, another journalist who examined the Reagan administration in the early 1980s, provided evidence that gives credence to Dugger's charge that Reagan attacked Social Security from within the Oval Office. Barrett documented that presidential aides knew that the massive Social Security cuts included in Reagan's proposals in 1981 were more than double any that could have been needed to ensure the system's solvency. In addition, the proposals called for massive reductions in benefits.[7] Although, as mentioned above, public reaction to such excesses did force the administration to halt its overt attacks on Social Security and to restore the minimum benefit to those who previously were receiving it, that benefit vanished for future beneficiaries; since that time, retirees with extremely low earnings have no guaranteed minimum payment. President Reagan's rush to soothe the public and to promise that there would be no more cuts to Social Security was a political necessity, but it must have been as painful to him as loss of the minimum benefit had been to a poverty-stricken retiree.

If any questions remain about the administration's intentions or about Reagan's preferences, Reagan's own budget director, David Stockman, set them to rest. As the designer of "Reaganomics," Stockman authored much of the Reagan economic policy. He admitted that the phrase "future savings to be identified," the phrase he used to "explain" the more then $40 billion in unspecified cuts in the initial budget that Reagan proposed to Congress, was nothing other than "a euphemism for 'We're going to go after Social Security.'"[8] Barrett said that when Reagan took office, he could not resist taking "one more whack at the Social Security system," even though it was clear that he would have to pay a political price to do so.[9]

REAGAN'S LEGACY: THE WAR AGAINST SOCIAL SECURITY

Reagan had a genius for appealing to the people and for portraying himself as "reasonable." When he secured the Republican presidential nomination, the public appeared quickly to forget that almost immediately before he became a candidate of a major party and within a year of his becoming president, Reagan had represented the far-right fringe of American politics. As president, he had to abandon some of his right-wing agenda. He failed to achieve his long-term goal of eliminating Social Security. In fact, he had to shift tactics to abandon direct attacks and advocate more subtle restrictions.

By this shift of tactics, however, Reagan did achieve some of his goals, including some benefit reductions. He also managed to manipulate America's system of taxation to reduce progressivity in income taxes and to secure a drastically lower level of income taxation for upper-income taxpayers. As Kevin Phillips, then a Republican political analyst, reported, Social Security taxes rose to 36 percent of federal tax receipts from 31 percent, and the share of income taxes dropped from 47 percent to 45 percent.[10]

Reagan paved the way for the vastly more drastic cuts in the administration of the second George Bush, who came into office with a budget surplus bequeathed to him by the administration of Bill Clinton. Bush argued that a surplus meant taxes were too high, necessitating cuts. Shortly, though, Bush had succeeded in eliminating the surplus and returning the United States to deficit financing. His argument, in effect, then became that tax cuts were necessary because there was a deficit; cuts were essential to stimulate business activity. The only consistent theme was that taxes, especially on the most wealthy, must be reduced, regardless of any other circumstance.

There were other consequences of Reagan's efforts as well, and it is these that we see in today's discussions of Social Security. Reagan's rhetoric and that of his followers had an effect. Those who had always opposed the principle of social insurance with its government involvement had begun for the first time to have some success in influencing others with their arguments, sometimes even others who were supporters of Social Security. Many of the arguments were misleading at best, and they were deliberately so. It is clear to those who look that, even so, they have had enormous effect.

Reflecting the influence of Reagan's success, the mainstream of American politics moved sharply to the right. As the twenty-first century got under way, the dominant themes from Washington were the social agenda of the evangelical Right, privatization of everything possible, and, above all, continuous reduction of taxes on the wealthy. Encouraging the early efforts to privatize Social Security was the skillful use of misleading political rhetoric designed to generate conflict among different age groups, squeezing Social Security in the middle. In 1984, a Republican senator from Minnesota, David Durenberger, working in concert with conservative activists, founded Americans for Generational Equity (AGE). One may debate Durenberger's sincerity or whether his partners were using him, but AGE's purpose was clearly to create questions about the "prudence, sustainability, and fairness of federal old age programs."[11]

Within a few years, Durenberger's own financial irregularities brought him into disrepute, bringing censure from the Senate and disbarment, and AGE disbanded. Before vanishing, however, the organization accomplished substantial mischief and demonstrated that well-funded propaganda can influence the news media to take even the most nonsensical notion seriously. Regardless of the elusive nature of the notion of "generational equity" (or inequity)—after all, people move with absolute regularity from one age group to another, and a "generation" is hardly a homogeneous, or even a precise, grouping—AGE's propaganda created the illusion that there was some substance to the idea.

During the administration of the first President Bush, the thoughtful scholar Jill Quadagno argued that because of the strength of the perception that AGE created, all future policy choices would have to "take generational equity into account."[12] As a matter of fact, neither she nor anyone else at the time would likely have been able to foresee the extent to which naked self-interest would come to dominate the rhetoric of American politics in the new century. As a result, concern for any sort of equity faded, while the political rhetoric of those in power tended to appeal to individual selfishness.

At any rate, AGE was sufficiently powerful in the latter 1980s that its demise in 1990 left a political vacuum. Into that vacuum stepped investment banker Peter Peterson, a former secretary of commerce in the administration of Richard Nixon and an anti–Social Security zealot. In 1992, Peterson was instrumental in founding the Concord Coalition, which crafted its appeal so skillfully that it attracted support from some well-meaning figures from both political parties. For example, former Republican senator Warren Rudman and the late Paul Tsongas, a former Democratic senator, joined with Peterson to be listed as Concord's cofounders. Peterson hit the equity issue hard. Prior to founding Concord, he had even made the preposterous charge that Social Security was "a direct cause of our federal budget deficit."[13] Undoubtedly, the Concord Coalition contained, and continues to contain, many members of ability and good will. Regardless, the organization was created to be Peterson's tool in his strenuous efforts to undermine Social Security, and it continues under his dominance.

Some of the most perceptive analysts of social policy in the United States have made explicit the true nature of the Concord Coalition:

> Nominally dedicated to the purpose of educating Americans about the hard financial choices the nation will be confronting, the coalition reiterates the conservative position that government spending favors older, more affluent Americans at the expense of a younger generation that is already under financial distress. In addition to encouraging younger Americans to see themselves as needy and to see the elderly as an affluent group not deserving of public support, the coalition is not . . . [above] the use of scare tactics. It has warned, for example, that the failure to transform Social Security may bring on a generational war. And given their own residualist political agenda, Peterson and other coalition members have been ready to lead it.[14]

Peterson and his coalition members are not alone. Two clearly defined groups have been at the heart of the effort to eliminate Social Security. The Cato Institute, a libertarian think tank and activist group, joined with Third Millennium, Citizens for a Sound Economy (CSE), and others to provide ideological fervor from a dedicated cadre of activists who simply do not believe that government should be involved in social welfare or large-scale social policies. Funding comes from Wall Street. Brokerage houses and investment firms would stand to reap untold billions of dollars in fees and commissions if even a small portion of Social Security were to become private. Some time ago, Trudy Lieberman exposed the nature of the financial power arrayed against Social Security. Her article in the *The Nation* was one of the first revealing portrayals, and it received too little attention.[15]

As Lieberman reported, Leila Bate of Citizens for a Sound Economy was candid about the group's aims. It planned to spend "millions" in order to encourage privatization. When CSE "educated" congressional interns at a "youth summit" on Social Security during the Clinton administration in 1996, the interns left the sessions, Bate reported, with a "sense of the need to reform the system." She has remarked that it is important to have the "average American" accept the idea that Social Security must be radically revised if the group is to be successful.[16]

Jeanette Nordstrom of the National Center for Policy Analysis, another group that has attacked Social Security since the late 1980s, echoed her comments. The center spends hundreds of thousands of dollars on seminars, forums, and various media activities that Nordstrom has described as parts of a "product line." The approach is purely a sales pitch: appeal on the one hand to greed and, on the other, to fear, fear that Social Security faces a crisis "and needs a radical makeover." She has remarked that "the same clear, concise message must come from every direction." Undoubtedly, it has done so. As she put it, one of the aims of that message is "to break the strong tie between the taxes employees pay during their working years and their right to a pension later on."[17]

Third Millennium was a small organization purporting to speak for the young; in reality, it was a front group for wealthy organizations endorsing privatization. It had only a handful of employees, but they flooded the media with monographs and op-ed pieces. One of its largest contributors was—no surprise this—Peter Peterson.

It was from Third Millennium that the media were bombarded with the "finding" from a poll designed for it by the Republican pollster Frank Luntz and by Mark Siegel that young people were more likely to believe in UFOs than they were to believe that they would ever collect Social Security. The well-publicized assertion, however, was a fraud, consistent with many of Luntz's later efforts on behalf of George W. Bush. Two respected scholars of public opinion, Lawrence Jacobs and Robert Shapiro, demonstrated conclusively the fraudulent nature of the UFO propaganda.[18] It is worthwhile to quote from their study extensively:

The Third Millennium's UFO survey has become the flagship for the presumption that confidence in Social Security has collapsed. The UFO survey, however, has been falsely sold. Journalists conveyed the impression that respondents had weighed the relative likelihood of UFOs existing and Social Security surviving and concluded that UFOs were more probable. In fact, the survey never offered respondents a direct comparison; instead, it offered two separate questions, with the Social Security question appearing fifth and the UFO question fourteenth (as the survey's last substantive question before some standard demographic items).

A 1997 survey by the Employee Benefit Research Institute (EBRI) offered respondents the direct choice that Third Millennium falsely claimed to have posed. EBRI asked, "Which do you have greater confidence in: receiving Social Security benefits after retirement or alien life exists in outer space?" EBRI found that Americans overwhelmingly sided with Social Security over UFOs by a whopping margin of 71 percent to 26 percent. (Even among Generation X, respondents aged 33 or younger, the margin remained a stunning 63 percent to 33 percent).

Third Millennium not only misrepresented its results on UFOs and Social Security but also recounted an old story about public opinion. Confidence in Social Security's future has been low since the late 1970s.[19]

But, Jacobs and Shapiro say, "Despite their low confidence, the public's support has remained strong, according to available trend data."[20]

Another group directing its appeal to the young is Sam Beard's Economic Security 2000. Beard until recently spread his message with support from wealthy donors, some obviously misguided. He was notorious for alleging that privatization would enable workers earning a mere $8,000 a year (this was in the 1990s) to retire with almost a half million dollars in investments—"minimum-wage millionaires," he called them. It takes no imagination whatever to recognize how fanciful was the math (not to mention the other assumptions) behind his calculations. Beard, by the way, is fond of portraying himself as a "liberal" because he once worked for Robert Kennedy.[21] The same reasoning, of course, could lead to strange (and, fortunately, most misleading) classifications for Kennedy, himself, since as a young lawyer he once worked for the unspeakable senator Joseph R. McCarthy.

The J. M. Kaplan Fund and the Stuart and John M. Olin foundations have poured thousands of dollars into anti–Social Security groups. Similarly, the Investment Company Institute (ICI) has made lavish campaign contributions to members of Congress.[22] Former senator Robert Kerrey, a Democrat from Nebraska, was one of the loudest voices calling for "reform." ICI made contributions to Kerrey and even had him as keynote speaker for one of its conventions. President Clinton appointed Kerrey to chair the Bipartisan Commission on Entitlement and Tax Reform, apparently as the price of Kerrey's support for the 1993 budget with its tax increase.[23] That budget passed by a razor-thin majority that included a tie-breaking vote by Vice President Al Gore in the Senate and not a single Republican vote in either house of Congress. Its passage was fortunate. It contributed substantially to the achievement of a balanced budget, demonstrating clearly to the antitax zealots that, contrary to their predictions, a thriving economy is not dependent upon tax cuts. Kerrey could take pride in his vote, however reluctant he was to cast it. Sadly, Clinton's successor, George W. Bush, adopted policies that depended upon sharp reductions in taxes. As was obvious, huge deficits resulted, eliminating the surplus that he inherited from the Clinton administration.

Michael Hiltzik, then business columnist for the *Los Angeles Times*, in 2005 wrote an excellent book outlining the attack on Social Security. He discussed the "privateers," as he artfully called them, and noted that they frequently adopted "unexceptionable, reassuring, and even uplifting names, like the National Taxpayers Union, the Center for Freedom and Prosperity, Freedom Works, and the Alliance for Worker Retirement Security." Who, he asked, could be opposed to that?[24]

The "privateers" are conduits for the Bush White House and promise—as does Bush himself—a future so rosy that it would bring prosecution for any securities salesman who even hinted at claims so extravagant. A website for the Council for Government Reform echoed Sam Beard and promised citizens that they could retire as millionaires. Hiltzik said that "dozens of such organizations have collected beneath one big tent in the name of privatizing Social Security. As the plot against Social Security unfolds, they are spending lavishly on issue advertising, drawing from a slush fund of as much as $200 million raised with the help of White House operatives."[25] Hiltzik has done a public service by identifying the complex network of corporations and naming names of wealthy figures working in a coordinated manner to unravel Social Security and to return America to the days of "tough; you're on your own!" It bears repeating that the most prominent attacker of America's most successful and popular program is the president himself, George W. Bush, aided and abetted by Republican leaders in both houses of Congress.

Although the anti–Social Security groups portray themselves as representing the grass roots and profess to have mass membership—USA Next, for example, formerly the United Seniors Association with Art Linkletter as its spokesman, or the National Taxpayers Union—in reality they speak for wealthy special interests, and the same names appear on one list of contributors after another. Their names tend to be designed to mislead—Derrick Max's COMPASS, for example, seeks to eliminate social insurance, but its name cynically stands for Coalition for the Modernization and Protection of America's Social Security—and to disguise the fact that they represent banks, insurance companies, and other corporations. Conservative think tanks and evangelical religious spokesmen also figure prominently, the latter apparently having forgotten that Jesus admonished them to speak for the downtrodden rather than for the economic elites that they now have joined. To be sure, not all Republicans oppose Social Security, but the clear fact is that the attackers and their groups are nearly always Republican.

One of the most energetic, but more honest, of the groups opposing Social Security is the Cato Institute. It freely advocates privatization and does not attempt to hide behind misleading language. Cato's libertarian principles commit it to the most minimal government, regardless of the consequences. To that end, it employs José Piñera, at one time labor minister for the former dictatorship of Augusto Pinochet in Chile, to speak around the country touting Pinochet's privatized plan as a model for the United States. "Workers can become capitalists," or "Every Worker a Capitalist," is his refrain. For a time, contributions to Chile's system did indeed bring a high rate of return, but recent years have seen it drop sharply. Moreover, administrative costs in Chile's privatized system are astronomical, especially when compared with the extraordinarily efficient American Social Security system, which costs far less than 1 percent of income to administer. High administrative costs, of course, reduce the amount available to pay benefits.

Chilean officials now report that half of the working population will be unable to pay into the system enough to cover the guaranteed minimum benefit. They say that although the system has strengthened the economy, it has been disastrous for the citizens. One indication that all might not be well was apparent at the beginning when Pinochet's army imposed privatization on the country. The army was the privileged elite, and military leaders were shrewd enough to keep within the public system and stay away from private accounts. Now, military pensions still come from a public retirement system; they are far higher than the meager payments that civilians receive under the privatized system. One should keep in mind that this poor system deprives the Chilean people of a decent retirement, and it is this system that Cato and its spokesman Piñera, along with their enthusiastic convert, the ideological and poorly read president of the United States, George W. Bush, would impose upon the American people.

Cato's efforts to portray its paid spokesman as an expert, rather than as an ideologue, are only a small part of its extensive "Project on Social Security Choice." Until Republicans objected, Cato had called its program the "Project on Social Security Privatization." The director of this project, whatever its name, is Michael Tanner. It also includes William Shipman of State Street Global Advisors of Boston's State Street Bank, which has financed extensive advertising in favor of privatization.

In 1997, I debated the issues with Tanner on a panel in Kansas City. In those perhaps less complex and certainly less expensive days, I pointed out that Cato had a $2 million propaganda campaign to undermine Social Security. He corrected me smugly, and proudly. The figure, he said, was $3 million.

With the great diversity of American news media, one might have expected some skepticism about the sudden announcements of impending doom to a program that had been so successful for so long. Instead, with rare exceptions, the media accepted the propaganda uncritically. Even worse, many reported the special-interest propaganda as if they had uncovered it as "news." One newspaper, for example, the *Kansas City Star*, for a time almost completely turned its editorial page over to the Concord Coalition. It sponsored and coordinated Concord's "DebtBusters" game, played throughout the metropolitan area, convincing many players that the problems were simple and required only simple common sense to solve. Of course, the players could make "decisions" without having to live with their consequences. A *Star* editorial alleged that there really was no budget surplus. It then asked, "How should the big federal entitlement programs—Social Security and Medicare—be reformed?" There was an answer: "The Concord Coalition has the solution," the writer gushed. "A new edition of its handy booklet, '10 Questions Voters Should Ask Their Candidates.' The free booklet," he wrote, "includes not only suggested questions but clear, concise explanations of the key budget issues." A highly biased description of Concord followed: "The Concord Coalition is a national, non-partisan organization that provides information about the federal budget to the public and advocates fiscal responsibility in Washington." The editorial then urged voters to obtain the booklet by calling the coalition and published both local and national telephone numbers, stressing once more that the booklet provided a "good, simple solution" and "balanced information" on "Social Security reforms under discussion."[26]

The *Star*'s willing seduction by the Concord Coalition was so extreme that a professor from the University of Kansas (KU), David Eckerdt, made it the subject of a scholarly study.[27] Eckerdt, a distinguished scholar who heads KU's Gerontology Center, clearly revealed the manner in which a determined campaign can mislead even thoughtful people of good will and produce widespread public misunderstanding.

To give credit where it is due, I must report that the *Star* in recent years has become considerably more balanced and has even solicited op-ed pieces on Social Security from me. This was not always the case, however, for the *Star* or for the rest of America's mainstream media. The *Star* did print opposing op-ed pieces once from Michael Tanner and me, but it was long reluctant otherwise to publish anything in its editorial pages that questioned the conventional wisdom of doom and gloom about Social Security. Officials from the Social Security Administration (SSA) told me off the record in the late 1990s that they had tried repeatedly, and unsuccessfully, to persuade the *Star* to print their corrections to some of the more outrageous misrepresentations that then were gracing *Star* editorials. The *Star* was not alone, of course.

When *New York Times* reporter Robert Pear wrote an extensive piece quoting economist Dean Baker in praise of Social Security, the *Pittsburgh Post-Gazette* ran the story. When it appeared in Pear's own paper, though, the *Times* had cut all references to Baker and his criticism of those who would undermine Social Security. As Baker said at the time, "The media have closed off discussion."[28]

To its credit, in 1998 the *Times* did publish an early instance of a thoughtful analysis of Social Security. Fred Brock, one of its own editors, wrote "Save Social Security? From What?" in the business section.[29] Brock remarked that when the Congress assembled in 1999, it would be tackling the issue of Social Security. "Politicians talk crisis and issue dire warnings about the graying of America and the threat of generational warfare," he wrote. "Journalists toss off phrases like 'looming insolvency.' There is little wonder that a survey this year showed that 68 percent of Americans think that 'fixing' Social Security is very important." In striking contrast to nearly all other reports of the time, however, Brock then pointed out that the system, even under the most pessimistic forecasts regarding economic growth, is "rock solid for the next 30 years or so—and, with some minimal changes, for 40 years after that."

Under more likely scenarios, "even if economic growth over the next 75 years slows to half the annual average of 3.5 percent over the past 75 years, the Social Security system will do just fine." That, he said, was the view of economist Mark Weisbrot, research director of a Washington think tank. (Weisbrot is also coauthor with Dean Baker of a fine 1999 book with an excellent title, *Social Security: The Phony Crisis*.) Brock quoted Weisbrot as saying, sensibly, that "the most important thing we could do to protect Social Security right now is to leave it alone." Of course, that is no longer as easy as it was then; now, it is important to protect it from George W. Bush.

Given the economic facts, why, Brock asked, had there been such a fuss? "Think hidden agendas," he answered, "on all sides": "Wall Street would love to get its hands on at least some of the billions of dollars in the Social Security trust fund. And many ultraconservative Republicans want to privatize the system fully. But knowing that the idea won't fly politically, they are pushing for partial privatization, in which individuals would invest a portion of their contributions in the stock market, all in the name of rescuing the system." Brock quoted Weisbrot as saying that there is "a kind of gentlemen's agreement" in Washington not to acknowledge the "basic fact that we don't really need to be talking about Social Security." The whole notion of generational conflict, he argued, is purely a "smoke screen." In 2020, he said, the median age of the country will have risen from thirty-five, but only to thirty-eight, and that was then the median age in Florida. The aging of the population will come slowly, and in any case, younger people want their elderly relatives to "have a secure retirement."

Brock's article cut through the lavishly financed propaganda barrage and was one of the first to do so. As heartening as it may have been to find it in the country's "newspaper of record," though, it was more disheartening to discover how little the ideas it contained influenced the editorial policy of the paper that published it. In the very same issue that contained Brock's article, the lead editorial remarked that "the next Congress will have to deal with nothing less than shoring up the global economy and devising a plan to save Social Security in the next generation."[30]

When the *Washington Post* did run an op-ed piece by Henry Aaron, an economist from the Brookings Institution, who presented evidence that the portrayal in the media of a "crisis" in Social Security was nonsense, then senator Robert Kerrey, a Democrat, blasted Aaron in the pages of the *Congressional Record*.

Television network news was no better. In general, the media seemed to have concluded that there was nothing to say about Social Security except to speculate about the proper ways to "save" it. Tanner crowed that Social Security's supporters were caught "flat-footed" and that the debate was over, that the public was convinced that Social Security could not survive without radical restructuring and a change in the system's principles.

Although Tanner overstated his case, it was commonplace to hear that Social Security unfairly transferred wealth to the elderly from the rest of the population or that it was a "middle-class" entitlement. Previously, it had been considered—correctly—to be a program that protected nearly the entire population, regardless of age or class, in a variety of ways. Defining the middle class and the elderly as "special interests," the opponents commanded attention when they demanded that Social Security incorporate a means test (or as Peterson would have it, an "affluence test") to limit it to those who "need" it.

The coordinated propaganda campaign against Social Security was proceeding fully as the 1990s began and continued strongly until weakened by the crumbling of the second Bush's presidency. In 1993, for example, the "middle-class entitlement" theme was the substance of a representative attack in an article entitled "Many Retirees Don't Want Aid" by Lawrence A. Benenson in the *Christian Science Monitor* for February16. Benenson asserted that he had money enough without getting any more "from the government." He attacked the American Association of Retired Persons for its support of Social Security, although he carefully identified himself as a member. Payments to people who do not "need" them, he argued, were "immoral." Another of his criticisms was that he received more than a welfare mother. That, of course, was irrelevant and said nothing about Social Security, although it might have spoken volumes about the welfare system.

Consider a more widely distributed component of the campaign against Social Security. The Sunday supplement magazine *Parade*, which cautiously tends to support a conservative agenda and accompanies the Sunday newspapers in a huge number of cities throughout the country, published an article by Jack Anderson, formerly a highly popular columnist. His eye-catching title was, "Why Should I Pay for People Who Don't Need It?"[31] He cited the alarming, but largely irrelevant, fact that a declining number of workers will be supporting an increasing number of retirees. Moreover, he said, "Social Security is not a 'trust fund.'" That, of course, depended upon what he meant. The trust funds are invested in government securities, and they do, indeed, need to be paid back. The same is true for government bonds held by private sources. As noted previously, to say there is no money in the trust funds is no different from saying that there is no "money" in one's safety-deposit box full of government bonds.

Without acknowledging them as a source of his ideas, Anderson echoed the calls from the 1960s by Goldwater and Reagan to convert Social Security into a private system. Like his predecessors, he disregarded coverage for disability, Medicare, and survivors. Oddly, Anderson did undercut the complaints of Social Security's enemies and destroyed much of his own case by admitting that "Social Security neither has caused our financial woes nor is it leading us into bankruptcy."

One of the more strident examples of the propaganda that year was a *Newsweek* article by one Rich Thomas.[32] Because he recognized that "entitlement" had become a pejorative term, Thomas included Social Security in the same discussion with other "entitlements," although it is completely different. He referred to "the elderly on Social Security, the poor on food stamps, the sick on Medicare or Medicaid," but he carefully avoided mentioning that Social Security is self-supporting and was then—and still is—running a comfortable surplus. He did admit that "some entitlements are more worthy than others. The aging poor need social security," he wrote, but "the aging rich do not."

No one then or later has explained why "need" should be a factor any more than it is with a pension for corporate executives, although it may have a superficial plausibility. As discussed earlier, one major reason for Social Security's success is that it in fact does include virtually everyone and pays benefits by right, not on the basis of need. A requirement to undergo humiliating means tests to receive the benefits for which one has deferred consumption throughout his or her working career would quickly cause political support for the program to dwindle and die.

And why would that be the case? Everyone would continue to pay into the system, but only a minority would receive benefits. Would that be equitable? When support dried up, so would the program. It would die—and that is exactly the goal of the opponents. A retired executive may not "need" his or her corporate pension, but no one suggests easing the burden on corporate profits by withdrawing it (that option is limited to the corporations' workforce). A wealthy widow might not "need" the proceeds of her late husband's life insurance policy, but no one suggests relieving the company on that account of its obligation to pay, even if it is in financial trouble, which the Social Security system (apart from possible future difficulties facing Medicare, to be discussed later) is not.

Social Security is different from the other "entitlements," but they are important to the social fabric of the country as well. The rising cost of Medicaid is one of the greater economic threats. Do we merely cut it? "Yes," said Rich Thomas. At what cost? The removal of medical care for the poor. Should we cut food stamps? "Yes," said Thomas. At what cost? Lessening the amount of food for the poor, not to mention impairing the income of some farmers.

This is not merely an academic issue. For example, in 2004, a young, inexperienced, and highly ideological Republican in his early thirties, Matt Blunt, was elected governor of Missouri (his election benefited from the fact that his father, Roy Blunt, was majority whip of the U.S. House of Representatives and the Blunt family received strong support from evangelical groups). Immediately upon assuming office, Governor Blunt announced that the primary goal of his governorship would be no tax increases. He added, as though it were an afterthought, that, oh yes, that would mean that somewhat more than ninety thousand Missourians would be removed from Medicaid and, thus, would cease receiving health care.

Is the conservatives' answer the only possibility for our wealthy society? Aggravating their plight damages far more than the poor. Disregarding the moral and ethical issues, such an approach presents a direct threat to the middle and upper classes also. We progressively retreat into the suburbs, behind our security systems, and fear for our children, if not for ourselves. Encouraging social unrest is shortsighted policy that does not help economically—and certainly not ethically. It could easily be the greatest threat of all to "family values."

In any case, whatever the attitudes toward the other entitlements may be, the public appropriately continues to see Social Security in a different light. The barrage of anti–Social Security propaganda and the uncritical media coverage of the issue have resulted in some loss of confidence; fortunately, however, the reality of the public's attitude is not so simple as Social Security's enemies would wish. Despite their off-the-cuff answers, people do seem to believe that they will receive Social Security. The same polls that report loss of confidence in Social Security also report that more than 90 percent of the respondents expect it to be a significant source of their retirement income. Results from focus groups conducted over a decade reveal that early in the groups' discussions, people often said "matter-of-factly that Social Security would not 'be there' in the future. Later, having the groups talk about Social Security forced people to think about what they were saying." Frequently, their attitudes changed as it "became clear that the matter-of-fact 'it won't be there' statement was not based on any sort of judgment. It was simply a reaction."[33]

THE ROLE OF "THE MEDIA" AND THE CHANGE IN PUBLIC UNDERSTANDING OF SOCIAL SECURITY

If there is any doubt about the quality of public information available in the 1990s, the Cato spokesman's comments should eliminate it. Tanner candidly said that the media had become "very sympathetic." So they had. It was distressing to see newspapers simply running Concord Coalition faxes as editorials or op-ed pieces. Martha Phillips as Concord's executive director acknowledged happily that "the *Baltimore Sun* ran one on Medicare practically verbatim. Concord's DebtBusters game," she said, "shows up on newspaper editorial pages." As we have seen, she was not exaggerating. She gave special praise to the leading newspaper of the nation's capital, saying "We like the *Washington Post* editorials today." When Concord began its campaign, the *Post's* editorials "weren't singing our tune," but after meetings with the *Post's* staff, "it's like they're reading right out of our playbook."[34]

Now, a decade later, even though some major media outlets (*Time* and *Newsweek*, for example, as well as the *New York Times* and other newspapers, including the *Washington Post* and the *Wall Street Journal* in their news pages) have run some pieces examining critically the conventional wisdom about Social Security, most of the information being published or discussed on television remains highly biased. The *Post* continues to print editorials on the subject that not only contradict some of their own news items but that directly reflect talking points from the Republican National Committee.

As late as August 4, 2006, the *Post* criticized Democrats for referring to "the Social Security reform that President Bush pushed last year" as privatization. Yes, said the editorial, Bush's plan involved "personal retirement accounts. But it did not involve 'privatization.'" Really? "Privatization" was exactly what Republicans previously called their proposals. Even President Bush frequently used the term for his ideas. GOP media czars abruptly changed their terminology, although not their plans, after discovering that people rejected privatization but might be (they hoped) more receptive to "personal accounts." Note that the Republicans (and apparently the *Post's* editorial writers) now also reject even the term "private accounts"—that is too close to "privatization."

Although the phrase "the liberal media" has become so common as to be tiresome, it is nonsense. The *Post* is often the target of those decrying "liberalism" in the media, but it frequently repeats the arguments of the Bush administration, adopting them as its own. In fact, its editorial positions in general have moved decisively to the right. When Senator Joseph Lieberman lost his primary election to a challenger, for example, the *Post* praised Lieberman and supported his announced decision to flout the rules of the game and run as an independent, even though his party in Connecticut had rejected him and chosen another candidate. Lieberman is a conservative Democrat who frequently supports Republican policies. The *Post* thus explicitly aligned itself with Lieberman's other supporters, nearly all of whom are administration spokesmen and conservative commentators, rather than with the more liberal nominee, Ned Lamont. The *Post* justified its position by calling for bipartisanship. True bipartisanship, though, requires two parties willing to cooperate, not merely one party that accedes to the positions of the other. In recent years, Republican leaders have been unwilling to compromise. House leaders, for example, insisted on operating only with a "majority of the majority," and when George W. Bush appointed a "bipartisan" advisory commission on Social Security, he appointed only those who had committed themselves in advance to privatization—or, as the Republicans and the *Post* would have it, to "personal retirement accounts." Refusing to consider any position other than one's own is hardly "bipartisan"; nor is it likely to result in sound public policy.

The charge that the media are dominated by liberal bias dates back to the Nixon administration. Vice President Spiro T. Agnew vigorously attacked any news reporting that failed to present the administration in a favorable light. So eager were journalists to guard their objectivity that since that time, they have been exceedingly cautious about criticizing conservatives. Conservatives are quick to mobilize a chorus of opposition to news coverage of which they disapprove.

Liberals, though, are fair game. Criticizing them appears to be a demonstration by the media that they do not reflect "liberal bias." It is never enough, though, to blunt the persistent charges. Both the *Post* and the *New York Times* were quick to give front-page space to the most lurid charges against the Clintons and "Whitewater." Neither paper apologized when the Whitewater charges were demonstrated to be false and evaporated. To its credit, the *Times* did apologize for having permitted itself to be misled by administration spokesmen regarding weapons of mass destruction in Iraq, whereas the *Post* has never done so. Nevertheless, there is a loud voice from explicitly conservative media, such as the *Washington Times*, the editorial page of the otherwise excellent *Wall Street Journal*, the Fox News Channel, and nearly the whole of talk radio. Liberal examples, by contrast, are mere whispers. Recent studies and reports have made this plain—the most direct is Eric Alterman's *What Liberal Media? The Truth about Bias and the News*—but they have yet to dispel the misconception that conservatives continue to foster.[35]

This helps explain why the public that once understood Social Security quite well now accepts many misconceptions (although public understanding of the program is still probably better than its opponents would wish). Some of the misconceptions, to be sure, result from the increasingly complex nature of the programs. In large part, however, they stem from deliberate efforts to undermine social insurance in the United States and uncritical media that fail to examine the issues adequately. After many years, the underground grumbling of those who believe the government has no place in ensuring the welfare of its citizens, riding the success of Reaganism and the even greater extremism of George W. Bush, coalesced into a persistent campaign against what arguably is the most popular and beneficial program this country has ever enacted.

How different all this negativity about Social Security is from the atmosphere that existed when I went to work for the Social Security Administration as a young management intern in 1959. After running out of funds, I was faced almost literally with the prospect of becoming a starving graduate student (I was at the University of Minnesota). I therefore found it a distinct pleasure to accept the position in Baltimore at the headquarters of Social Security. I was even willing to accept the status of "government bureaucrat," despite still being a most conservative Republican. I also had developed the rather cynical attitude typical in the academic world. Nevertheless, I was impressed with much that I found. The Social Security Administration was widely accepted as a model government agency. Its employees, from the lowest to the highest, prided themselves on providing service to the public. They had no doubt that they deserved to be considered top-notch. Certainly not all was perfect, but the employees were dedicated and efficient. They prided themselves on humanizing an enormous bureaucracy, especially in its dealings with the public.[36]

The public, too, accepted Social Security with pride as an earned benefit, not a "handout." It was not "welfare" but had become part of the "American way of life." Brochures from the SSA explaining the program even stressed that elderly actor and comedian Eddie Cantor had qualified for benefits in one month during which he had no earnings, although he was a millionaire and earned large amounts in other months that year. If even he could apply, surely there could be no stigma involved. The agency made strenuous efforts to seek out those who were eligible and to ensure that they received benefits.

The cuts of the 1980s came long after I had left government service in the 1960s. The Social Security Administration became a target of Social Security's opponents. Eroding the agency was one way of attacking Social Security without arousing public ire. Morale plummeted as employees became overworked and underappreciated.

When letters brought tardy, if any, response, telephones went unanswered, callers were put on hold for lengthy periods, or claims took a seemingly interminable time to process, the public was encouraged to blame "government bureaucrats," not the elected officials who for twelve years had worked directly and diligently to undermine Social Security in the United States. The official attitude appeared to be that the primary function of the agency was to deny funds to those who were ineligible, rather than to make great efforts to provide them to those who qualified.

There was definite improvement under President Clinton and, to some extent, even under the first President Bush. The cutbacks, though, largely remained. Even though Social Security programs are far larger now than in the 1960s, the SSA still has fewer employees than it had then.

An especially disturbing development under the presidency of the second Bush has been the politicizing of the agency. Earlier, even under the Reagan administration, the SSA was a source of neutral and expert information. Its website during the Clinton years was a model source of information. The current Bush administration, however, has converted the website into a forum for propaganda that forecasts a dire future for the program if something substantial is not changed. The SSA website still makes excellent historical and other information available, but one must delve beyond the first material encountered to find it. The move to politicize the sources of public information has proceeded so far that now even the annual statements that citizens receive regarding their Social Security reflects administration propaganda.

We should remember that in the view of Social Security's enemies, those "who are not eligible" would and should include nearly all of us. The central figure among those enemies until the second Bush was Ronald Reagan. Just how striking a departure from tradition his role was becomes even clearer when we consider his predecessors. George W. Bush has gone far beyond even Reagan, but Reagan's administration and policies, supported by the most hardcore of his followers, provided the foundation for Bush and made it possible for him to attack Social Security openly with less of a firestorm of protest than would have existed before Reagan's accomplishment in shifting the political center far to the right.

The role of American presidents has been crucial in developing and maintaining Social Security. Their support was uniform from FDR through Jimmy Carter and included both conservatives and liberals, Republicans and Democrats. In the next chapter, I take a close look at the language they used to support Social Security and contrast it to Reagan's language as he attacked and sought to undermine the entire notion of social insurance.

NOTES

1. Max J. Skidmore, *Medicare and the American Rhetoric of Reconciliation* (Tuscaloosa: University of Alabama Press, 1970), 131.

2. Kurt Ritter, "Ronald Reagan and 'The Speech': The Rhetoric of Public Relations Politics," *Western Speech* 32, no. 1 (winter 1968), reprinted in Max J. Skidmore, *Word Politics: Essays on Language and Politics* (Palo Alto, CA: James E. Freel and Associates, 1972), 110–18.

3. The text of the Phoenix speech, "Encroaching Control," is available at the Reagan Collection of the Hoover Institution at Stanford University. It is virtually the same as the Orange County speech, "Encroaching Control: Keep Government Poor and Remain Free," in *Vital Speeches of the Day* 37 (September 1, 1961): 678.

4. Ronald Reagan, "Free Enterprise," *Vital Speeches of the Day* 39 (January 15, 1973): 200–201.

5. Ronnie Dugger, *On Reagan: The Man and His Presidency* (New York: McGraw-Hill, 1983), 49–50.

6. Dugger, *On Reagan*, 43.

7. Laurence I. Barrett, *Gambling with History: Ronald Reagan in the White House* (Garden City, NY: Doubleday, 1983), 156.

8. David A. Stockman, *The Triumph of Politics* (New York: Avon Books, 1987), 175.

9. Barrett, *Gambling with History*, 63.

10. Kevin Phillips, *The Politics of Rich and Poor* (New York: Random House, 1990), 80.

11. Annual Report (Washington, DC: Americans for Generational Equity, 1990), 2.

12. Jill Quadagno, "Generational Equity and the Politics of the Welfare State," *Politics and Society* 17, no. 3 (1989): 2.

13. Peter Peterson and Neil Howe, *On Borrowed Time: How the Growth of Entitlements Threatens America's Future* (San Francisco: Institute for Contemporary Studies, 1988), 43.

14. Theodore R. Marmor, Fay Lomax Cook, and Stephen Scher, "Social Security Politics and the Conflict between Generations: Are We Asking the Right Questions?" in *Social Security in the 21st Century*, ed. Eric R. Kingson and James H. Schulz (New York: Oxford University Press, 1997), 204.

15. Trudy Lieberman, "Social Insecurity: The Campaign to Take the System Private," *The Nation* 264, January 27, 1997, 11–18.

16. Lieberman, "Social Insecurity," 14.

17. Lieberman, "Social Insecurity," 13.

18. Lawrence R. Jacobs and Robert Y. Shapiro, "Myth and Misunderstandings about Public Opinion and Social Security," in *Framing the Social Security Debate*, ed. R. Douglas Arnold, Michael J. Graetz, and Alice Munnell (Washington, DC: National Academy of Social Insurance, 1998), 355–88.

19. Jacobs and Shapiro, "Myth and Misunderstandings," 364.

20. Jacobs and Shapiro, "Myth and Misunderstandings," 357.

21. See, e.g., Beard's website at www.network-democracy.org/social-security/nd/rt/beard.html.

22. Lieberman, "Social Insecurity," 13.

23. Lieberman, "Social Insecurity," 15–18.

24. Michael Hiltzik, *The Plot against Social Security* (New York: Harper Collins, 2005), 125.

25. See Hiltzik, *The Plot*, ch. 8; the following paragraph draws from this chapter, and the quotation above is from p. 126.

26. Stephen Winn, "Despite the 'Surplus,' Our National Debt Still Grows," *Kansas City Star*, October 4, 1998, 12.

27. See David J. Ekerdt, "Entitlements, Generational Equity, and Public-Opinion Manipulation in Kansas City," *Gerontologist* 38, no. 5 (1998): 525–36.

28. Lieberman, "Social Insecurity," 16.

29. Fred Brock, "Save Social Security? From What?," *New York Times*, November 1, 1998, 12.

30. "The Impeachment Breather," *New York Times*, November 1, 1998, 14.

31. Jack Anderson, "Why Should I Pay for People Who Don't Need It?" *Parade*, February 21, 1993.

32. Rich Thomas, "Why Cutting Entitlements Makes Sense," *Newsweek*, May 31, 1993.

33. Virginia P. Reno and Robert B. Friedland, "Strong Support but Low Confidence," in *Social Security in the 21st Century*, ed. Eric R. Kingson and James H. Schulz (New York: Oxford University Press, 1997), 188.

34. Lieberman, "Social Insecurity," 16.

35. Eric Alterman, *What Liberal Media? The Truth about Bias and the News* (New York: Basic Books, 2003); see also, e.g., Joe Conason, *Big Lies: The Right-Wing Propaganda Machine and How It Distorts the Truth* (New York: St. Martin's Press, 2003), and David Brock, *Blinded by the Right* (New York: Crown Books, 2002); see also Brock's blog, "Media Matters," an explicitly liberal website that identifies conservative bias in the media or the unthinking use of conservative metaphors and Republican "talking points." http://mediamatters.org.

36. See Max J. Skidmore, "Public Integrity: Perspectives from Home and Abroad," *Public Integrity Annual* (Council of State Governments/American Society for Public Administration) 1 (April 1996): 107–14.

9

Presidential Attitudes toward Social Security: "Only Desperate Men with Their Backs to the Wall"

The individualistic nature of American thought and traditions creates a large reservoir of antigovernment attitudes. These attitudes can make it difficult for the government to act positively. They place fewer restraints on the power of the government to act negatively—they can even encourage it. This is especially so with regard to the government's major actor, the president.

For decades, the prevailing opinion among political scientists regarding the presidency reflected the approach of Harvard political scientist Richard Neustadt, who argued that the presidency is inherently a weak office. The power of a president, he argued, depended upon the incumbent's ability to use his position, and especially his personality, to create coalitions, to persuade, and thus to secure broad support for his policies.[1] Although a president's skill and personality undoubtedly are important, Neustadt consistently underestimated the power of the office itself.

Until recently, a president's ability to take direct action has largely escaped the notice of both the public and the academy, yet as Kenneth Mayer has made clear, "throughout U.S. history presidents have relied on their executive authority to make unilateral policy without interference from either Congress or the courts."[2] More recently, George W. Bush's extraordinary use of "signing statements"[3] (often going so far as to contravene the intent of Congress, sometimes to the extent of using them as though he had the power of the line-item veto) has become so flagrant that it has even attracted public attention.

So the power of the presidential office is great, but the greatest power of all that a president can exercise is to restrain action, to reduce programs, to slow movement, or to keep things going as they are. This negative power is considerably greater than the positive power to expand existing programs or to innovate. To achieve significant progressive policies, the times must be right in order to overcome the inherent resistance of the American ideology and its political system. There must also be a president in office willing and able to lead in a progressive direction, one with the ability to craft appeals with a sensitivity to America's values and political symbols.

Such times have been rare in American political history. In the 1930s, there was a most uncommon confluence of factors. There was urgent and recognized need, while at the same time there was a sitting president who inspired trust and was able to create programs to meet that need. The most important of the many results of that unique and difficult period was Social Security. It was as great a departure from tradition as any program in American history, so it was essential first to tailor the program to fit American conditions and needs, then to demonstrate how its departure from tradition enhanced, rather than violated, American values.

By any measure, the programs that the Social Security Act of 1935 created and inspired are among the most ambitious and successful activities ever undertaken by the American political system—or by any political system anywhere. Presidential rhetoric alone can accomplish little or nothing, but it was a key ingredient in Social Security's implementation and the dramatic expansion of its coverage and benefits. It also has been crucial in educating the people and developing public attitudes toward the program. Social Security has been highly popular and remains so, despite the attacks upon it and despite its striking inconsistency with American notions of individualism as traditionally interpreted.

Much of the credit for the initial wide acceptance of Social Security must go to Franklin D. Roosevelt for the brilliant manner in which he used traditional American language to associate the Social Security Act with American values and to defend it against charges that it was alien or foreign. "One of the most interesting features of the acceptance speeches of President Carter and Governor Reagan in 1980," for instance, "was their dispute about who should be able to claim the mantle of Franklin Roosevelt."[4] Roosevelt set the tone, and at least until Reagan, his successors followed his lead, through good times and bad, both reflecting and generating popular support.

Roosevelt's artistry in the use of political rhetoric, his ability to meld change with continuity in a nonthreatening manner, was extraordinary. Take, for example, his famous "Four Freedoms" declaration. Freedom, of course, had been the central tenet of America's political ideology since the American Revolution. Thus, he was thoroughly in accord with the country's tradition when he proclaimed as central to his program the "freedom of speech" and the "freedom of religion." When he proceeded to add "freedom from want" and "freedom from fear," however, he was enlarging upon that tradition. He added "two parts security under the label of 'freedom' to the idea of freedom in the 'classic liberal sense.'"[5]

Roosevelt's skill at using rhetoric to bring support for innovation without discarding tradition characterized his approach to the New Deal in general and to the Social Security Act in particular. "Even the most precedent-breaking New Deal projects reflected capitalist thinking and deferred to business sensibilities. Social Security was modeled, often irrelevantly, on private-insurance systems."[6] By including private insurance principles in the Social Security Act, it was possible to lessen the burden of individual responsibility without doing violence to traditional beliefs regarding the place of the individual and the role of government.

There was also another political reason: it is well known that Roosevelt wished the program to be designed in such a manner as to protect it from future politicians who might be tempted to reduce or eliminate it. The "insurance-company model" would create within the public a sense of ownership, and a separate trust fund would protect both the program—since such a trust fund would be visible and call attention to any attacks upon it—and the general treasury.[7] He made his intention clear in a speech in New York a year after the adoption of the Social Security Act.

Speaking at Madison Square Garden on October 31, 1936, in response to the well-orchestrated "pay-envelope campaign," the president said,

> Only desperate men with their backs to the wall would descend so far below the level of decent citizenship as to foster the current pay-envelope campaign against America's working people. [Boos] . . . They tell the worker that his wage will be reduced by a contribution to some vague form of old-age insurance. But they carefully conceal from him the fact that for every dollar of premium he pays for that insurance, the employer pays another dollar. That omission is deceit. . . .
> But they are guilty of more than deceit. When they imply that the reserves thus created . . . will be stolen by some future Congress—diverted to some wholly foreign purpose—they attack the integrity and honor of American Government itself. Those who suggest that are already aliens to the spirit of American democracy. Let them emigrate and try their lot under some foreign flag in which they have more confidence. [Applause][8]

Roosevelt thus reassured Americans as to the safety of Social Security, and he also warned future politicians against attempts to divert funds from the program. He also managed at the same time to describe an attack upon a government program as an attack not upon government but upon "working people." Additionally, his rhetoric was strictly conventional. Americans understood "premiums," "insurance policies," and even "contributions." Such language is thoroughly consistent with private enterprise and sounds in no manner as if it is "socialistic," "alien," or even governmental. In fact, in adopting language that assumed the "American" character of the programs under the act, Roosevelt was able to turn the tables upon opponents

and associate them with forces alien "to the spirit of American democracy."
He thus linguistically created a symbol that portrayed a government innovation as an outgrowth of American tradition and suggested that those
who opposed it were the ones under foreign influence.

Although the tone was of course different, Roosevelt's rhetoric describing
the program itself remained consistent with his comments upon signing the
Social Security Act more than a year earlier on August 14, 1935. At that time,
he had spoken of protection for citizens whose lives had tended to become
insecure because of industrial changes, conceding that it would never be
possible to insure the entire population against all of the "hazards and vi-
cissitudes of life." He referred to the beginnings of Social Security as a "cor-
nerstone in a structure which is being built but is by no means complete"
and described the program as one that also would be beneficial to the country's economy. It would protect "the Government against the necessity of
going deeply into debt to furnish relief to the needy" and would provide "a
law to flatten out the peaks and valleys of deflation and of inflation—in
other words, a law that will take care of human needs and at the same time
provide for the United States an economic structure of vastly greater soundness."[9]

It is ironic that FDR succeeded grandly by invoking traditional values for
a truly innovative program. President Bill Clinton, on the other hand, more
than a half-century later, failed when he proposed a plan for health coverage that, for the most part, actually did reflect American traditions: it would
have relied essentially on private insurance plans that workers would have
received from their employers (see chapter 10 for a more extended discussion). The Clinton plan failed primarily because opponents portrayed it as
alien and "un-American." Many even accused Clinton (absurdly, but effectively) of attempting to "socialize one-seventh of the U.S. economy."

As for FDR, the themes he sounded were outgrowths of ideas he had long
advocated. In August of 1931, he spoke as governor to the New York legislature, saying that government must extend aid to the unemployed "not as
a matter of charity but as a matter of social duty."[10] Previously, in discussing
a New York pension bill, he had asserted that "our American aged do not
want charity." Rather, he said, they sought "old age comforts to which they
are rightfully entitled by their own thrift and foresight in the form of insurance." As for the bill itself, "we can only hope," he said, "that this will be a
forerunner of a proper system of security against old-age want in the years
to come."[11] When he accepted the Democratic nomination for president in
1932, he cited "work and security" as prime goals of the party. Somewhat
more than a year later, he declared that security for individuals and families
would be the foremost objective of his administration, and he called for social insurance as the mechanism to provide it, with funds to be contributed
by workers and employers to a program that would be national in scope.[12]

So effective has Roosevelt's rhetoric been in influencing both public policy and public attitudes that it can be difficult to recognize the extent to which his views were different—strikingly different—from those preceding him. When Ronald Reagan, and later Newt Gingrich and the new crop of zealous Republicans, began echoing those pre-FDR ideas, many people received them as fresh, new, and innovative.

By the time of the State of the Union address of 1935, FDR's emphasis on security and reform had become so strong that many scholars have seen in his policies the beginnings of a second New Deal.[13] His rhetoric had stressed "the average man" to demonstrate that the New Deal had not forgotten, and would not forget, ordinary people (the reference was to the late sociologist William Graham Sumner's "The Forgotten Man"). By the time of his second inaugural address, however, Roosevelt's emphasis had expanded to include those whose income was far lower than average. Achieving a poetic flair, he said that he saw "one third of a nation ill-housed, ill-clad, ill-nourished" and added that "we are determined to make every American citizen the subject of his country's interest and concern; and we will never regard any faithful, law-abiding group within our borders as superfluous."[14] He clearly and directly stated the new obligations of government in his 1938 State of the Union address when he said that "Government has a final responsibility for the well-being of its citizenship."[15] Such a thought, announced so directly, would have been nothing short of startling a few brief years earlier. By 1938, however, the public was receptive, partly—perhaps in large part—because of FDR's skillful nurturing of the idea.

Nevertheless, at no time did Roosevelt fail to pay homage to traditional values or to associate his innovations with those values. In his fifth State of the Union message (January 3, 1938), FDR demonstrated that his rhetorical skill remained undiminished and that he had not lost sight of the need to keep his ties to American values. "As a nation," he said, "we have rejected any radical revolutionary program. For a permanent correction of grave weaknesses in our economic system we have relied on new applications of old democratic processes."[16] This example supports the observation that in order to implement an innovation, a president generally must describe the new program, however radical a departure from traditional values it may be, as the embodiment of those values.

Despite the pressures of World War II, Roosevelt did not permit preoccupation with the conflict to cause him to forget domestic social issues. In chapter 1, I discuss FDR's bold, and to date unanswered, call for an Economic Bill of Rights. He spoke out for social justice on numerous occasions. On February 5, 1944, for example, he held a press conference at the White House for the Negro Newspaper Publishers Association. He declared himself to be "for extension of the system of social security, which recognizes the right of the individual to self-development, protection against the hazards of illness, unemployment and want, and promotes the orderly development of the nation's resources."[17]

He kept the rhetoric alive. In a campaign speech in Washington later that year on September 23, speaking before the Teamsters, he accused the Republicans of appropriating that rhetoric. "I got quite a laugh," he said, "when I read this plank in the Republican platform. . . . 'The Republican party accepts the purposes of the National Labor Relations Act, the Wage and Hour Act, the Social Security Act and all other Federal statutes designed to promote and protect the welfare of American working men and women, and we promise a fair and just administration of these laws.'" His comments provoked laughter, and he proceeded to charge the Republicans with having worked to fight each of those programs, saying that they "would not even recognize these progressive laws, if they met them in broad daylight."[18] The laughter increased.

Although FDR's successor as president, Harry S. Truman, made no effort to duplicate Roosevelt's rhetorical heights, his language reflected the same themes. Certainly, he was fully his predecessor's equal in the strong support he provided for Social Security and in his efforts to expand the minimal program that the new Deal had provided. In his combative manner, he continued to associate Social Security with insurance and to stress its beneficial effects. In 1948, for example, speaking before the Greater Los Angeles Press Club on June 14, he said,

> I've been asking the Congress to broaden the base of Social Security so more people could benefit from the Social Security Act. . . .
>
> Now, do you know how Congress has broadened the base of Social Security? They've just taken 750,000 people off Social Security and sent me a bill to that effect and tied a rider onto it increasing the old-age assistance, hoping I'd take the bait and let them get away with tearing up Social Security. I didn't do it. I vetoed that bill this morning. I've told the Congress that if they would pass the bill in the proper form I'd be happy to sign it, and they have plenty of time to pass it in the proper form—don't think they haven't.[19]

In the same talk, he called for a major addition, one unprecedented in the United States and affecting the average citizen: "I wish the Congress would go into this health situation and pass an intelligent health bill for the benefit of the whole country, so that everybody could get medical care at a reasonable price when he needs it. . . . There are only two classes of people who can get the proper medical care nowadays, and that is the indigent and the very rich."[20] His proposal, of course, elicited tremendous opposition and was not seriously considered. In fact, the Republican Congress overrode Truman's veto of the Social Security bill the very day he cast his veto, and by record margins.[21]

Nevertheless, Truman missed no opportunity to call for expansion of Social Security benefits. In fact, he went so far as to urge Congress to adopt a full program of national health insurance, something Theodore Roosevelt had advocated as early as 1912 but that conservatives had consistently managed to block for almost a century. In his State of the Union message on January 5, 1949, shortly after his reelection, Truman said,

> The Government has still other opportunities—[*sic*] to help raise the standard of living of our citizens. These opportunities lie in the fields of social security, health, education, housing and civil rights.
> The present coverage of the social security laws is altogether inadequate, and benefit payments are too low. One third of our workers are not covered. Those who receive old age and survivors insurance benefits receive an average payment of only $25 a month. Many others who cannot work because they are physically disabled are left to the mercy of charity.
> We should expand our social security program, both as to the size of the benefits and extent of coverage, against the economic hazards due to unemployment, old age, sickness, and disability.
> We must spare no effort to raise the general level of health in this country. In a nation as rich as ours, it is a shocking fact that tens of millions lack adequate medical care. We are short of doctors, hospitals, and nurses. We must remedy these shortages. Moreover, we need—and we must have without further delay—a system of pre-paid medical insurance which will enable every American to afford good medical care.[22]

Although the style differed, the populist spirit that had infused FDR's rhetoric remained. So did the stress on the average citizen's needs. At least by implication, Truman's rhetoric also continued Roosevelt's association of social insurance with American values and traditions. In fact, in countering his critics, he explicitly raised the issue of rhetoric. For example, in a speech at the Allegheny County Fair in Pittsburgh, Pennsylvania, on September 5, 1949, he belligerently attacked those who opposed social welfare and the expansion of Social Security:

> These propagandists do not argue the merits of our program. They know that the American people will always decide against the selfish interests if all the facts are before them. So they have adopted an age-old device to hide the weakness of their case.
> This is the device of the "scare word" campaign.
> It is a device that has been used in every country and every age by the propagandists for selfish interests. They invent slogans in an effort to scare the people. They apply frightening labels to anything they happen to oppose. These scare words are intended to confuse the people and turn them against their own best interests.

Scare words change with the times.

When Franklin Delano Roosevelt and the New Deal saved our country from the great depression, the selfish interests raised the scare words of "socialism" and "regimentation."

But the American people didn't scare.

Year after year the selfish interests kept up their refrain. They tried new words—"bureaucracy" and "bankruptcy."

But the American people still didn't scare.

Last November the people gave the selfish interests the surprise of their lives. The people just didn't believe that programs designed to assure them decent housing, adequate wages, improved medical care, and better education were "socialism" or "regimentation."

So the selfish interests retired to a back room with their high-priced advertising experts and thought things over. They decided that the old set of scare words had become a little mildewed. Maybe it was time for a change.

So they came up with a new set of scare words. Now they're talking about "collectivism," and "statism," and "the welfare state."

The selfish interests don't know—and in fact they don't care—what these words mean. They're using those words only because they want to turn the American people against the programs which the people want, and need, and for which the people voted. . . .

The people want a better social security system, improved education, and a national health program. The selfish interests are trying to sabotage these programs because they have no concern about helping the little fellow, and so they call this the "welfare state."

Well, we don't care what they call it.[23]

By describing the rhetoric of his opponents as empty propaganda, Truman attempted to establish clearly that government programs to assist citizens economically were indeed consistent with individualism, freedom, and a limited state. It is noteworthy that at this time public fear of "socialism" and government programs was joining with apprehension regarding the expansion of Marxism-Leninism to produce the beginnings of what soon came to be called McCarthyism, a name Truman himself used with relish.

Truman continued such themes—and his belligerency—throughout his presidency. Speaking before a political group at a Jefferson-Jackson Day dinner in Washington in March 1952, he announced that he would not be a candidate for reelection, and he attacked what he called the "dinosaur school of Republican strategy." Those of the dinosaur school, he argued, were saying, "Let's stop beating about the bush—let's say what we really believe. Let's say we're against social security—and we're against the labor unions and good wages . . . that we're against the Government doing anything for anybody except big business." Truman conceded that he had some sympathy for this group because they were urging their party to tell the truth, but their prescription would not be good for the country. He said it would not be good for their party either, because if it told the truth, it would receive nothing but the "dinosaur vote."[24]

Rather than the truthful "dinosaur strategy," he warned, the Republicans would adopt a "white is black" campaign. "First of all they will try to make people believe that everything the Government has done for this country is socialism. They will go to the people and say: 'Did you see that Social Security check you received the other day—you thought that was good for you, didn't you? That's nothing in the world but socialism.'"[25]

Such rhetoric from the president may have helped protect Social Security, if protection indeed were needed at the time for such a popular program. It may even have helped bring about an expansion of coverage in 1950 to include most of the self-employed, as well as the benefit increases of 1951 and 1952. It did not, however, appreciably advance the fortunes of Truman's proposal for health care; nor did it prevent the strong Republican victory in 1952 that brought the very popular General Dwight D. Eisenhower to the White House, along with Republican majorities in both the House and Senate.

Far from being a disaster for the program, though, the Republican victory showed just how much a part of the American way of life Social Security had become. Eisenhower assumed the presidency at the height of McCarthyism, during a time of growth and prosperity. It could have been a time conducive to an attack on Social Security, but Eisenhower continued the pattern of support set by his two predecessors, differing from them essentially only in emphasis. He accepted Social Security, even if he did add a "Yes, but" note.

To illustrate, Eisenhower campaigned against "too much government." He proposed a "middle way" that he said "assumes that all Americans of all parties have now accepted and will forever support what we call social gains, the security that people are entitled to in their old age and to make certain that they are adequately cared for, insured against unemployment, equal opportunities for everybody regardless of race, religion, where he was born or what is his national origin." He said that social gains were to provide a solid floor, "but on top of that floor, let's not interfere with the incentive, the ambition, the right of any of you to build the most glorious structure on top of that floor you can imagine."[26] Eisenhower's rhetoric thus continued language combining individualism with support for Social Security, but it added a note of caution. Despite the cautionary tone, the Republican Party had plainly accepted Social Security.

Eisenhower did not mention Social Security in his inaugural address on January 20, 1953.[27] This did not mean, though, that he had left it off his agenda. The following month, he delivered his first State of the Union message. Using language that could have been from FDR or Truman, he called for significant expansion of Social Security:

> This Administration is profoundly aware of two great needs born of our living in a complex industrial economy. First: the individual citizen must have safeguards against personal disasters inflicted by forces beyond his control. Second: The welfare of the people demands effective and economical performance by the Government of certain indispensable social services.
>
> In the light of this responsibility, certain general purposes and certain concrete measures are plainly indicated now.
>
> There is urgent need for greater effectiveness in our programs, both public and private, offering safeguards against the privations that too often come with unemployment, old age, illness, and accident.
>
> The provisions of the old age and survivors insurance law should promptly be extended to cover millions of citizens who have been left out of the Social Security System.[28]

Eisenhower's proposal made plain that Social Security had become a nonpartisan issue and had indeed been accepted by the polity as a whole. The next year, he devoted a portion of his State of the Union address to reiterating his call for expansion. His rhetoric describing the system had come to differ little from that of the New Dealers. On January 7, 1954, he said,

> Our basic social security program, the old-age and survivors insurance system, to which individuals contribute during their productive years and receive benefits based on previous earnings, is designed to shield from destitution. Last year I recommended extension of the social insurance system to include more than 10 million additional persons. I ask that this extension soon be accomplished. This and other major improvements in the insurance system will bring substantial benefit increases and broaden the membership of the insurance system, thus diminishing the need for Federal grants-in-aid for such purposes.[29]

He even built into his address recognition of the inadequacies of the health-care system. "I am flatly opposed to the socialization of medicine," he said, and stressed that the needs were best met through private efforts. On the other hand, he noted the rising costs of medical care and the hardships that were resulting. "The Federal Government can do many helpful things," he remarked, "and still avoid the socialization of medicine." Among the things he mentioned were assistance to research and to hospital construction.[30]

In his 1955 State of the Union message, Eisenhower boasted of the "notable advances" in certain "functions of government" during his administration. "Protection of old-age and survivors insurance was extended to an additional ten million of our people," he said.[31] The following year, he again noted the extension of coverage and the increase in benefits with pride, calling for yet further expansion:

> Under the 1954 amendments to the old-age and survivors insurance program protection was extended to some ten million additional workers and benefits were increased. The system now helps protect nine out of ten American workers and their families against loss of income in old age or on the death of the breadwinner. The system is sound. It must be kept so. In developing improvements in the system we must give the most careful consideration to population and social trends and to fiscal requirements. With these considerations in mind the Administration will present its recommendations for further expansion of coverage and other steps which can be taken wisely at this time.[32]

The reelection campaign saw President Eisenhower continuing to speak as glowingly of Social Security as any New Dealer. "We made coverage virtually complete," he said, "and we put through the biggest real increase in benefits in the program's history."[33] It is also significant that during the Eisenhower administration, in 1956, came the addition of disability benefits, an enormously important expansion of the Social Security system. Although Eisenhower did not mention Social Security in his notable Farewell Address (January 17, 1961),[34] he did take time in his final State of the Union message once again to point out that "the coverage of the Social Security Act has been broadened since 1953 to make 11,000,000 additional people eligible for retirement, disability or survivors benefits for themselves or their dependents, and the Social Security benefits have been substantially improved."[35]

To be sure, the parties did vary in their emphases, but there can be no doubt that both the Democratic and Republican parties had accepted Social Security as an American institution. The contrast with the post-Reagan Republican Party, and especially with the second George Bush, is little short of astounding.

With the election of John F. Kennedy, despite the pressures of the Cold War, Social Security again emerged at the top of the political agenda. This time it was in the form of a strong effort to secure passage of health benefits for the elderly. Because of such fervent opposition from many quarters, including, among others, the insurance industry, the U.S. Chamber of Commerce, the pharmaceutical manufacturers, and especially the American Medical Association (AMA) (discussed in chapter 5), Kennedy's program generated a furious rhetorical battle.[36] His language remained firmly within the pattern established by his predecessors, and, following their lead, he used the State of the Union address to call for action. On January 11, 1962, he said to the Congress and the American people that "in matters of health, no piece of unfinished business is more important or more urgent than the enactment under the social security system of health insurance for the aged."

He proceeded to say, "Social Security has long helped to meet the hardships of retirement, death, and disability. I now urge that its coverage be extended without further delay to provide health insurance for the elderly."[37] He was sincere and threw the full energy of his office behind what came to be called Medicare. The struggle was under way.

In a major address to the National Council of Senior Citizens in New York on May 20, 1962, Kennedy cited examples of the need for government health-care provisions and said, "We say that during his working years [the worker] will contribute to Social Security, as he has in the case of his retirement." He praised physicians but criticized the proposal's opponents and condemned what he termed the misinformation they disseminated. He denied that such provisions would in any way interfere with freedom or provide a "handout." He spoke of "great unfinished business in this country" and conceded that "while this bill does not solve our problems in this area, I do not believe it is a valid argument to say this bill isn't going to do the job. It will not, but it will do part of it." He reminded his listeners that "all the great revolutionary movements of the Franklin Roosevelt Administration in the Thirties we now take for granted" and used his trademark metaphor of moving this country forward.[38] Thus, Kennedy associated revolutionary (radical) actions with individual freedom. Such rhetoric was congenial to Americans because of their reverence for the American Revolution. The effect was to praise the New Deal's programs and their extensions as supports for individualism.

The year 1962 was one of stormy controversy, with charges, countercharges, and threats flying back and forth in a rapid and confusing manner. Physicians' groups threatened boycotts; the AMA alleged that "Medicare" would be a "cruel hoax" for the poor and that the U.S. Treasury was being "looted to help subsidize the biggest lobbying campaign this nation has ever seen" in support of the proposal. In March, Democratic National Chair John M. Bailey called the AMA an "ally of the John Birch Society in a surgical mask."

Kennedy himself had commented during a news conference on May 23 that the AMA had been one of the chief opponents of Social Security in the 1930s. AMA president Leonard Larson said that Kennedy's charge was "entirely incorrect" and that the AMA had never taken a position on the legislation. Kennedy retorted by referring to the 1939 *Journal of the American Medical Association (JAMA)* editorial saying that "all forms of security, compulsory security, even against old age and unemployment, represent a beginning invasion by the state into the personal life of the individual, represent a taking away of individual responsibility, a weakening of national caliber, a definite step toward either communism or totalitarianism." As noted earlier, the AMA's position was that only resolutions by its House of Delegates reflected official AMA policy. To bolster his charges, Kennedy reminded the AMA of the resolution by its House of Delegates in 1949, saying that "so-called 'Social Security'" was in fact "socialism," that it had failed everywhere it had been tried, and that it always "served as the entering wedge for establishment of a socialistic form of government control over the lives and fortunes of the people."[39]

Kennedy had devoted a huge amount of effort to Medicare's passage. His assassination did not diminish the effort—far from it. Lyndon B. Johnson made Medicare, along with aid to education, civil rights, and a general "war on poverty," top priorities in his new administration.

In his State of the Union message on January 8, 1964, Johnson said,

> Let this session of Congress be known . . . as the session which declared all-out war on human poverty and unemployment in these United States; as the session which finally recognized the health needs of all of our older citizens. . . . We must provide hospital insurance for our older citizen financed by every worker and his employer under Social Security . . . to protect him in his old age in a dignified manner, without cost to the treasury against the devastating hardship of prolonged or repeated illness. . . . Every American will benefit by the extension of Social Security to cover the hospital costs of their aged parents.[40]

Thus, he launched the battle by adopting a ringing martial rhetoric incorporating the same symbols employed by Roosevelt at the beginning of Social Security: dignity, unmet needs, financing by workers without strain to the Treasury, and widespread benefit to all. He included strong reference to Social Security in his speech accepting the 1964 Democratic nomination in Atlantic City, New Jersey, portraying it as a mainstay of human freedom. "Most Americans," he said, "want medical care for older citizens, and so do I. . . . For more than 30 years, from Social Security to the war against poverty, we have diligently worked to enlarge the freedom of man."[41]

Johnson's opponent that year was Senator Barry Goldwater, who represented the most conservative wing of the Republican Party. For the first time since the 1930s, comments from a major party's presidential candidate led to concern that he might, if elected, move to make Social Security a voluntary system, thus changing it completely and, most experts believed, destroying it. Goldwater went down to a crushing defeat, as LBJ won by a popular-vote margin still unexcelled in American history. Most observers believed that the perception that Goldwater was hostile to Social Security was one of several major factors in his defeat.

Johnson won his victory with nurturing rhetoric, such as "We seek to care for the old through medical care under Social Security."[42] On January 4, 1965, after the election, he devoted time in his State of the Union message to the subject. He adopted rhetorical symbols of justice, dignity, and struggle. "Let a just nation," he said, "promise: To the elderly . . . hospital care under Social Security and . . . raising benefit payments to those struggling to maintain the dignity of their later years."[43]

The Congress responded to Johnson's patient and determined urging. After years of effort by dedicated supporters, Congress approved legislation adding Medicare to the Social Security system. Johnson, though, did not stop. In his 1967 State of the Union message, he boasted of bringing "medical care to older people" and said that "three and one-half million Americans have already received treatment under Medicare since July." Nevertheless, he said, "we should raise Social Security payments," and "I will ask that you raise the minimum payment by 59 percent . . . to guarantee a minimum benefit of $100 a month for those with a total of 25 years of coverage." Furthermore, "we should extend Medicare benefits that are now denied to 1,300,000 permanently and totally disabled Americans under 65 years of age."[44]

Throughout his presidency, LBJ continued to point with pride to the many people who had received treatment through Medicare. He also faulted those who had been in opposition, especially Republicans. "In the Congress," he said, "some closed their ears and their ranks" to the need; "93 percent of the House Republicans voted to kill the Medicare Bill."[45] In his 1968 State of the Union address on January 17, he boasted that "last year, Medicare, Medicaid and other new programs brought better health to more than 25 million Americans."[46] The Great Society programs—Medicare, civil rights, aid to education, and the War on Poverty—were LBJ's fondest accomplishments, even as the Vietnam War wore him down both physically and emotionally, causing him to relinquish the presidency.

In his final State of the Union message, delivered on January 14, 1969, Johnson kept pressing, taking this last opportunity to use careful rhetoric to craft symbols on behalf of Social Security. He noted, "Medicare, that we were unable to pass for so many years, is now a part of American life." Moreover, "since the enactment of the Social Security Act in 1935, Congress," he said,

> has recognized the necessity to "make more adequate provision for aged persons . . . maternal and child welfare . . . and public health."
>
> And that is the words of Congress.
>
> The time has come, I think, to make it more adequate and I think we should increase social security benefits and I am so recommending. . . .
>
> Our nation is rightly proud of its medical advances. But we should remember that our country ranks 15th among the nations of the world in its infant mortality rate.
>
> I think we should assure decent medical care for every expectant mother, and for their children during the first year of their life in the United States of America.
>
> I think we should protect our children and their families from the costs of catastrophic illness.[47]

Lyndon B. Johnson must have felt despair when foreign policy not only consumed his administration but diverted the country from his Great Society. Thurgood Marshall and others have mentioned that it destroyed him. Nevertheless, he did not permit any despair he felt to prevent him from presenting a final grand rhetorical picture of a caring country, one that had moved toward his vision of a Great Society, as he relinquished the presidency to his successor, Richard M. Nixon.

President Nixon did not stress Social Security in his inaugural address or his first State of the Union message. On December 2, 1969, however, he startled the country with a plan that in many respects went considerably beyond the Social Security system. At a 1969 White House Conference on Food, Nutrition, and Health, although he did not refer specifically to Social Security, Nixon proposed "for the first time, this new Family Assistance Plan" that "would give every American family a basic income."[48] The plan did not succeed, but it demonstrated Nixon's willingness to speak the same language as his predecessors with regard to social issues. That Nixon, the Republican, could even think about, let alone propose, such a radical plan demonstrates the extent to which Reagan began and the second Bush completed the destruction of America's consensus regarding the need for effective government and caring policies.

The Nixon administration in general did not give Social Security a position of top priority, but when the president did speak of social insurance and related matters, he used the supportive rhetoric that had become more or less traditional. In his State of the Union message on January 22, 1971, for example, although Nixon did not stress Social Security, he outlined six "great goals," the fourth of which was to "offer a far-reaching set of proposals for improving America's health care and making it available more fairly to more people. I will propose," he said, "a program to insure that no American family will be prevented from obtaining basic medical care by inability to pay." The program included aid to medical schools, incentives to those who delivered health services, some new encouragements for preventive medicine, and a $100 million effort to fight cancer.[49] This was not a Social Security proposal; nor was it a call for universal health coverage to be guaranteed by government. Nevertheless, it was related. The rhetoric could have been taken directly from speeches on Social Security by earlier presidents, even New Deal Democrats.

Similar rhetoric permeated Nixon's acceptance speech on August 23, 1972, after receiving renomination. "And while we are talking about welfare," he said, "let us quit treating our senior citizens in this country like welfare recipients. They have worked hard all their lives to build America. And as the builders of America, they have not asked for a handout. What they ask for is what they have earned—and that is retirement in dignity and self-respect. Let's give that to our senior citizens."[50]

Nixon won the election, crushing the decent and misrepresented Midwestern candidate, the decorated World War II bomber pilot Senator George McGovern, in one of history's greatest landslides. Nixon's victory could hardly have been in doubt, even though conservatives lately have begun to reconsider and some even concede that McGovern would have been the better choice by far. In 2006, for example, *The American Conservative* could publish "Come Home America," an article concluding that what is now needed is "a bracing shot of McGovernism."[51]

Despite Nixon's almost assured victory, he sought assistance from the popularity of Social Security.

> A president can judiciously time economic benefits to interest groups or certain segments of the electorate to ensure their support on election day. Timing of Social Security increases provides a classic example of this point. Checks went out in October 1972, one month before the elections, with the following memo enclosed and personally approved by President Nixon to each of the 24.7 million Social Security recipients:
>
> Your social security payment has been increased by 20 percent starting with this month's check by a new statute enacted by Congress and signed into law by President Richard Nixon on July 1, 1972.
>   The President also signed into law a provision which will allow your social security benefits to increase automatically if the cost of living goes up.
>
> This example from the Nixon administration is hardly unique.[52]

As this quotation indicates, adjusting the timing of benefit increases, before they became automatic, was fairly common. This instance, though, had a unique, characteristically Nixonian aspect. (To be sure, by the standards of some later administrations, especially that of the second Bush, it now seems almost quaint.)

What was unusual here—and, one might observe, especially hypocritical for the time—is that President Nixon had approved the benefit increase entirely because he had no choice: Democrats attached it to a bill that Nixon considered to be essential. He had favored an increase but only a small one; in fact, he had threatened to veto the increase that he ultimately signed—and for which he then took credit—because he believed it to be too great. Thus, things in politics frequently are not what they seem.

In Nixon's defense, he did favor a benefit increase, even if not the large one, so his threat of a veto should not be taken to mean that he was hostile to social insurance. His supporters could point out that fears of a cash-flow shortage did in fact emerge during his administration. Those fears led, after Nixon left office, to a delay in the automatic adjustment of benefits. Therefore, these supporters could argue, Nixon had been correct in opposing the larger benefit. They could not, however, seriously dismiss the allegation of hypocrisy.

Regardless of the extent to which Nixon may have lacked enthusiasm for the large Social Security increase, he clearly accepted the Social Security system. His rhetoric was traditionally supportive, and at no time did he demonstrate anything resembling opposition. Like his predecessor, Lyndon Johnson, he boasted of increases and system expansion. Speaking over the radio on February 24, 1973, Nixon said, "Social security cash benefits for the elderly and the disabled in fiscal year 1974 will be twice what they were four years ago. Next year, five million additional poor, aged, and disabled persons will receive health benefits."[53] Nixon had joined the succession of presidents, Republican as well as Democrat, who, however their emphases may have varied, accepted and supported the Social Security system and described it with symbolically similar rhetoric.

When Gerald Ford, a decent man who became a decent president, replaced Richard Nixon, he followed his predecessors in supporting Social Security and even in calling for expansion and benefit increases. Like some of the others, he did not place matters relating to the program at the top of his agenda. Also, he faced inflation, which caused him concern. Accordingly, he sounded an unusual note. In his State of the Union message of January 15, 1975, speaking not exclusively of Social Security, he charged that "we have been self-indulgent. For decades, we have been voting ever increasing levels of government benefits—and now the bill has come due. . . . One characteristic of these programs is that their cost increases automatically every year because the number of people eligible for most of the benefits increases every year." Ford outlined several cost-cutting mechanisms, then said, "As an additional step toward putting the Federal Government's house in order, I recommend a 5 percent limit on Federal pay increases in 1975. In all Government programs tied to the Consumer Price Index—including Social Security, Civil Service and military retirement pay, and food stamps—I also propose a one-year maximum increase of 5 percent."[54]

The purpose of imposing ceilings was to combat inflation, but the move suggested that Social Security might at some time face actual reduction because of a budget revision that Lyndon Johnson had inaugurated in 1968. At that time, he and the Congress accepted a recommendation to include receipts and disbursements from "the Social Security, Medicare, highway and other trust funds" with the ordinary budget for purposes of accounting.[55] Note that this did not, as a wildly inaccurate Internet charge indicates (see appendix B), do away with the trust funds; nor did it mingle the funds with general revenues. It was purely an accounting device to reflect total government income and outgo realistically. Nevertheless, it did create misunderstandings that could in the long run be detrimental to Social Security, especially if the government continues to deny itself needed revenues by adopting tax cuts regardless of need.

It is significant in this regard that 1968 was the last fiscal year in which the budget was reported to be in balance until the second term of the Clinton administration (the Clinton surpluses, of course, vanished with the second Bush's war and tax reductions). The problem for Social Security has been that when deficits grow, as they escalated under Reagan and the Bushes, the pressure to hold down Social Security increases to counter inflation could become pressure to reduce benefits in order to reduce the deficit. Exactly that has happened under George W. Bush. Certainly, though, as their rhetoric indicated, neither Johnson, Nixon, Ford, nor, subsequently, Jimmy Carter had any such intention; nor were their deficits large enough to encourage it. Johnson's move did, though, create a potential for application of the well-known law of unintended consequences.

Regardless of his concern for inflation, Ford joined the traditional pattern of encouraging increases to Social Security. In his 1976 State of the Union message on January 17, he proposed "catastrophic health insurance for everybody covered by Medicare. . . . I propose improving the Medicare and other health programs," he said, "to help those who really need more protection: older people and the poor." As for the basic Social Security program, his rhetoric could have come from FDR or LBJ. "Our Federal Social Security system for people who have worked hard and contributed to it all their lives is a vital part of our economic system. Its value is no longer debatable. In my budget for fiscal year 1977 I am recommending that the full cost of living increase in Social Security benefits be paid during the coming year."[56]

Ford, like all the presidents back to and including Franklin Roosevelt, described Social Security, at least by implication, as part of the American way of life. He suggested that it was an integral and traditional component of the economic system, one that rewarded the thrift and hard work of individual Americans. In other words, Ford, like those who occupied the White House before him, described Social Security in the language of American individualism.

In one respect, Ford did break with tradition in that he injected a cautionary note. "I am concerned," he said, "about the integrity of our Social Security trust fund that enables people—those retired and those still working who will retire—to count on this source of retirement income. Younger workers watch their deductions rise and wonder if they will be adequately protected in the future." There was a challenge, he said, but "we must meet this challenge head on." He saw a Social Security trust fund that was "headed for trouble" and called for quick action. "Unless we act soon to make sure the fund takes in as much as it pays out, there will be no security for old or young." His solution was not privatization; nor was it to reduce benefits. In a sensible proposal, though one that these days would seem astonishing coming from a Republican, Ford recommended a tax increase on both employers and employees to take effect the following year.[57] The rhetoric therefore remained consistent. Ford used the same symbols that had justified increase and expansion to justify protection and preservation.

In his acceptance speech on August 19, 1976, following his nomination in Kansas City, Ford included Social Security, emphasizing both improvement and protection of the program. "We will ensure the integrity of the social security system," he said, "and improve Medicare so that our older citizens can enjoy the health and happiness that they have earned. There is no reason they should go broke just to get well."[58] Social Security and Medicare thus were individual benefits earned by hard work—the American Way. Those who had produced all their lives deserved a decent life as a reward and to be protected from exploitation.

President Ford's acceptance address reflected his acceptance of the essential pattern that the New Deal established, as well as of the rhetoric that the New Deal pattern had inspired. Social programs with their roots in the New Deal were nevertheless neither his foremost consideration nor among his major concerns. In his final State of the Union speech,[59] he did not refer to Social Security among his list of accomplishments; nor did he include it in his recommendations to his successor, Jimmy Carter.

Although he was a Democrat, President Carter spoke less about Social Security than did his predecessors. He did not stress the program in his acceptance speech, his inaugural address, or his State of the Union messages, although he did propose expanded health-care coverage. Social Security did not change notably during Carter's administration, except for revisions to the formula for indexing benefits to the cost of living and the adoption in 1979 of a schedule of tax increases for many years to come. It is safe to conclude that the program was not among his foremost priorities, but Carter did support social insurance, and when speaking of it, he did continue the traditional rhetoric.

As the election of 1980 neared, Carter began to emphasize Social Security more than before, no doubt because of the long-held hostility of his opponent, Ronald Reagan, to the popular program. Carter engaged in a bitter battle with Senator Edward Kennedy but was ultimately successful in gaining renomination. In his acceptance address before the Democratic National Convention in New York on August 14, 1980, he referred to the "make-believe" world of the Republicans. "In their fantasy," he charged, "American, inner-city people and farm workers and laborers do not exist. Women, like children, are to be seen but not heard. The problems of working women are simply ignored. The elderly do not need Medicare." He accused the Republicans, now led by Reagan, of presenting proposals that were "an attack on everything that we've done in the achievement of social justice and decency that we've won in the last 50 years, ever since Franklin Delano Roosevelt's first term. They would make social security voluntary," he said presciently.[60]

Ronald Reagan did not mention Social Security in his inaugural address or in some early televised speeches, but he did reply to his critics in his first State of the Union message. On February 18, 1981, he said that he regretted fears that "unfounded stories have caused," fears that Social Security checks would be taken away from beneficiaries. "We will continue to fulfill the obligations that spring from our national conscience. Those who through no fault of their own must depend on the rest of us, the poverty-stricken, the disabled, the elderly, all those with true need can rest assured that the social safety net of programs they depend on are exempt from any cuts. The full retirement benefits of the more than 31 million Social Security recipients will be continued along with an annual cost of living increase. Medicare," he added, "will not be cut."[61]

The rhetoric may have sounded familiar to those who did not listen carefully, and certainly Reagan designed it to be comforting. He spoke of "obligations that spring from our national conscience," a phrase that could easily have come from FDR, Truman, Kennedy, or LBJ. A thoughtful person listening closely, though, could have noted a sharp difference in tone from the language of earlier presidents. There was no mention of reward for work or of earned benefits. Reagan in no way conceded that Social Security might be based upon American traditions. Instead, he spoke of those who could not care for themselves and who needed help through no fault of their own. While pretending to soothe those who feared his policies toward Social Security, he actually spoke only of preserving a needs-based program for the poor. Implicit in his words was his long-held belief that Social Security was, indeed, "welfare," not a universal program that paid benefits based upon an earned right to those benefits. Reagan provided assurances, but he craftily limited those assurances to current beneficiaries, and he was careful not to mention Social Security for future generations. Heralded by some and deplored by others, "Reaganism" had arrived to the United States.

From Franklin D. Roosevelt through Jimmy Carter, presidential comments about Social Security showed a remarkable consistency, regardless of whether the president was conservative or liberal, Democrat or Republican, and regardless of the condition of the country. Reagan broke that pattern. His rhetoric in office questioned the foundation of Social Security, even though at the same time he sought to reassure those who depended upon the system.

Reagan's precandidate rhetoric had been overtly a frontal assault upon every principle of social insurance; yet, he cleverly adopted the same rhetorical symbols that others had used in support to form the basis for his attack. Social Security and related programs, he had argued, were incompatible with individualism, the prime symbol of the time in American discourse. They threatened American liberty by discarding the country's tradition of limited government.

Rarely are the effects of the spoken word and the written word the same. Franklin Roosevelt was a master speaker, and his written words retain their force. John Kennedy similarly excelled in both media. In Lyndon Johnson's case, his words in writing often were powerful, usually more powerful than when he spoke them, even though he could be a compelling speaker. In Reagan's case, the effects were sharply different. On paper, Reagan's rhetoric is flat and uninspiring. As a speaker delivering a prepared text, he was unexcelled. His powerful rhetoric developed an undercurrent of support throughout the country at the same time that his ideas brought ridicule (that ridicule by and large vanished once he became the presidential candidate of a major party and quickly faded from most people's memories). Reagan's delivery on the AMA's recording for "Operation Coffeecup" has to be heard to experience its intensity and effectiveness. His masterful performance for Goldwater in 1964 was owing entirely to the sound of his words, not their content. The content was a typical presentation of "the Speech," which moved millions when spoken but affected only the true believer in print.

All presidents since FDR have had some effect upon Social Security. The rhetoric that Roosevelt inspired led to the implementation of the program and continued to justify protecting and expanding it. Reagan was the first to differ. He often adopted the rhetoric of his predecessors but used it skillfully to reverse its previous effect: to question, to undermine, and to suggest alternatives. He made a president such as George W. Bush possible. Clinton had deftly used Social Security to prevent many of the devastating cuts in social programs that the Republican Congress was eager to implement. "Save Social Security first" was his rallying cry, and even when he was under fierce attack, he held off Social Security's enemies. Clinton's successor, the second George Bush, going beyond even Reagan, has attacked Social Security directly from the White House. Thus far, Bush has failed in his attacks. The sweeping victories of the Democrats in the congressional elections of 2006 brought them renewed majority status in both House and Senate. Thus, Bush's failure will be permanent. Given the history of Social Security's opposition, though, even with Bush gone there will continue to be danger until Americans finally awaken to the nature of the campaign against their social insurance protections.

NOTES

1. See, e.g., Richard E. Neustadt, *Presidential Power and the Modern Presidents* (New York: Free Press, 1991).

2. See Kenneth J. Mayer, *With the Stroke of a Pen: Executive Orders and Presidential Power* (Princeton, NJ: Princeton University Press, 2001); p. 4.

3. The most impressive scholarly work on the subject is by Portland State University political scientist Phillip J. Cooper, most recently in "George W. Bush, Edgar Allan Poe, and the Use and Abuse of Presidential Signing Statements," *Presidential Studies Quarterly* 35, no. 3 (September 2005): 515–32.

4. John Zvesper, "The Liberal Rhetoric of Franklin Roosevelt," in *Rhetoric and American Statesmanship*, ed. Glen Thurow and Jeffry Wallin (Durham, NC: Academic Press and Claremont Institute for the Study of Statesmanship and Philosophy, 1984), 87.

5. David Potter, *People of Plenty: Economic Abundance and the American Character* (Chicago: University of Chicago Press, 1954); quoted in Max J. Skidmore, *Medicare and the American Rhetoric of Reconciliation* (Tuscaloosa: University of Alabama Press, 1970), 4. The next few paragraphs draw extensively upon this latter work.

6. William E. Leuchtenburg, *Franklin D. Roosevelt and the New Deal, 1932–1940* (New York: Harper and Row, 1963), 165.

7. See Jill Quadagno, *The Transformation of Old Age Security: Class and Politics in the American Welfare State* (Chicago: University of Chicago Press, 1988), 121.

8. Franklin D. Roosevelt, *Franklin D. Roosevelt: Selected Speeches, Messages, Press Conferences, and Letters*, ed. Basil Rauch (New York: Rinehart and Co., 1957), 161–62.

9. Roosevelt, *Selected Speeches*, 144–45.

10. Robert H. Bremner, "The New Deal and Social Welfare," in *Fifty Years Later: The New Deal Evaluated*, ed. Harvard Sitkoff (Philadelphia: Temple University Press, 1985), 69.

11. Bremner, "The New Deal," 77.

12. Bremner, "The New Deal," 77.

13. A good capsule discussion is included in Frank Freidel, *The New Deal in Historical Perspective* (Washington, DC: Service Center for Teachers of History of the American Historical Association, 1959), 3–14.

14. Bremner, "The New Deal," 88–89.

15. See William E. Leuchtenburg, "The Achievement of the New Deal," in *Fifty Years Later: The New Deal Evaluated*, ed. Harvard Sitkoff (Philadelphia: Temple University Press, 1985), 220.

16. Fred L. Israel, ed., *The State of the Union Messages of the Presidents*, vol. 3 (New York: Chelsea House Publications, 1967), 2840 ff; also readily available at http://janda.org/politxts/State%20of%20Union%20Addresses/1934-1945%20Roosevelt/FDR38.html.

17. Roosevelt, *Selected Speeches*, 351.

18. Roosevelt, *Selected Speeches*, 363–64.

19. *Vital Speeches of the Day* 14 (July 1, 1948): 196.

20. *Vital Speeches of the Day*, 552.

21. Harry S. Truman Library, Bill File, 1948, June 11–17, Box No. 37.

22. *Vital Speeches of the Day* 15 (January 15, 1949): 196; also readily available at http://janda.org/politxts/State%20of%20Union%20Addresses/1945-1952%20Truman/HST49.html.

23 *Vital Speeches of the Day* 15 (September 15, 1949): 707.

24. *Vital Speeches of the Day* (September 15, 1949): 387

25. *Vital Speeches of the Day* (September 15, 1949): 387.

26. Dwight D. Eisenhower "The Middle Road," an address delivered in Boise, Idaho, on August 20, 1952; *Vital Speeches of the Day* 18 (September 1952): 677.

27. See *Vital Speeches of the Day* 19 (February 1, 1953): 252–54; available also at www.yale.edu/lawweb/avalon/presiden/inaug/eisen1.htm.

28. *Vital Speeches of the Day* 19 (February 15, 1953): 264.

29. *Vital Speeches of the Day* 20 (February 1, 1954): 230.

30. *Vital Speeches of the Day* 20 (February 1, 1954): 231.

31. *Vital Speeches of the Day* 21 (January 15, 1955): 966.

32. *Vital Speeches of the Day* 22 (February 1, 1956): 231.

33. Dwight D. Eisenhower "What Is the Job to Be Done?" Address to a Lexington, Kentucky, rally on October 1, 1956, in *Vital Speeches of the Day* 23 (October 15, 1956): 3.

34. *Vital Speeches of the Day* 27 (February 1, 1961): 226–27; available at http://mcadams.posc.mu.edu/ike.htm.

35. *Vital Speeches of the Day* 27 (February 1, 1961): 237.

36. See Skidmore, *Medicare*, 96–167.

37. *Vital Speeches of the Day* 28 (February 1, 1962): 231.

38. *Vital Speeches of the Day* 28 (June 1, 1962): 515–16.

39. See Skidmore, *Medicare*, 129–31; as noted earlier, in the 1930s, the AMA took no position in its official testimony before Congress regarding passage of the Social Security Act.

40. *Vital Speeches of the Day* 30 (January 15, 1964): 194–95.

41. *Vital Speeches of the Day* 30 (September 15, 1964): 709–10.

42. Lyndon Johnson, "The Wants of the People," Labor Day address in Detroit, Michigan, on September 7, 1964, in *Vital Speeches of the Day* 30 (October 1, 1964): 742.

43. Lyndon Johnson, "The Great Society," *Vital Speeches of the Day* 31 (January 15, 1965): 196.

44. *Vital Speeches of the Day* 33 (February 1, 1967): 226–28.

45. Lyndon Johnson, "Speech to AFL-CIO Convention, Bal Harbour, Florida, 12 December 1967," *Vital Speeches of the Day* 34 (January 1, 1968): 162–63.

46. *Vital Speeches of the Day* 34 (February 1, 1968): 228.

47. *Vital Speeches of the Day* 35 (February 1, 1969): 228.

48. *Vital Speeches of the Day* 36 (January 1, 1970): 162.

49. *Vital Speeches of the Day* 37 (February 1, 1971): 227.

50. *Vital Speeches of the Day* 38 (September 15, 1972): 707.

51. Bill Kauffman, "Come Home America: Liberals Need Another George McGovern and Perhaps Conservatives Do Too," *American Conservative* (January 30, 2006), www.amconmag.com/2006/2006_01_30/print/articleprint.html.

52. Frank Kessler, *The Dilemmas of Presidential Leadership: Of Caretakers and Kings* (Englewood Cliffs, NJ: Prentice Hall, 1982), 313–14.

53. *Vital Speeches of the Day* 39 (March 15, 1973): 325–26.

54. *Vital Speeches of the Day* 41 (February 1, 1975): 227.

55. See Johnson's comment in his State of the Union message on January 17, 1968, in *Vital Speeches of the Day* 34 (February 1, 1968): 229.

56. *Vital Speeches of the Day* 42 (February 1, 1976): 228.
57. *Vital Speeches of the Day* 42 (February 1, 1976): 228.
58. *Vital Speeches of the Day* 42 (September 15, 1976): 708.
59. *Vital Speeches of the Day* 43 (February 1, 1977): 226–30.
60. *Vital Speeches of the Day* 46 (September 15, 1980): 706–10.
61. *Vital Speeches of the Day* 47 (March 15, 1981): 323.

10

The Special Problem of Health Care: The Fortunes to Be Made

If we are to understand why Medicare has special problems—although they are less frightening than the critics allege, they nevertheless are real—it is necessary to understand the problems of the American health-care delivery system in general. The health-care system in the United States historically involved certain irrationalities that are peculiar to it. First, practitioners, generally physicians and dentists, provided services and collected a fee for each specific service. Second, hospitals, where physicians provided care for serious illness, emerged as predominantly nonprofit institutions, most likely under the sponsorship of public, religious, or philanthropic organizations. Nursing homes tended to be an exception to the nonprofit rule; generally, for the most part, they have always been proprietary institutions.

Medical economics dealt a blow to each of these factors. Fee-for-service medicine proved too expensive to dominate in a modern competitive marketplace; it simply could not, and cannot, compete efficiently in a capitalistic economy. Moreover, it tends to ignore wellness; that is, rather than promoting healthy lifestyles and preventive care, it concentrates on curing pathologies after they develop. With a fee charged for each service, there are economic incentives for providers to require numerous procedures and to order a maximum number of diagnostic tests. Economic pressures to maximize profits similarly encourage the selection of the most expensive procedure when several are available.

For decades, there have been fortunes to be made by investing in nursing homes. In recent years, hospitals have come to present the same dynamic. In a development too little noticed by the public, nonprofit hospitals have almost completely lost out in the marketplace to proprietary—that is, profit-making—institutions. The few nonprofit hospitals remaining often

behave the same as those run for profit. The same market forces have destroyed many nonprofit group-practice plans that have been converted into
proprietary HMOs.

Just as specialization has come to dominate American medicine, so has
specialization affected hospitals. The tendency now is for those institutions
to emphasize profitable services and eliminate those that nonprofit hospitals once operated as a community service. Hospitals have become so profitable that they compete vigorously for patients—and for investors. Nonprofit institutions in general, and teaching hospitals in particular, are an
endangered species.

Fee-for-service private medicine plus burgeoning technology began at
least by the 1930s to force the costs of medical care to rise considerably far
more quickly than the general cost of living. Blue Cross plans emerged to
provide the insurance principle as protection against rising hospitalization
costs. Adopting the principle of community rating, Blue Cross guaranteed
hospital care as needed for those who paid a monthly fee. The fee was equal
for every member in a given region. Thus, those who were elderly or in ill
health could be protected for the same cost to the patient as those who were
young and healthy.

In the absence of regulation, such a situation could not continue in the
American economy. Private insurance companies recognized the huge
profit to be made in offering coverage to young, healthy persons at rates below those of Blue Cross. They were able to keep their expenditures low by
refusing to issue policies to anyone who presented higher risk. As private
companies persuaded those presenting the lowest risk to switch from Blue
Cross to their own policies, Blue Cross plans were left increasingly with
high-risk, therefore high-cost, members. In order to survive in any form,
Blue Cross had no alternative but to abandon the community rating that
had shared risk among all and to adopt the practices of the insurance companies. Thus, the unregulated market succeeded in destroying Blue Cross as
it originally existed, that is, as a plan to provide prepaid hospital coverage
for the entire community at a reasonable cost to all.

The Blue Cross experiment had failed, resulting in a Blue Cross that in
practice differed little from the companies that had attacked it. American
health care came increasingly to be provided through insurance companies
offering coverage at reasonable rates to those who need it least and prohib-
itively expensive coverage, if any at all, to everyone else. Because large
groups can negotiate lower rates, numerous employers came to offer health
insurance as a fringe benefit to their employees. Health insurance as a fringe
benefit of employment came ultimately to be the only possibility of coverage for most Americans.

The resulting dynamic not only caused an increase in the numbers of
people with no coverage—individual policies became too expensive for

nearly everyone, and small employers rarely could or would provide insurance for their employees—but also forced the costs of health care to rise at an even more rapid rate. There came to be little or no connection between cost and the patient. A third party, the insurance company, paid nearly all the cost. The insured patient generally had no concern for the size of his or her bills because "insurance covered it." The many without insurance often obtained no care or sometimes received care in hospital emergency rooms, which by law could not turn them away. Emergency room services are the most expensive care possible. When such patients could pay no more or could pay nothing, hospitals had to find payment elsewhere. They therefore increased their other charges to compensate, thus raising health costs and insurance premiums still higher.

Competition among hospitals has reflected a similar dynamic. Consider the following example. To compete, hospitals have sought to obtain every piece of equipment, necessary or not. If a community has, for example, four hospitals but needs only one enormously expensive piece of equipment (such as an MRI or CAT scan machine), each hospital nevertheless feels it must have its own for competitive reasons. As the trend accelerated, some hospitals even sought to have multiple pieces of equipment for extra convenience. As a matter of fact, the community with four hospitals likely has more hospitals than it needs. Communities now are very often overbuilt because of competition among huge health-care companies that seek to increase their profits and the enormous salaries of their executives (these salaries do not include those of their physicians and certainly not of their nurses). When there are too many hospitals, too many beds remain unoccupied, and the cost per bed rises sharply.

Quality of care is also an issue. The mobility of the population and the shifting among insurance plans work to discourage long-term relationships between patients and health-care providers. Without the prospect of continued relationships, there are no economic incentives for providers to adopt expensive technology and procedures that would increase the likelihood of greater life expectancy for their patients. All of these factors have worked to reduce quality of care and to increase the number of medical errors. Despite the prevailing propaganda that America has the world's best medical care, by most objective measurements, this simply is not true. Some countries that many Americans would dismiss as "backward" appear to provide better care with fewer errors than does the health-care system in the United States. These countries not only provide better care, but they are able to do so at far less cost—and they cover their entire populations.

This is the system that America, virtually alone in the world, developed. We provide less care than other developed countries, and the care we provide is often lower in quality than would be the case elsewhere. And it is always is far more expensive.

The system provides nearly all health care through profit-making institutions and caregivers, financing most of that profit through another profit-making institution, the insurance company. Such companies are notoriously inefficient. Long ago, for example, it was reported that one company in one limited jurisdiction, Massachusetts Blue Cross, employed more clerks than did the entire health-care delivery system in Canada.

For the general population, this is the way things remain; Medicare, Medicaid, and programs of the Veterans' Administration now provide a considerable amount of health care, but not to the citizenry at large. America's health care costs far more for each citizen than does health care anywhere else in the world—at the same time that America has a higher proportion of citizens with no coverage than is the case in any other industrialized country.

There are those who argue that America cannot afford to do more for its people, but the truth is that doing more, if done correctly, almost assuredly would cost less. No other country receives so little for every dollar it spends for health care as the United States does. The people pay for health care in ways that often are hidden. News items for years have pointed out that automobile manufacturers in the United States pay more for health insurance for their workers than they pay for steel. That, of course, drives up the cost of automobiles. The large amount added to the price of a car is only one of the more dramatic examples. It is certainly not the only one or the costliest one.

This was the situation that encouraged President Bill Clinton on November 20, 1993, to propose his plan for providing health-care coverage to the entire population. It was an opportunity for the United States to adopt a program that it desperately needs. America missed the chance and, so, remains alone among advanced countries in failing to provide health care for all its citizens. Such opportunities for progressive reform are extraordinarily rare in the United States, hardly ever coming more than once in a lifetime, or even a century.

Clinton failed, but he at least made a sincere and vigorous attempt. The situation has worsened considerably since then, but George W. Bush's response has been consistently, and characteristically, that of an ideologue. He has ignored public need, while at the same time working diligently for political gain. He permitted the health insurance and pharmaceutical industries to craft a prescription-drug benefit for Medicare (Part D) that is cumbersome and extraordinarily expensive. In fact, Part D assists those industries far more than it assists Medicare recipients, huge numbers of whom gain nothing or even lose. For example, many low-income Medicare recipients previously could have full drug coverage under Medicaid, but now they cannot; many others had prescription drug coverage under retirement health plans, but many of those plans now, because of "Part D," have dropped such coverage. Unfortunately, because the most conservative and ideologically rigid elements of the Republican Party had control over all branches of the national government, Bush succeeded.

The Clinton plan was cumbersome, but it would have provided health coverage—including drug coverage—to the entire population. Rejecting the single-payer plan as politically infeasible, Clinton would have established coverage for most of the population through regional alliances. States would have established the alliances, which would have contracted with several plans to produce a comprehensive benefits package.

The Clinton proposal would therefore have retained the elements of the traditional system: private practice of medicine and coverage through insurance companies. It also would have permitted citizens to choose among several options. Each alliance would have had varied programs, including managed-care plans and those offering coverage based on traditional fee-for-service payment to health-care providers.[1] To have charged that the plan was "socialism," or even more absurdly that Clinton sought to "socialize one-seventh of the entire economy of the United States," as many writers and commentators did, reflected either ignorance, malice, or both. It clearly would not have been socialism; nor did Clinton seek to socialize any part of the economy.

In retrospect, Clinton probably should have gone the single-payer route; doing so would have avoided the complexity that burdened his proposal and would have been vastly more efficient than either the plan under his proposal or the existing system. His plan did have many virtues. It avoided radial approaches that nearly always terrify Americans. It would have been consistent with previous practices, taking care to avoid upsetting the fundamental elements of America's health-care delivery system. It would have provided virtually universal coverage, and it had some cost-containment provisions. In short, in many ways it was brilliantly constructed.

Nevertheless, it also had many weaknesses. Some of these were the same as its virtues. In avoiding radical approaches, it retained the worst elements of America's health-care delivery system. Alliances and managed care, to be sure, would have increased efficiency and reduced some costs, but retention of insurance companies as the primary payment mechanisms meant retention of gross inefficiencies. Similarly, the system had to generate profits to operate, profits not only to health-care providers but also to insurance companies and investors.

Initially, even opponents of the Clinton plan assumed something would pass and that, at most, they could modify it so that it would be less to their disliking. After all, the public feared loss of coverage, and there was strong pressure for reform. Ultimately, however, the support fell apart because of a combination of factors. Special-interest lobbies spent almost unlimited funds to defeat the plan. They portrayed it as a government takeover of the health-care system, something that it obviously was not and something that the Clinton administration had worked strenuously and successfully to keep it from being. As a matter of fact, as indicated above, the proposal would have been stronger had there been greater government involvement and more governmental control.

In response to Clinton's proposal, small businesses, insurance companies, and other special interests fought fiercely. The Clinton administration was new and inexperienced, and Clinton was unwilling to compromise. Republicans saw their chance. William Kristol, who had been an aide to Vice President Dan Quayle and who had become recognized as a Republican spokesman, urged the party to stand firm and reject any health plan. The "echo-chamber" of conservative talk radio generated an avalanche of opposition messages, including hysterically perpetuating the falsehood mentioned above that Clinton was trying to socialize one-seventh of the economy. A number of Republicans recognized the need and had supported health care, but all recognized that success would give Clinton an FDR-like aura and ensure his reelection. They assumed that if he failed to secure health care, Clinton would certainly be a one-term president. Any health program then adopted after his departure would come under the Republican who replaced him. As it turned out, in 1996 Clinton won reelection. Republicans, though, had secured control of both houses of Congress as a result of the 1994 off-year elections. The new majority in both chambers, especially the House, was under the firm control of a new breed of Republican, one sympathetic neither to any program such as health coverage from the government nor to compromise in any respect.

The effort against health care by special interests and the entire Republican Party was enormous and unprecedented. Clinton's inflexibility contributed to the sad result since, hitherto, Washington had rarely, if ever, worked without flexibility and compromise. In the end, Congress did not vote against the Clinton plan—the plan did not even make it to a vote. It died, truly, with no bang but with a whimper.

Journalists Haynes Johnson and David Broder wrote a remarkable study of the plan's failure and how that failure reflected American politics and society. They based *The System: The American Way of Politics at the Breaking Point*[2] on careful observation and on interviews with all the major figures who participated in the battle. It amply documents the administration's errors, the pernicious political tactics of the extremists who had captured the Republican Party, the timidity of some Democrats, and the pervasive effect of the vast sums of money that numerous interests successfully devoted to defeating the plan and to dominating American public policy.

Certainly, the defeat of the Clinton plan contributed to the startling turnaround in Congress. Republicans had not controlled the full Congress for four decades. After they achieved their majority, the Republicans treated failure of the universal plan as a great victory. Rather than proposing their own plan, they expressed alarm at the high costs of Medicare and sought to place tight restrictions on the program's growth. The party's overwhelming emphasis came to be on cutting taxes, regardless of any other considerations. When George W. Bush assumed the presidency, they realized their fondest dreams.

Johnson and Broder had harsh words for many of the players in the system and for the demise of the Clinton health proposal. They quoted Paul Starr, who summed up the tragedy superbly:

The story of the life and death of health reform shines a harsh light on the way The System—and the men and women in it—succeeds or fails. As Paul Starr, the Princeton scholar and author who played a major part in designing the Clinton health-care reform, ruefully said later, "the collapse of health care reform in the first two years of the Clinton administration will go down as one of the great lost political opportunities in American history. It is a story of compromises that never happened, of deals that were never closed, of Republicans, moderate Democrats, and key interest groups that backpedaled from proposals they themselves had earlier co-sponsored or endorsed. It is also a story of strategic miscalculations on the part of the President and those of us who advise him." He also accurately said, "The Republicans enjoyed a double triumph, killing reform and then watching jurors find the President guilty. It was the political equivalent of the perfect crime."[3]

David Gergen is a Republican who served in the Clinton White House and can therefore provide an unusual perspective. Writing in *U.S. News and World Report*, he noted that even Johnson and Broder, who followed the health-care plan's defeat as closely as anyone, seemed "startled by the power and skill of the most influential players on the field: national lobbyists."[4] That power unquestionably increased under the presidency of the second Bush, but as Gergen made clear, it already was huge. After having been snubbed in their efforts to compromise, he said, the Health Insurance Association of America and the National Federation of Independent Business mobilized against the Clinton plan. They spent "at least $100 million (and perhaps three times that), greatly exceeding the combined amount all candidates spent running for president of the United States in 1992, a year that marked a record for campaign spending." He, Johnson, and Broder agreed that the lobbies had become "crypto-political parties of their own—unelected and unaccountable." It is important, Gergen noted, that we begin paying closer attention to them.[5]

Sadly, instead of closer public attention, there came to be even less, and things became much worse. The new leadership of Newt Gingrich and Tom DeLay came to exert unprecedented control over the House of Representatives and over the lobbyists themselves. Their "K Street project" required lobbying firms to employ only Republicans and to contribute only to Republicans. Their tactics outlasted Gingrich and DeLay themselves and, particularly with the advent of the George W. Bush/Dick Cheney presidency, effectively merged that "third party" of lobbyists into the Republican power structure.

Some observers, including Gingrich, saw the failure of health-care reform as evidence that the system worked. Arguing that inaction was the best outcome, they pointed to changes occurring in the marketplace. Not all observers were so sanguine. Even Bill Gradison of the Health Insurance Association of America, an association that worked fervently to kill the Clinton health plan, remarked a year after the plan's defeat that one could argue that government's failure gave the private market "a chance to develop without major hurdles. On the other hand," he said, "there are actions which only the government can take which are really needed." For example, he added, "I told my members when Congress went home in 1994 that there were no winners and a lot of losers in the great health care debate. The problems were still there. The number of uninsured was already at unacceptable levels and was going to rise. The level of health care inflation, while moderating, was still too high. These things require action. That is still my view." Johnson and Broder said it was their view as well.[6]

Gradison's pessimism was well grounded. Even his hopeful view that the private market might "develop without major hurdles" has become a nightmare. By every measure, the health-care delivery system's troubles in 1994 have sharply increased a dozen years later. Moreover, there is still no government plan to help. The Bush administration portrayed its inexcusably clumsy "drug benefit" under Medicare Part D as helping citizens, but on balance it merely adds to the turmoil while assisting drug manufacturers and insurance companies far more than it aids citizens.

Many of the developments that critics charged would emerge if the Clinton plan were adopted did emerge, changing the face of American medicine—without the Clinton plan. Potentially, HMOs can provide superb care, but the primary emphasis in managed care is not the patient's benefit; rather, it is suppressing costs and maximizing profit. Managed care now dominates the health-care industry. The charge that the Clinton plan would have effected a "government takeover of medicine" was patently absurd. The charge that it would have eliminated patient choice was equally ridiculous. That plan would have preserved a private fee-for-service option, which Americans traditionally equate with freedom of choice.

Freedom of choice, however, insofar as it ever really existed, has now largely become a thing of the past. This took place without additional government involvement in health care. Even the rather limited freedom of choice that previously existed has now fallen victim to the industry's rush toward managed care. All evidence, both statistical and anecdotal, increasingly demonstrates that emphasis upon investor profits works to deprive patients of needed, oftentimes essential, treatment. Congressional hostility toward trial lawyers and punitive damages has gone so far as to make it impossible in most instances for patients, however mistreated, to bring suit against their health maintenance organizations, known now to all by the dreaded initials "HMO."

The country faces this situation at the same time that ideologues holding high position tell its people that Medicare cannot survive as currently constituted. The issue purports to be one of medical economics. Medicare pays the full cost for a wide range of health services. Traditionally, the cost of modern health services has escalated rapidly, and it appears that it will continue to increase as the techniques of managed care reach their limits.

Certainly, much of the perceived crisis reflects considerations more political than economic. Dire predictions were rife even when the Clinton administration achieved the substantial budget surplus that it bequeathed to the incoming administration of George W. Bush. Such predictions continued and escalated, of course, after Bush quickly succeeded in eliminating the surplus and restoring an enormous deficit. The heavily publicized assertions that Medicare would go "bankrupt" (a notion, remember, that simply is not applicable to a program of the federal government) and that the trouble would come in seven years or so are merely links in a long chain of such predictions spreading back for decades—predictions each time that the system had only seven years left. The public became aware of the predictions for political, not economic, reasons. Citizens became concerned because opponents of Medicare and social insurance in general hammered gloomy forecasts into public consciousness in order to justify their assaults on the program.

Currently, the discussion centers almost entirely on Medicare, a program the Bush administration works eagerly to privatize. Of course, though, it is private health care, not government health care, that has created the trouble. If one limits consideration to how Medicare may be "reformed," there can be only one of three options. A large infusion of money must come into the system, or expenditures must be reduced in one of two ways. Either benefit levels must be reduced, or additional numbers of people must be denied coverage.

In the minds of the "reformers," increased funding is not feasible. Taxes are always to be lowered, never raised or restored to previous levels. Reducing the number of beneficiaries is certainly the most appealing to the administration because it could be achieved by imposing a means test. A means test would convert Medicare into "welfare," which would put it in the way of ultimate extinction, thus fitting into the anti–social insurance ideology (the Bush administration actually has made a move in this direction by adopting a differential fee schedule for Medicare Part B; those with higher incomes pay more for this optional program than others do). A means-tested program would require millions of taxpayers to fund a system that would limit its benefits to others. This, of course, would wind up causing public support to dwindle and vanish.

The only true solution is to forget about "reforming," or revising, Medicare itself. Instead, consider the whole of the American health-care delivery system. Other industrial countries provide comprehensive health care for all their citizens. America is far wealthier than they, yet we have become convinced that it is too expensive to do as they do. We already spend more than those countries. Surely we could provide their benefits with what we already spend. In any case, it is nonsense to say that among the world's advanced industrial countries, only the wealthiest, America, has too few resources to care for its entire population.

This country absolutely does not need any "reform," or any policy that would increase the number of people who have no coverage for health care. To provide the coverage that other countries provide, and to provide it at lower cost, can almost certainly be done. It is not fundamentally a question of economics but rather one of priorities, of political will. It cannot by done, however, by simply "saving" Medicare. Ultimately, to "save" Medicare will require a basic reform of America's health-care delivery system.

This could come in several ways. The federal government could mandate that states provide comprehensive health-care systems. This might help eliminate the tax-limitation measures that have caused such mischief in a number of states. Alternatively, there could be some combination of federal and state systems. Most efficient would be a single-payer system at the federal level. As I discussed in chapter 1, this could come in the form of an expanded Medicare as suggested by former senator George McGovern and others, or this could be combined with a great expansion of the system that currently provides this country's best health care, the Veterans' Administration system.

It is clear that reform, in whatever guise it comes, must eliminate as much inefficiency as possible. It must restructure the fee system that rewards certain specialists inordinately as compared with internists, pediatricians, family practitioners, and others who provide general care; it must discover ways to provide comprehensive coverage of high quality to the entire population and reduce the use of emergency rooms; it must eliminate the current hemorrhaging of funds from the system into exorbitant profits; and if there are fees involved, they must incorporate the original Blue Cross principle of community rating in order to keep costs reasonable on a per capita basis.

In all probability, it will be necessary to restructure the delivery system by emphasizing the nurse practitioner as the primary care provider. As for concerns regarding quality, nurse practitioners are highly trained professionals who recognize their limitations and who, within the limitations of their practice, as a rule have considerably more "hands-on" patient experience than physicians. They can provide excellent care at considerably less cost than most physicians. HMOs, managed-care plans, and individual physicians whose practices extend over broad geographic areas that limit their availability already utilize nurse practitioners extensively. The result has been very favorable, with nurse practitioners frequently becoming patients' preferred primary practitioners.

The point is that some of the critics' concerns are legitimate. Many of them are based on genuine conditions that do require change. Medicare, though, is only the most obvious part of the picture. American medicine is already undergoing changes and certainly must change more. Medicare is part of the broad pattern of American medicine, and it is best not to consider it in a vacuum. More important than "saving" Medicare—and this bears repeating—is reform of the entire American system of health-care delivery.

Changes are indeed taking place, but at this time the changes seem hardly to be improvements. We must put aside political differences and respond to reality, not to ideology. A great opportunity passed in 1993. Clearly, no such opportunity can again occur until after January 2009 at the earliest, but it may be coming.

The Bush administration has so thoroughly discredited itself that a golden opportunity may develop. It appears as if the reactionary movement that began with Ronald Reagan's victory may finally have played itself out. The public seems to be recognizing that electing those who demean government, whose philosophy of governing is to oppose government, inevitably results in very poor government. Government under control of such officials cannot perform well and cannot provide essential services of quality.

There is a good chance that in 2008 the country will reject those who have caused it so much damage on all fronts and will instead elect enlightened and competent leaders. The process began with the off-year elections of 2006. If it continues, America at last can find progress.

Anticipating the crisis and averting it by reforming medical practice itself would be the rational, and probably the easier, approach. We can do it if we choose the skilled political leadership required to counter those who believe that government has no role to play in bettering the lives of Americans. This was precisely the situation that brought us Social Security, the most successful income-maintenance program in history.

Thus, the argument here is that it is essential—and possible—to establish universal health coverage for Americans while increasing quality and reducing costs. This should be done by creating a dual system that would provide a choice. Those who wish to remain in a standard program based on American traditions should have the choice of enrolling in Medicare, which should be expanded to be available to the entire population. It should include some reforms in benefits, including long-term care and a meaningful prescription-drug coverage, rather than the outrageous "Part D" that pharmaceutical and insurance companies, with their henchmen in the White House and Congress, foisted on the American people.

Alternatively, those who want complete coverage with no copays or additional expenses could enroll in a fully governmental program patterned on the Veterans' Health Administration. In either case, government would be the single payer and must, for the sake of efficiency, pay directly, not through insurance companies.

Wealthy people who want luxury care could continue to purchase private insurance or to self-insure and seek private care if they wish. The population, however, would have complete coverage without the inefficiencies and exorbitant profits that now are characteristic of America's health-care delivery system.

The American people, working together, have accomplished great reforms before when needed and when they have had skillful and enlightened political leaders. Assuming that they once more will have such leaders, they can do it again.

In the meantime, the immediate challenge before us is to avoid the efforts to destroy Social Security and Medicare. The challenge at the moment is simply to preserve America's extraordinarily successful income-maintenance program. To that challenge, my final chapter returns.

NOTES

1. For additional details about the Clinton plan, see Max J. Skidmore, *Social Security and Its Enemies: The Case for America's Most Efficient Insurance Program* (Boulder, CO: Westview Press, 1999), 141–43; for complete details, see Beth C. Fuchs and Mark Merles, *CRS Report for Congress: Health Care Reform: President Clinton's Health Security Act* (Washington, DC: Congressional Research Service, Library of Congress, November 22, 1993).

2. Haynes Johnson and David S. Broder, *The System: The American Way of Politics at the Breaking Point* (New York: Little, Brown), 1996.

3. Johnson and Broder, *The System*, 602.

4. David Gergen, "And Now, the Fifth Estate?" *U.S. News and World Report*, April 28, 1996, 84.

5. Gergen, "And Now, the Fifth Estate?" 84.

6. Johnson and Broder, *The System*, 603.

11

Some Final Words to Sum It All Up

Thus far, to its credit, the public has resisted the more extreme arguments of Social Security's enemies. *Securing America's Future* has sought to assist the public by providing information to offset the confusion and misinformation that those enemies have deliberately fostered as they worked to generate the controversy about social insurance. It describes how Social Security actually works, and reveals how the critics have distorted its operation, its financing, and its future role in protecting Americans.

Additionally, in countering the charges of the opponents, this book points out that—in contrast to allegations from the "privateers"—what really would be "a bad deal" for the country would be to shrink Social Security, or damage it in any manner. What America actually needs is Social Security's expansion.

Along with expanding Social Security, the country vitally needs true and efficient universal health coverage with the government as single payer. *Securing America's Future* suggests a way to achieve such coverage that would be more economical than our current chaotic system, while greatly improving quality of care.

Finally, this book outlines a unique, simple, and commonsense plan to introduce progressivity into Social Security's financing. Social Security already provides a progressive benefit structure. Now, in view of the tiny minimum wage, the low prevailing earnings for the majority of the workforce, and the unfair restructuring of the tax structure under Reagan and especially under Bush, the time has come to make Social Security's financing—as well as its benefit structure—progressive. It can be done easily and with virtually no pain. *Securing America's Future* explains how.

The following items of information should be sufficient for informed judgment regarding the true details of the Social Security system and an understanding of needed reforms that will strengthen, not weaken, our protections.

THE TRUTH ABOUT SOCIAL SECURITY

- The intermediate projections of the trustees (their alternative II projections) are based on pessimistic assumptions that the economy in the decades to come will fare far worse than it ever has over a comparable period. Their optimistic projections (alternative I) are more realistic; they have been more consistent with actual economic developments.

  The respected consulting actuary David Langer has even suggested that "(1) the high cost projection [Alternative III] is so far off that it deserves to be discarded, (2) the intermediate cost projection [Alternative II] should be redesignated as high cost, (3) the low cost projection [Alternative I], since it is on target, merits promotion to the intermediate level, and a new low-cost basis needs to be developed."[1] Regardless of the propaganda, there will be a higher proportion of the population in the workforce in 2030 than there was in 1965, and no projection shows that proportion ever again dropping to the 1965 levels. Pressure from baby boomers will be partially offset by reduction in the number of younger beneficiaries, and in any case, the boomers ultimately will pass from the scene.

  The average life span has increased since Social Security began paying benefits but not as dramatically as the propaganda asserts. The average life expectancy for a woman at age sixty-five is fewer than five years longer now than it was in 1940; for a man, it is fewer than three years longer. Moreover, raising the age for full retirement from sixty-five to sixty-seven has compensated for two of those years of increase.
- Money in the trust funds is invested in government securities, which pay interest back into the funds. The government has not misappropriated the money. Government bonds do represent value, just as currency does. They represent a claim on the resources of the U.S. Treasury, and the government provides them with its "full faith and credit."
- Those who popularize the idea of privatization distort their calculations to favor their point of view. Even when their math is accurate, their assumptions and representations are not. They ignore the loss of disability and survivors benefits, which together represent over three-quarters of a million dollars in benefits, as well as of Medicare. They select a single worker as the example so that they can ignore benefits for a spouse. They also select a highly paid worker, whose benefits are

proportionally less (in relation to that worker's contributions to the system) than the benefits of a lower-wage worker would be. They ignore the huge advantage of Social Security's inflation protection; in contrast to earnings from private investments, Social Security protects the purchasing power of its benefits when prices increase. Above all, they ignore economic reality: in a private system, some people will lose their money. A rising stock market, even if it were to rise forever, would not mean that all stocks would rise in value. Privatized systems in other countries have fallen short of what Social Security provides in America. The praise for those systems is misleading. A securities salesperson who promises what "privatizers" do would be subject to prosecution. Social Security's record is established. It has never failed to provide its checks when due. Private industry cannot truthfully make the same claim.

- All objective studies, contrary to the propaganda of its enemies, demonstrate that Social Security represents excellent value to the worker for the money paid in and will continue to do so.
- Means-testing Social Security would change its nature and destroy the system. Universal coverage, regardless of need, is one of Social Security's strong points. Millionaires do receive benefits, but they also pay into the system. Their benefits represent a smaller return on what they pay in than do the benefits of lower-paid workers. Covering the wealthy actually benefits the system.
- Social Security bears no relation to a Ponzi scheme (or pyramid scheme). See appendix C for a discussion.
- Social Security operates at a level of administrative efficiency that is far higher than that of any private program. That is, it operates at a far lower administrative cost and puts more of its resources into benefits than any private program can manage.
- The idea of "intergenerational inequities" as applied to Social Security is a fraudulent notion designed as political propaganda, not economics or ethics. Social Security provides protection to all age groups and to all economic classes.
- All complex projections over any great length of time are questionable; they are educated guesses. Using long-term projections as the basis for making radical changes in a vital program that has served the country well and is continuing to do so would be the height of folly.
- The issues surrounding Social Security's viability are not economic. Rather, they are questions of political priorities and political will. There is no question that America's economy, the most powerful in history, is easily able to support a comprehensive program of social insurance, including Social Security, Medicare, or even a comprehensive system of health care for all.

- Any changes that may be implemented should be based upon sound advice from disinterested parties. Pleas from special interests, from those who have ideological points to score, or who have fortunes to be made should be analyzed impartially. Objective analysis will lead to quick rejection of the special pleading from such groups or figures. Virtually all of the information about Social Security that has inundated the country for nearly two decades is propaganda from two groups: the ideologues and the selfish.

MAKING SOCIAL SECURITY EVEN BETTER (SEE CHAPTER 7)

- Free the first $20,000 in wages from Federal Insurance Contributions Act (FICA) taxes on the worker but not the employer. This would lower taxes for the vast majority of workers.
- Follow the Medicare precedent and remove the cap on wages subject to FICA taxes. This would reverse the system that currently requires low-income workers to pay a higher percentage of their earnings as FICA taxes than very high earners pay. The cap has already been removed for Medicare taxes, which are levied on one's full wages, regardless of how high.
- Adopt an estate or inheritance tax, exempting the first $5 million or so, and devote the proceeds to Social Security's trust funds.
- For more affluent beneficiaries, include all Social Security benefits in income for purposes of calculating income tax; currently, those beneficiaries may exempt 15 percent of their benefits. Dedicate the additional income tax received to the trust funds. Retain the provision that frees Social Security benefits from income taxes completely for beneficiaries with low incomes.
- Direct additional resources to the trust funds by increasing the interest rate the government pays on the bonds the funds hold and by directing to the funds that portion of the personal income tax that results from a "tax on a tax," that is, on the amount of tax paid that results from levies on FICA amounts.
- Devote amounts borrowed from trust fund surpluses to paying down the national debt, instead of using them for general expenses.

MAKE AMERICA'S PEOPLE SECURE BY
MAKING SOCIAL SECURITY COMPREHENSIVE

- Discard the notion of the "three-legged stool" and expand Social Security by increasing its benefits sufficiently to be a complete retirement and social insurance system. Companies would no longer have the burden of providing for and administering retirement systems. Workers would have complete portability from one job to another, and they and their dependents would be protected against inflation, deprivation in retirement, and disability.

• Provide the American population with comprehensive health coverage as other industrial countries do, thus increasing Americans' access to health care of quality, freeing business from any obligation to provide health care to their workers, and providing a healthy workforce—in fact, creating a healthy American population. Do this by providing Americans a choice between enrolling on the one hand in a fully government program patterned on that of the Veterans' Health Administration or, on the other, enrolling in Medicare made available to all. The expanded Medicare program should include a few benefits now missing, such as long-term care and a true prescription-drug benefit.

NOTE

1. David Langer, "Scrapping Social Security's Intermediate Cost Projections" (letter to the editor), *Society of Actuaries* (March 2004), www.davidlanger.com/article _c67ahtml (accessed January 28, 2007).

Appendix A: Text of Recording of "Operation Coffeecup"

RONALD REAGAN SPEAKS OUT
AGAINST SOCIALIZED MEDICINE

My name is Ronald Reagan. I have been asked to talk on the several subjects that have to do with the problems of the day. It must seem presumptuous to some of you that a member of my profession would stand here and attempt to talk to anyone on serious problems that face the nation and the world. It would be strange if it were otherwise.

Most of us in Hollywood are very well aware of the concept or the misconception that many people, our fellow citizens, have about people in show business. It was only a generation ago that people of my profession couldn't be buried in the churchyard. Of course, the world has improved since then. We can be buried now. As a matter of fact, the eagerness of some of you to perform that service gets a little frightening at times.

Now back in 1927 an American socialist, Norman Thomas, six times candidate for president on the Socialist Party Ticket, said the American people would never vote for socialism. But he said under the name of liberalism the American people would adopt every fragment of the socialist program.

There are many ways in which our government has invaded the precincts of private citizens, the method of earning a living. Our government is in business to the extent of owning more than 19,000 businesses covering 47 different lines of activity. This amounts to a fifth of the total industrial capacity of the United States.

But at the moment I'd like to talk about another way because this threat is with us and at the moment is more imminent. One of the traditional methods of imposing statism or socialism on people has been by way of

169

medicine. It's very easy to disguise a medical program as a humanitarian project. Most people are a little reluctant to oppose anything that suggests medical care for people who possibly can't afford it. Now, the American people, if you put it to them about socialized medicine and gave them a chance to choose, would unhesitatingly vote against it. We have an example of this. Under the Truman administration it was proposed that we have a compulsory health insurance program for all people in the United States, and, of course, the American people unhesitatingly rejected this.

So, with the American people on record as not wanting socialized medicine, Congressman Forand introduced the Forand Bill. This was the idea that all people of social security age should be brought under a program of compulsory health insurance. Now, this would not only be our senior citizens, this would be the dependents and those who are disabled, this would be young people if they are dependents of someone eligible for social security. Now, Congressman Forand brought the program out on that idea for that particular group of people. But Congressman Forand was subscribing to this foot-in-the-door philosophy because he said, "If we can only break through and get our foot inside the door, then we can expand the program after that." Walter Reuther said, "It's no secret that the United Automobile Workers are officially on record as backing a program of national health insurance." And by national health insurance he meant socialized medicine for every American.

Well, let's see what the socialists themselves had to say about it. They say, "Once the Forand Bill is passed this nation will be provided with a mechanism for socialized medicine capable of indefinite expansion in every direction until it includes the entire population." Well, we can't say we haven't been warned. Now Congressman Forand is no longer a congressman of the United States Government. He has been replaced, not in his particular assignment, but in his backing of such a bill, by Congressman King of California. It is presented in the idea of a great emergency that millions of our senior citizens are unable to provide needed medical care. But this ignores the fact that in the last decade, 127 million of our citizens, in just ten years, have come under the protection of some form of privately owned medical or hospital insurance.

Now, the advocates of this bill, when you try to oppose it, challenge you on an emotional basis. They say, "What would you do, throw these poor old people out to die with no medical attention?" That's ridiculous and of course no one has advocated it. As a matter of fact, in the last session of Congress a bill was adopted known as the Kerr-Mills Bill. Now, without even allowing this bill to be tried to see if it works, they have introduced this King Bill which is really the Forand Bill. What is the Kerr-Mills Bill? It is a frank recognition of the medical need or problem of our senior citizens that I have mentioned. And it is provided from the Federal Government money to the states and the local communities that can be used at the discretion of the state to help those people who need it. Now what reason could the other people have for backing a bill which says we insist on compulsory health insurance for senior citizens on a basis of age alone regardless of whether they are worth millions of dollars, whether they have an income, whether they're protected by their own insurance, whether they have savings. I think we could be excused for believing that, as ex-Congressman Forand said, this was simply an excuse to bring about what they wanted all the time: Socialized medicine. James Madison, in 1788, speaking to the Virginia Convention, said: "Since the general civilization of mankind I believe there are more instances of the abridgement of the freedom of the people by gradual and silent encroachment of those in power than by violent and sudden usurpations."

They want to attach this bill to social security and they say, "Here is a great insurance program, now instituted, now working." Let's take a look at social security itself. Again, very few of us disagree with the original premise that there should be some form of saving that would keep destitution from following unemployment by reason of death, disability, or old age. And to this end social security was adopted. But it was never intended to supplant private saving, private insurance, pension programs of unions and industries. Now, in our country under our free enterprise system we have seen medicine reach the greatest heights that it has in any country in the world. Today the relationship between patient and doctor in this country is something to be envied any place. The privacy, the care that is given to a person, the right to choose a doctor, the right to go from one doctor to the other. But let's also look from the other side at the freedom the doctor loses. A doctor would be reluctant to say this. Well, like you, I'm only a patient so I can say it in his behalf. The doctor begins to lose freedom. It's like telling a lie and one leads to another. First you decide that the doctor can have so many patients. They are equally divided among the various doctors by the government. But then doctors were equally divided geographically. So a doctor decides he wants to practice in one town and the government has to say to him, You can't live in that town. They already have enough doctors. You have to go someplace else. And from here it's only a short step to dictating where he will go. This is a freedom that I wonder whether any of us have the right to take from any human being. I know how I'd feel if you, my fellow citizens, decided that to be an actor I had to become a government employee and work in a national theater. Take it into your own occupation or that of your husband. All of us can see what happens once you establish the precedent that the government can determine a man's working place and his work methods, determine his employment. From here it's a short step to all the rest of socialism to determining his pay. And pretty soon your son won't decide when he's in school, where he will go or what he will do for a living. He will wait for the government to tell him where he will go to work and what he will do.

In this country of ours took place the greatest revolution that has ever taken place in world's history, the only true revolution. Every other revolution simply exchanged one set of rulers for another. But here for the first time in all the thousands of years in man's relation to man a little group of men, the Founding Fathers, for the first time established the idea that you and I had within ourselves the God-given right and ability to determine our own destiny. This freedom was built into our government with safeguards. We talk democracy today and, strangely, we let democracy begin to assume the aspect of majority rule is all that is needed. Well, majority rule is a fine aspect of democracy, provided there are guarantees written into our government concerning the rights of the individual and of the minorities. What can we do about this? Well, you and I can do a great deal. We can write to our congressmen and to our senators. We can say right now that we want no further encroachment on these individual liberties and freedoms. And at the moment the key issue is: We do not want socialized medicine. Now, you may think when I say write to the congressman or the senator that this is like writing fan mail to a television program. It isn't. In Washington today 40,000 letters, less than 100 per congressman, are evidence of a trend in public thinking. Representative Halleck of Indiana has said, "When the American people want something from Congress, regardless of its political complexion, if they make their wants known, Congress does what the people want." So write. It's as simple as finding just the name of your congressman or your senator, and then you address your letter to that individual's name. If he's a congressman to the House Office Building, Washington, D.C.; if he's a senator to the Senate Office Building, Washington, D.C. And if this man writes back to you and tells you that he, too, is for free enterprise, but we have these great services and so forth that must be performed by government, don't let him get away with it. Show that you have not been convinced. Write a letter right back and tell him that you believe in government economy and fiscal responsibility, that you know that governments don't tax to get the money they need, governments will always find a need for the money they get, and that you demand the continuation of our traditional free enterprise system. You and I can do this. The only way we can do it is by writing to our congressman even if we believe that he's on our side to begin with. Write to strengthen his hand. Give him the ability to stand before his colleagues in Congress and say, I heard from my constituents and this is what they want. If you don't, this program, I promise you, will pass just as surely as the sun will come up tomorrow. And behind it will come other Federal programs that will invade every area of freedom as we have known it in this country. Until one day, as Norman Thomas said, we will awake to find that we have socialism. And if you don't do this and if I don't do it, one of these days you and I are going to spend our sunset years telling our children and our children's children what it once was like in America when men were free.

SOCIALIZED MEDICINE AND YOU

[Male voice, unidentified]

Mr. Reagan's concern is very real. And all of us who are equally concerned should follow his advice. Now you may wonder just what sort of letter to write to your congressman. The answer is almost any letter, so long as it reflects your thinking, your convictions, your feelings. And so long as you use your own words, and put them in your own handwriting.

Perhaps a little background on the subject of socialized medicine will prove helpful to you. To begin with, socialized medicine simply means compulsory national health insurance, medicine controlled and administered by the federal government, financed through compulsory taxation. For many years, an attempt has been made to socialize the practice of medicine through the Social Security tax mechanism. The American people, and Congress, have rejected overwhelmingly these attempts.

Last year, Representative Forand attempted to establish the principle of socialized medicine by applying it only to the elderly—at first. He, and others like him, counted on the concern we all feel for those of the aged in need of help. The Forand Bill failed. But this year, another congressman has stepped forward to lead the forces of socialized medicine. Representative King, of California. It is his measure, H.R. 4222, or the King Bill, that now threatens the free practice of medicine.

The supporters of the King Bill contend that most of the aged are in poor health and that most of the aged are financially unable to pay for their own medical care. The fact is that most of the aged are in reasonably good health. And most are in reasonably good shape financially. Surveys prove both points.

However, I'm sure that we all recognize that some of our older people are in poor health and some can't afford to pay for the health care they need. That's why the doctors of America strongly supported the legislation passed during the last Congress: the so-called Kerr-Mills Law. They felt, and have always felt, that people who need medical help should get it, but that tax dollars should not be used to pay the medical and hospital bills of those who are perfectly able to pay their own.

Physicians favored the Kerr-Mills Law because it would help those of the elderly who need help, help them quickly, and effectively, and do so without wasting either the taxpayer's money or destroying the basic American freedoms involved in our system of medical practice. The Kerr-Mills Law is now being put into effect. It permits the individual states to guarantee to every American over sixty-five who needs help the health care he requires. It benefits all older persons unable to meet the cost of a serious or chronic illness. It specifically allows the individual states to run their own programs. It provides for local administration and local determination of need, and is financed from both the federal and state general tax funds.

Without even giving this program a chance to prove what it could do, the King Bill, H.R. 4222, was introduced. Here's how it would work. The federal government would buy a limited amount of hospitalization, nursing home care, home-health services, and outpatient hospital diagnostic services for all eligible to receive Social Security retirement payments, regardless of their financial needs. The number of days the beneficiary could receive these services is limited. And the patient would be required to pay ten dollars a day for the first nine days spent in a hospital, and twenty dollars for each complete diagnostic study made. Physicians' services in the fields of radiology, pathology, physiatry, and anesthesiology would be included, plus the services of interns and residents and those serving the outpatient clinics.

There is little doubt but what the program would soon be expanded to include all physicians' services, as well as to cover the entire population, thus completely socializing medicine in the United States. The federal government would set up the rules and regulations under which the program would operate. And every one who pays Social Security taxes would help pay the bill, because taxes would be raised beyond the nine percent of taxable payroll already scheduled in the years ahead.

I'm sure many of you are wondering why there's any objection to using the Social Security system to finance medical care for the aged. Well first of all, it is a misnomer to think of Social Security as being insurance. In the *Nestor v. Fleming* case heard before the Supreme Court in 1959, the Department of Justice in its brief said, "The OASI [Old-Age and Survivors Insurance] program is in no sense a federally-administered insurance program under which each worker pays premiums over the years and acquires at retirement an indefeasible right to receive a fixed monthly benefit. The contributions exacted, are a tax."

Many people also have the mistaken impression that Social Security benefits are paid out of accumulated reserves, similar to private insurance programs, when in truth the program is financed almost entirely on a pay-as-you-go basis, with the benefits paid out of current income. Pay-as-you-go means that the government raises, through current taxes, just enough money to pay the cost of the benefits currently due. No one prepays his own benefits. Today's taxpayers pay for today's beneficiaries.

The acceptance of the King Bill would actually mean that our children and grandchildren will be asked to pay ever increasing Social Security taxes to finance the medical-care needs of the previous generations. With growing families, young people have enough difficulty trying to make ends meet without assuming the additional obligation of paying higher taxes to pay for the medical-care needs of all over sixty-five, many of whom are in better financial shape than those paying the tax.

Now this is the choice we're faced with: on the one hand, we can help those who need help while preserving the right of the self-reliant to finance their own care. Or we can legislate a compulsory national health scheme for the aged, regardless of whether they need it or not.

To put this choice in even sharper focus, Americans are being asked to choose between a system of medicine practiced in freedom and a system of socialized medicine for the elderly which will be expanded into socialized medicine for every man, woman, and child in the United States.

Your letter will help determine the outcome of this struggle. Remember what Ronald Reagan said:

[Reagan's voice]

Write those letters now. Call your friends, and tell them to write them. If you don't, this program I promise you will pass just as surely as the sun will come up tomorrow. And behind it will come other federal programs that will invade every area of freedom as we have known it in this country, until one day, as Norman Thomas said, we will awake to find that we have socialism. And if you don't do this, and if I don't do it, one of these days, you and I are going to spend our sunset years telling our children, and our children's children, what it once was like in America when men were free.

Appendix B: Internet Nonsense about Social Security

EXAMPLE 1

Much that bounces around on the Internet is nonsense. Some of it is possibly well intentioned but based on wrong information. The following excerpt is an actual example from early 2007 that may fall into this category; it certainly is wrong. Although it is impossible to tell (and this is a charitable interpretation), it could have resulted purely from false information, rather than from intent to deceive.

PETITION FOR: President Bush,
   Gov. Schwarzenegger and Congressman Dana Rohrbacher
   Mr. President and Gentlemen:
   The petition below is a protest against what the Senate voted on recently which allows illegals to access our social security! We demand that you and all congressional representatives require citizenship for anyone to be eligible for social services in the United States. We further demand that there not be any amnesty given to illegals, and NO free services or funding, or payments to and for illegal immigrants. We are fed up with the lack of action about this matter and are tired of "paying" for services to illegals! Tell Señor Fox to pay for his own people!

Of course, by 2007 Vicente Fox was no longer President of Mexico. There also had been no such congressional action, and in any case, immigrants have always qualified for Social Security benefits exactly as everyone else does: they pay into the system and receive benefits only if they qualify. As a system with virtually universal coverage, Social Security covers all workers in the United States who have jobs in covered employment.

The assumption of this Internet plea is that illegal immigrants receive benefits when American citizens could not; that is, they do not have to qualify as citizens do. That is absurd.

Noncitizens qualify just as citizens do but only if they, too, pay into the system for most of their working lives. One disadvantage they face is that, under most circumstances, they can receive benefits only if they continue to live in the United States after they retire. If they return to their home countries, as many immigrants do, they can no longer qualify for benefits. American citizens, in contrast, can retire abroad and continue to receive their Social Security (although in most situations, they do not receive Medicare unless they are in this country).

In a strange and counterintuitive twist, it is often illegal immigrants who benefit the Social Security system the most. People cannot work legally in the United States without a Social Security number. Those who are here illegally cannot qualify to receive one. Frequently, therefore, they use a fraudulent account number. They and their employers pay Federal Insurance Contributions Act (FICA) taxes that go into the Social Security trust funds, but since the illegal workers have no valid accounts, they can never receive benefits: they pay into the system, strengthening it, but never take anything out.

EXAMPLE 2

Another recurring Internet message, one that is no more accurate, has been around in various forms since at least 2000. It spreads just before elections, but this one also seems to reflect more a prevailing suspicion of Congress and "politicians" than any real hostility toward Social Security. A gullible acceptance of misinformation and a willingness to believe the worst, rather than any intent actually to deceive, more likely generated it and keep it going.

As is customary with such messages, it is a call to action:

Our Senators and Congressmen don't pay in to Social Security, and, of course, they don't collect from it. The reason is that they have a special retirement plan that they voted for themselves many years ago. For all practical purposes, it works like this: When they retire, they continue to draw their same pay, until they die, except that it may be increased from time to time, by cost of living adjustments. For instance, former Senator Bradley, and his wife, may be expected to draw $7,900,000, with Mrs. Bradley drawing $275,000 during the last year of her life. This is calculated on an average life span for each.

This would be well and good, except that they paid nothing in on any kind of retirement, and neither does any other Senator or Congressman. This fine retirement comes right out of the General Fund: our tax money. While we who pay for it all, draw an average of $1,000/month from Social Security. Imagine for a moment that you could structure a retirement plan so desirable that people would have extra deducted so that they could increase their own personal retirement income. A retirement plan that works so well, that Railroad employees, Postal Workers, and others who aren't in it, would clamor to get in. That is how good Social Security could be, if only one small change were made. That change is to jerk the Golden Fleece retirement out from under the Senators and Congressmen, and put them in Social Security with the rest of us. Then watch how fast they fix it. If enough people receive this, maybe one or some of them along the way, might be able to help. How many can YOU send it to?

The main trouble with this message is that it is completely wrong. No member of Congress receives a congressional salary after leaving office. Members of Congress, both representatives and senators, do pay into Social Security, and they get the same benefits from the program as anyone else. It is true that they do have another retirement system, but it is the Federal Employees' Retirement System (FERS), and it also requires contributions. Its benefits are based upon salaries and years of service; they do not come from "the General Fund" and by law cannot exceed 80 percent of the member's salary. Moreover, they are not payable until the former member reaches retirement age, and a member who serves too few years to qualify receives nothing from FERS and only his or her Social Security.

Undoubtedly, many inflammatory messages are certainly malevolent; they are designed to confuse, distort, and manipulate political opinion. The Left has its share of crackpots that generate messages. The one asserting that the Social Security Administration secretly assigns Social Security numbers on the basis of race may be one of these. This, of course, is not only untrue but completely absurd. Race is not a factor in the assignment of Social Security numbers.

Most of the devious political messages designed to mislead, though, come from the Right. I shall deal with two of the latter below. In any case, it is a good idea to refer to the website dealing with urban legends, www.snopes.com, to check on any shocking revelation that comes from the Internet. All of the examples in this appendix are covered thoroughly by snopes.com.

EXAMPLE 3

This example alleges that Social Security is an illegitimate program: FDR intended Social Security to be temporary, as an emergency measure to counter the Great Depression. This is completely untrue. No one at the time ever suggested, or even hinted at, such a thing. In any case, it would have been unworkable; it's silly on the face of it to think that a retirement system into which one pays throughout a lifetime of work could have been designed to be temporary.

EXAMPLE 4

This has been circulating for years and generally flourishes just before elections, when Democrats make an issue of Republican attacks on Social Security. Its purpose is obvious: to mislead voters into thinking that Social Security would fare better under Republicans than under Democrats.

SOCIAL SECURITY:
Franklin Roosevelt, a Democrat, introduced the Social Security (FICA) Program. He promised:

1. That participation in the Program would be completely voluntary,
2. That the participants would only have to pay 1% of the first $1,400 of their annual incomes into the Program,
3. That the money the participants elected to put into the Program would be deductible from their income for tax purposes each year,
4. That the money the participants [paid in would be] put into the independent Trust Fund rather than into the General operating fund, and therefore, would only be used to fund the Social Security Retirement Program, and no other Government program, and
5. That the annuity payments to the retirees would never be taxed as income.

Since many of us have paid into FICA for years and are now receiving a Social Security check every month—and then finding that we are getting taxed on 85% of the money we paid to the Federal government to "put away," you may be interested in the following:

Q: Which Political Party took Social Security from the independent "Trust fund" and put it into the General fund so that Congress could spend it?
A: It was Lyndon Johnson and the Democratically controlled House and Senate.
Q: Which Political Party eliminated the income tax deduction for Social Security (FICA) withholding?
A: The Democratic Party.
Q: Which Political Party started taxing Social Security annuities?
A: The Democratic Party, with Al Gore casting the tie-breaking deciding vote as President of the Senate, while he was Vice President of the U.S.
Q: Which Political Party decided to start giving annuity payments to immigrants?
A: MY FAVORITE: That's right! Jimmy Carter and the Democratic Party. Immigrants moved into this country, and at age 65, began to receive SSI Social Security payments! The Democratic Party gave these payments to them, even though they never paid a dime into it! Then, after doing all this thieving and violation of the original contract (FICA), the Democrats turn around and tell you that the Republicans want to take your Social Security away! And the worst part about it is, uninformed citizens believe it!

If enough people receive this, maybe a seed of awareness will be planted and maybe good changes will evolve.
How many people can YOU send this to?

This often comes in a version that purports to be written by friends of FDR's late son Elliott and his wife. It begins by describing a social setting in which Elliott condemns Social Security and says that his father would never have approved of what it has become. Elliott—conveniently for this Internet falsehood—died in 1990 and thus cannot comment.

The facts regarding the assertions are these:

1. The original legislation clearly made Social Security mandatory, and in no way did FDR ever say that the program would be voluntary. It could not have operated on a voluntary basis any more than road construction could depend on voluntary taxation.

2. FDR promised nothing about tax rates. The original legislation did provide for a 1 percent tax (matched by the employer), but it was on $3,000, not $1400, and even that original act provided for a gradual increase in the rate. It has since been raised beyond that (now, 6.2 percent + 1.45 percent for Medicare, which did not exist in the original act). The amount taxed for 2007 is $97,500 for Social Security, and there is no limit on the taxable amount for the Medicare portion.

3. FDR did not promise that FICA taxes would be deductible from income for income-tax purposes; in fact, the original legislation specifically provided that it would not be deductible.

4. FDR did say that the money would go into a trust fund and not the general fund—and that is what happened. It still does go into trust funds and not into the general fund. The trust funds invest money in government bonds for safety (required by law), and those bonds regularly mature and pay considerable interest back into the trust funds (I say "funds," plural, because there are three: Old-Age and Survivors Insurance, Disability Insurance, and Medicare). That does constitute borrowing from the funds, but the bonds bear the full faith and credit of the U.S. government, just as any treasury bonds do. If government did not borrow from the trust funds, it would simply borrow more from private sources (e.g., Japanese, Korean, and Chinese industrialists). Regardless of whether it issues bonds to Social Security, to China, or to a corporate pension plan that invests in them, it has to pay them back.

5. Social Security has never paid annuities. This no doubt means retirement payments or benefits in general. In any case, FDR did not promise that benefits would never be taxed, although it is correct that initially they were exempt. A portion of the benefits was first made taxable (except for beneficiaries of low income) as a result of changes resulting from the Greenspan Commission's recommendations that led to the 1983 amendments. That was under President Ronald Reagan and a Republican administration.

As for the correct answers to the questions above:

Which Political Party took Social Security from the independent "Trust Fund" and put it into the General fund? Neither, the trust funds still exist. The Lyndon B. Johnson administration was the one that began to count Social Security balances as part of the general budget, but this has nothing to do with Congress borrowing the funds. It always has done so when there has been a surplus.

Which Political Party eliminated the income tax deduction for Social Security (FICA) withholding? It was not the Democrats, as stated. In fact, as we have seen, neither party did so. FICA taxes have never been deductible; there has never been such a deduction from the time of the original Social Security Act until now.

Which Political Party started taxing Social Security annuities? It was not the "Democratic Party, with Al Gore casting the tie-breaking deciding vote." Instead, it was the Republican Party under Reagan with the 1983 amendments to the Social Security Act that subjected Social Security benefits (not "annuities") to taxation for the first time. That act exempted low-income beneficiaries but made half of the benefits taxable for others. There is perhaps legitimate basis for some confusion here. The 1993 budget act, with Vice President Al Gore casting the tie-breaking vote, did increase the portion of Social Security benefits that would be subject to tax. Reagan first taxed them, but the beneficiary still could exclude half, or 50 percent; under Bill Clinton, the portion subject to exclusion was reduced to 15 percent. That is, under Reagan, tax came to be levied against 50 percent of the benefits, and under Clinton that was raised to 85 percent. Some people are still confused and think that they pay an 85 percent tax on benefits—not so. A beneficiary in a 30 percent tax bracket, for example, would pay 30 percent of 85 percent of his or her benefits. That is, if the benefit were $10,000 per year, there would be a tax on $8,500 of the benefits. At 30 percent, the tax would be $2,550.

Which party "decided to start giving annuity payments to immigrants?" It was not the Democrats under Carter. Immigrants, whether citizens or not and just like citizens, have always been required to pay into the system and have always been eligible for benefits. However, they can receive benefits only while in this country. If they move back home, they cannot get them, and the system retains their contributions.

The message really mixes things up when it begins referring to Supplemental Security Income payments. Although SSI is part of the Social Security Act (just as workers' compensation and unemployment insurance are), it is not part of what most people mean when they say "Social Security." It is "welfare," and the states determine eligibility requirements. The requirements are quite strict. In Missouri, for example, one has to earn less than about $5,000 per year to get the payment, which is around $700 per month. Did the Democratic Party give this to immigrants even though they had never "paid a dime into it"? Well, no one ever pays into a fund to get

SSI. It's strictly welfare and not a contributory program at all. Thus, whoever wrote this completely misunderstood what he or she was talking about.

About the "thieving and violation of the original contract," again, this allegation is definitely not true. Both Republicans and Democrats have honored the law. It has changed through the years, but all the changes have been reasonably consistent with the intent of the original legislation.

The intention of this example of Internet nonsense is obviously political. It seeks both to undermine the current Social Security system and to persuade voters to cast their votes for Republicans. For some reason, this seems to be the case with most Internet nonsense regarding Social Security.

Do not be taken in by such political propaganda.

Appendix C: Social Security and Ponzi Schemes

Social Security is not a Ponzi, or pyramid, scheme; it bears no resemblance to one. Ponzi schemes are named for Carlo Ponzi, an Italian immigrant to the United States. Early in the twentieth century, he developed a plan that promised in ninety days to pay investors double the amount they had invested. He paid his initial investors with proceeds from those who came later. This is the "pyramid" scheme. The Securities and Exchange Commission explains on its website (www.sec.gov/answers/pyramid.htm) how such schemes work—or better yet, why they cannot work.

The website of the Social Security Administration (SSA) (www.ssa.gov) was long hailed as a reliable source of information about Social Security and as unusually helpful to the public. It still contains a wealth of useful information. Unfortunately, though, immediately after George W. Bush began his second term, his administration moved to politicize the site and incorporate political propaganda. The aim was to undermine Social Security by portraying its funding as inadequate and to assert the superiority of privatization, later defined as "personal accounts."

As reporter Robert Pear pointed out on the front page of the *New York Times*, many professionals in the Social Security Administration were upset at the Bush administration's efforts to use them as "conscripts" in a "political battle." At issue was a "tactical plan" to market the idea that Social Security is unsound and to portray private accounts as fundamental to any solution.[1] The employees argued that the administration was spending money from the trust funds to advance its political agenda.

Formerly, the SSA website had dealt with the Ponzi question and effectively demonstrated that Social Security was not a Ponzi, or pyramid, scheme. Under the current administration, the explanation to the question

185

"Is Social Security a Ponzi Scheme?"—which as recently as December 3, 2005, could be retrieved from the official SSA website—appears to have vanished.

One who has thoroughly exploded the notion that Social Security resembles a Ponzi scheme is the highly respected consulting actuary David Langer. Langer has written a series of articles, letters, op-ed pieces, and the like for a decade or so. Although his work has appeared in both popular and professional journals,[2] the strength of the propaganda campaign against Social Security has been so great that it seems to have drowned out his voice of sanity. Perhaps the results of the 2006 elections will enable his voice to be heard.

The trouble with a Ponzi, or pyramid, scheme is that the promised returns require a geometric increase in the number of investors at each level. In the initial wave, the first investor receives money from several others—for purposes of illustration, say ten others. In the second wave, those ten receive payment from one hundred others. In the third wave, there must be one thousand others to pay the previous hundred. After a few levels, the number of investors required to maintain the scheme exceeds the planet's entire population. Even if the initial investor receives payment from only two others, as in Ponzi's original scheme, the same principle applies. Obviously, such a scheme works only for a short time, if at all, and then collapses. That is why Ponzi schemes are illegal.

Now and then, someone will define a Ponzi scheme simply as one that pays investors from proceeds received from future investors. That is one element, to be sure, but there is far more to a Ponzi scheme than that. The key element is that a Ponzi scheme promises astronomical profits to investors, thus encouraging them to take great risks. Moreover, it is so constructed as to benefit only the architect of the scheme. There may be a tiny handful of initial investors who do profit, but they are incidental to the scheme. All investors other than the initial few lose their entire investments.

Social Security does not benefit a manipulator, it does not promise riches (and, in fact, makes no one wealthy), and it does not encourage risk. In fact, Social Security is not an investment plan at all. The American social insurance program turns the notion of a Ponzi scheme upside down; instead of impoverishing all but a few, for nearly three-quarters of a century it has provided extensive benefits to virtually the entire population. No pyramid scheme can operate over an extended period, providing benefits to nearly all who participate.

Social Security's enemies ignore this when they chortle with glee that economist and Nobel Laureate Paul Samuelson conceded in 1967 that Social Security was a Ponzi scheme, but one that worked.[3] He was referring to population growth and to increasing productivity when he quipped that the beauty of the system was that it worked, regardless of its financing. Samuelson had a keen sense of humor—as when he made a witty remark to the effect that economists had successfully predicted nine of the last five recessions. He clearly was joking about Social Security because Ponzi schemes do not and cannot work. Irony, though, tends to be lost on the deadly serious enemies of Social Security.

Allegations that Social Security is a Ponzi scheme reflect either ignorance or dishonesty; they are attempts to mislead. Numerous comments by the late economist Milton Friedman provide examples of the latter.[4] Peter Peterson has said similar things, but he is more easily dismissed. Friedman, along with Samuelson, was a Nobel laureate in economics, albeit one known far more for his stance as an ideologue than for humor. He surely knew the precise definition of "Ponzi scheme," what a Ponzi scheme is and what it is not. Nevertheless, he persisted in using the term inappropriately. At best, he slyly mentioned that "some people think" Social Security is a Ponzi scheme, implying that this was an accurate description.[5] At worst, he blatantly applied the term himself.

To repeat: Ponzi schemes are inherently unsustainable. They require a geometrically increasing income. Since this is impossible, they quickly collapse under their own weight. Social Security, by contrast, is merely one generation taking care of another; each generation pays benefits to its dependent population. This is sustainable indefinitely. In fact, in one form or another, every generation throughout history has supported its dependents—the previous and the next generations. Americans have merely discovered a far more efficient way to do so than ever before. That way is Social Security.

NOTES

1. Robert Pear, "Social Security Enlisted to Push Its Own Revision," *New York Times*, January 16, 2005.

2. A few of the many examples of Langer's work in popular journals would include a letter to the *Wall Street Journal* (March 13, 1998), "Ponzi Wouldn't Bother with Social Security," and an op-ed piece in the *Christian Science Monitor* (October 30, 2000), "Stalking Social Security." In the professional journal *Pensions and Investments*, he contributed an op-ed, "Social Fund Isn't Really a Ponzi Scheme of IOUs" (June 24, 1996), another, "Carl Ponzi Returns: The Privatization of Social Security Harkens Back to an Old Scheme" (April 14, 1999), and a follow-up letter, "Privatization and Ponzi" (August 23, 1999).

3. There are many examples, such as "Snares and Delusions," *The Economist*, February 14, 2002, www.economist.com/research/backgrounders.

4. See, for example, Milton Friedman's op-ed piece, "Social Security Chimeras," *New York Times*, January 11, 1999.

5. See Friedman, "Social Security Chimeras."

Bibliography

1991 Annual Report of the Board of Trustees of the Federal Old-Age and Survivors Insurance and Disability Insurance Trust Funds.

1998 Annual Report of the Board of Trustees of the Federal Old-Age and Survivors Insurance and Disability Insurance Trust Funds.

Adler, Eric. "I Do, I Do: Some Days It's Just One Wedding after Another for Courthouse Preacher." *Kansas City Star*, September 30, 1998, F2.

"Aldrich Assails Profit Tax Bill," *New York Times*, May 8, 1936.

Alterman, Eric. *What Liberal Media? The Truth about Bias and the News* (New York: Basic Books, 2003).

"The American Medical Association: Power, Purpose and Politics in Organized Medicine," *Yale Law Journal* 63 (May 1954), 937–1022..

Anderson, Jack. "Why Should I Pay for People Who Don't Need It?" *Parade*, February 21, 1993.

Anderson, Odin W. "Compulsory Medical Care Insurance, 1910–1950," *Annals of the American Academy of Political and Social Science* 273 (January 1951), 106–13.

Annual Report (Washington, DC: Americans for Generational Equity, 1990).

Asch, Steven M., et al. "Comparison of Quality Care for Patients in the Veterans Health Administration and Patients in an National Sample." *Annals of Internal Medicine* 141, no. 12 (December 21, 2004), 934–45.

"Asks Security Act to Be Voided by Court, Stockholder in Boston Suit Says It and State Jobless Law 'Seize Property,'" *New York Times*, May 8, 1936.

Baker, Dean and Mark Weisbrot. *Social Security: The Phony Crisis.*

Ball, Robert M., and Thomas N. Bethell. "Bridging the Centuries: The Case for Traditional Social Security." In *Social Security in the 21st Century*, ed. Eric R. Kingson and James H. Schulz, chapter 18. New York: Oxford University Press, 1997.

Banks, James, M. Marmot, Z. Oldfield, and J. P. Smith. "Disease and Disadvantage in the United States and in England." *Journal of the American Medical Association* 295, no. 17 (2006): 2037–45.

Barrett, Laurence I. *Gambling with History: Ronald Reagan in the White House* (Garden City, NY: Doubleday, 1983).

Benenson, Lawrence A. "Many Retirees Don't Want Aid," *Christian Science Monitor*, February 16, 1993.

Bernstein, Irving. *The Lean Years: A History of the American Worker, 1920–1933* (Boston: Houghton Mifflin, 1960).

Bosworth, Barry. "What Economic Role for the Trust Funds?" In *Social Security in the 21st Century*, ed. Eric R. Kingson and James H. Schulz, 156–77. New York: Oxford University Press, 1997.

Bremner, Robert H. "The New Deal and Social Welfare," in *Fifty Years Later: The New Deal Evaluated*, ed. Harvard Sitkoff (Philadelphia: Temple University Press, 1985).

Brewer, Benjamin. "Government-Funded Care Is the Best Health Solution: Multiple Insurers Create Expensive, Draining Hassle." *Wall Street Journal*, April 18, 2006.

Brewster, Agnes W. *Health Insurance and Related Proposals for Financing Personal Health Services* (Washington, DC: U.S. Department of Health, Education, and Welfare, Social Security Administration, 1958).

Brock, Fred. "Save Social Security? From What?," *New York Times*, November 1, 1998, p. 12.

———. *Blinded by the Right* (New York: Crown Books, 2002).

Cantril, Hadley, ed. *Public Opinion, 1935–1946* (Princeton, NJ: Princeton University Press, 1951).

Chambers, Clarke. *Seedtime of Reform* (Minneapolis: University of Minnesota Press, 1963).

Committee on Economic Security. *Social Security in America: The Background of the Social Security Act as Summarized from Staff Reports to the Committee on Economic Security* (Washington, DC: Government Printing Office, 1937).

Conason, Joe. *Big Lies: The Right-Wing Propaganda Machine and How It Distorts the Truth* (New York: St. Martin's Press, 2003).

Cooper, Phillip J. "George W. Bush, Edgar Allan Poe, and the Use and Abuse of Presidential Signing Statements," *Presidential Studies Quarterly* 35, no. 3 (September 2005): 515–32.

Davies, Laurence E. "Burden on Earner Held Lower Now," *New York Times*, December 30, 1939.

Denzer, Susan. "The Political Feasibility of Social Security Report" in *Framing the Social Security Debate: Values, Politics, and Economics*, ed. R. Douglas Arnold, Michael J. Graetz, and Alice H. Munnel, 420. Washington, DC: National Academy of Social Insurance, 1998.

Derthick, Martha. *Agency under Stress* (Washington, DC: Brookings Institution, 1990).

Douglas, Paul H. *Wages and the Family* (Chicago: University of Chicago, 1925).

———. *The Problem of Unemployment* (New York: The Macmillan Company, 1931).

———. *Social Security in the United States* (New York: McGraw-Hill, 1939).

Dugger, Ronnie. *On Reagan: The Man and His Presidency* (New York: McGraw-Hill, 1983).

Editorial, *Collier's*, November 28, 1936, 66.

Eisner, Robert. *Social Security: More, Not Less*. (New York: Century Foundation Press, 1998).

"Encroaching Control: Keep Government Poor and Remain Free," in *Vital Speeches of the Day* 37 (September 1, 1961).

Eisner, Robert. "What Social Security Crisis?" *Wall Street Journal*, August 30, 1966.

Ekerdt, David J. "Entitlements, Generational Equity, and Public-Opinion Manipulation in Kansas City," *Gerontologist* 38, no. 5 (1998): 525–36.

Epstein, Abraham. *Insecurity: A Challenge to America*, rev. ed. (New York: Harrison Smith and Robert Haas, 1936).

Epstein, Pierre. *Abraham Epstein: The Forgotten Father of Social Security* (Columbia: University of Missouri Press, 2006).

Ewing, Oscar. *The Nation's Health: A Ten-Year Program*. Washington, DC: Federal Security Agency, 1947.

Fishbein, Morris. *A History of the American Medical Association* (Philadelphia: W. B. Saunders, 1947).

Ford, Henry. *New York Herald Tribune*. November 2, 1936.

Freidel, Frank. *The New Deal in Historical Perspective* (Washington, DC: Service Center for Teachers of History of the American Historical Association, 1959).

Friedman, Milton. "Social Security Chimeras," *New York Times*, January 11, 1999.

Fuchs, Beth C., and Mark Merles. *CRS Report for Congress: Health Care Reform: President Clinton's Health Security Act* (Washington, DC: Congressional Research Service, Library of Congress, November 22, 1993).

Gergen, David. "And Now, the Fifth Estate?" *U.S. News and World Report*, April 28, 1996, 84.

Glassman, James K. "The Only Workable Solution for Social Security Is to Make It Private," *Kansas City Star*, September 10, 1995, J5.

"The Great Society," *Vital Speeches of the Day* 31 (January 15, 1965): 196.

Harry S. Truman Library, Bill File, 1948, June 11–17, Box No. 37.

Hicks, John D. *Republican Ascendancy* (New York: Harper and Row, 1960).

Hiltzik, Michael. "Undoing the New Deal." *Los Angeles Times*, June 26, 2005, www.latimes.com/business/investing/la-tm-hiltzik26jun26,1,714492.story.

———. *The Plot against Social Security*. (New York: Harper Collins, 2005).

"The Impeachment Breather," *New York Times*, November 1, 1998, 14.

Israel, Fred L., ed. *The State of the Union Messages of the Presidents*, vol. 3 (New York: Chelsea House Publications, 1967), 2840 ff; also readily available at http://janda.org/politxts/State%20of%20Union%20Addresses/1934-1945%20Roosevelt/FDR38.html.

"Issues, Principles, to Guide Business," *New York Times*, August 30, 1936.

Jacobs, Lawrence R., and Robert Y. Shapiro. "Myth and Misunderstandings about Public Opinion and Social Security," in *Framing the Social Security Debate*, ed. R. Douglas Arnold, Michael J. Graetz, and Alice Munnell (Washington, DC: National Academy of Social Insurance, 1998), 355–88.

Jacobson, Gary C. *A Divider, Not a Uniter: George W. Bush and the American People, the 2006 Election and Beyond* (New York: Pearson-Longman, 2007).

Johnson, Haynes, and David S. Broder. *The System: The American Way of Politics at the Breaking Point* (New York: Little, Brown, 1996).

Johnston, David Clay. "Talk of Lost Farms Reflects Muddle of Estate Tax Debate," *New York Times*, April 8, 2001.

Jones, Thomas W. "Social Security: Invaluable, Irreplaceable, and Fixable." *The Participant*, February 1996, 4.

Journal of the American Medical Association 181 (July 21, 1962), 265.

Kauffman, Bill. "Come Home America: Liberals Need Another George McGovern—and Perhaps Conservatives Do Too," *American Conservative* (January 30, 2006), www.amconmag.com/2006/2006_01_30/print/articleprint.html.

Kessler, Frank. *The Dilemmas of Presidential Leadership: Of Caretakers and Kings* (Englewood Cliffs, NJ: Prentice Hall, 1982).

Langer, David. "Carl Ponzi Returns: The Privatization of Social Security Harkens Back to an Old Scheme," *Pensions and Investments* (April 14, 1999).

———. "Privatization and Ponzi" (August 23, 1999).

———. "Scrapping Social Security's Intermediate Cost Projections" (letter to the editor), *Society of Actuaries* (March 2004), www.davidlanger.com/article_c67a.html (accessed on January 28, 2007).

———. "Social Fund Isn't Really a Ponzi Scheme of IOUs" *Pensions and Investments*, (June 24, 1996).

———. "Stalking Social Security," *Christian Science Monitor* (October 30, 2000).

———. *Wall Street Journal* (March 13, 1998), "Ponzi Wouldn't Bother with Social Security."

Leone, Richard C. "Stick with Public Pensions," *Foreign Affairs* 76 (July/August 1997): 41.

Leuchtenburg, William E. "The Achievement of the New Deal," in *Fifty Years Later: The New Deal Evaluated*, ed. Harvard Sitkoff (Philadelphia: Temple University Press, 1985).

Leuchtenburg, William E. *Franklin D. Roosevelt and the New Deal, 1932–1940* (New York: Harper and Row, 1963).

Lieberman, Trudy. "Social Insecurity: The Campaign to Take the System Private," *The Nation* 264, January 27, 1997, 11–18.

Longman, Phillip. "The Best Care Anywhere." *Washington Monthly*, January/February 2005, www.washingtonmonthly.com/features/2005/0501.longman.htlm (accessed April 3, 2005).

———. *Best Care Anywhere: Why VHA Health Care Is Better Than Yours* (Sausalito, CA: Polipoint Press, 2007).

Lynd, Robert, and Helen Lynd, *Middletown in Transition* (New York: Harcourt, Brace, and World, 1937).

Mannheim, Karl. Preface to *Diagnosis of Our Time* (New York: Oxford University Press, 1944).

Marmor, Theodore R., Fay Lomax Cook, and Stephen Scher. "Social Security Politics and the Conflict between Generations: Are We Asking the Right Questions?" in *Social Security in the 21st Century*, ed. Eric R. Kingson and James H. Schulz (New York: Oxford University Press, 1997), 204.

Mayer, Kenneth J. *With the Stroke of a Pen: Executive Orders and Presidential Power* (Princeton, NJ: Princeton University Press, 2001).

McGovern, George, and Max J. Skidmore. "Resurrecting Retirement," *Montana Professor* 18, no. 1 (Fall 2007), pp. 13–17.

McGovern, George *Social Security and the Golden Age* (Golden, CO: Fulcrum Publishing, Speaker's Corner Books, 2005).

———. "The Middle Road," an address delivered in Boise, Idaho, on August 20, 1952; *Vital Speeches of the Day* 18 (September 1952).

Moon, Marilyn. "Are Social Security Benefits Too High or Too Low?" In *Social Security in the 21st Century*, ed. Eric R. Kingson and James H. Schulz, 62–75. (New York: Oxford University Press, 1997).

Neustadt, Richard E. *Presidential Power and the Modern Presidents* (New York: Free Press, 1991).

"New Deal Blocking Jobs, Says Landon," *New York Times*, May 8, 1936.

New York Herald Tribune, November 2, 1936.

New York Herald Tribune, September 29, 1936.

Passell, Peter. "Can Retirees' Safety Net Be Saved?" *New York Times*, February 18, 1996, sec. 3, 1.

Pear, Robert. "Social Security Enlisted to Push Its Own Revision," *New York Times*, January 16, 2005.

Peterson, Peter G. "Will America Grow Up Before It Grows Old?" *Atlantic Monthly* 277, May 1996, 55–86.

Peterson, Peter, and Neil Howe. *On Borrowed Time: How the Growth of Entitlements Threatens America's Future* (San Francisco: Institute for Contemporary Studies, 1988).

Phillips, Kevin. *The Politics of Rich and Poor* (New York: Random House, 1990).

Piñera, José. "Retiring in Chile," *New York Times*, December 1, 2004, Op-ed, A31.

Porter, Eduardo. "Illegal Immigrants Are Bolstering Social Security with Billions," *New York Times*, April 5, 2005.

Porter, Kirk, and Donald Johnson. *National Party Platforms, 1840–1956* (Urbana: University of Illinois Press, 1956).

Potter, David. *People of Plenty: Economic Abundance and the American Character* (Chicago: University of Chicago Press, 1954).

PR Reporter (May 28, 1962).

"Press Briefing on the President's State of the Union Health Care Initiative." The White House. www.whitehouse.gov/news/releasesw/2007/01 (accessed January 28, 2007).

Pumphrey, Ralph E., and Muriel W. Pumphrey, eds. *The Heritage of American Social Work* (New York: Columbia University Press, 1961).

Quadagno, Jill. "Generational Equity and the Politics of the Welfare State," *Politics and Society* 17, no. 3 (1989): 2.

———. *The Transformation of Old Age Security: Class and Politics in the American Welfare State* (Chicago: University of Chicago Press, 1988).

Reagan, Ronald. "Encroaching Control: Keep Government Poor and Remain Free," *Vital Speeches of the Day* 37 (September 1, 1961).

———. "Free Enterprise," *Vital Speeches of the Day* 39 (January 15, 1973): 200–1.

Reno, Virginia P., and Robert B. Friedland. "Strong Support but Low Confidence," in *Social Security in the 21st Century*, ed. Eric R. Kingson and James H. Schulz (New York: Oxford University Press, 1997), 188.

Ritter, Kurt. "Ronald Reagan and 'The Speech': The Rhetoric of Public Relations Politics," *Western Speech* 32, no. 1 (winter 1968), reprinted in Max J. Skidmore, *Word Politics: Essays on Language and Politics* (Palo Alto, CA: James E. Freel and Associates, 1972), 110–18.

Rohter, Larry. "Chile's Retirees Find Shortfall in Private Plan," *New York Times*, January 27, 2005, A1.

———. "Chile Proposes to Reform Pension System," *New York Times*, December 26, 2006, A16.

Roosevelt, Franklin D. *Franklin D. Roosevelt: Selected Speeches, Messages, Press Conferences, and Letters*, ed. Basil Rauch (New York: Rinehart and Col, 1957), 161–62.

Rubinow, I. M. *Social Insurance* (New York: Henry Holt, 1913), 6.
———. *Standards of Health Insurance* (New York: Henry Hold, 1916).
———. *The Quest for Security* (New York: Henry Holt, 1934), 520–21.
Schlesinger, Arthur M., Jr. *The Age of Roosevelt: The Coming of the New Deal* (Boston: Houghton Mifflin, 1959).
"Scores Republicans on Security Attacks," *New York Times*, November 1, 1936.
Skidmore, Max J. "Operation Coffeecup: A Hidden Episode in American Political History," *Journal of American Culture* 12 (fall 1989): 89–96.
———. *Medicare and the American Rhetoric of Reconciliation* (Tuscaloosa: University of Alabama Press, 1970), 60 (now available online from Questia Media).
———. "Public Integrity: Perspectives from Home and Abroad," *Public Integrity Annual* (Council of State Governments/American Society for Public Administration) 1 (April 1996).
———. *Social Security and Its Enemies: The Case for America's Most Efficient Insurance Program*. Boulder, CO: Westview Press, 1999.
Skocpol, Theda. *Protecting Soldiers and Mothers* (Boston: Belknap Press, 1995).
"Snares and Delusions," *The Economist*, February 14, 2002, www.economist.com/research/backgrounders.
"Speech to AFL-CIO Convention, Bal Harbour, Florida, 12 December 1967," *Vital Speeches of the Day* 34 (January 1, 1968): 162–63.
Stockman, David A. *The Triumph of Politics* (New York: Avon Books, 1987).
Sunstein, Cass. *The Second Bill of Rights: FDR's Unfinished Revolution and Why We Need It More Than Ever*. New York: Basic Books, 2004.
Suskind, Ron. "Faith, Certainty, and the Presidency of George W. Bush," *New York Times Magazine*, October 17, 2004.
Thomas, Rich. "Why Cutting Entitlements Makes Sense," *Newsweek*, May 31, 1993.
U.S. Congress, *Health Services for the Aged under the Social Security Insurance System*, hearings before the Ways and Means Committee (Washington, DC: U.S. Government Printing Office, 1961).
Vital Speeches of the Day 14 (July 1, 1948).
Vital Speeches of the Day 15 (January 15, 1949): 196; also readily available at http://janda.org/politxts/State%20of%20Union%20Addresses/1945-1952%20 Truman/HST49.html.
Vital Speeches of the Day 15 (September 15, 1949).
Vital Speeches of the Day 19 (February 1, 1953); available also at www.yale.edu/lawweb/ avalon/presiden/inaug/eisen1.htm.
Vital Speeches of the Day 19 (February 15, 1953).
Vital Speeches of the Day 20 (February 1, 1954).
Vital Speeches of the Day 20 (February 1, 1954).
Vital Speeches of the Day 21 (January 15, 1955).
Vital Speeches of the Day 22 (February 1, 1956).
Vital Speeches of the Day 27 (February 1, 1961); available at http://mcadams.posc.mu .edu/ike.htm.
Vital Speeches of the Day 28 (February 1, 1962).
Vital Speeches of the Day 28 (June 1, 1962).
Vital Speeches of the Day 30 (January 15, 1964).
Vital Speeches of the Day 30 (September 15, 1964): 709–10.

Vital Speeches of the Day 33 (February 1, 1967): 226–28.
Vital Speeches of the Day 34 (February 1, 1968): 228.
Vital Speeches of the Day 34 (February 1, 1968): 229.
Vital Speeches of the Day 35 (February 1, 1969): 228.
Vital Speeches of the Day 36 (January 1, 1970): 162.
Vital Speeches of the Day 37 (February 1, 1971): 227.
Vital Speeches of the Day 38 (September 15, 1972): 707.
Vital Speeches of the Day 39 (March 15, 1973): 325–26.
Vital Speeches of the Day 41 (February 1, 1975): 227.
Vital Speeches of the Day 42 (February 1, 1976): 228.
Vital Speeches of the Day 42 (September 15, 1976): 708.
Vital Speeches of the Day 43 (February 1, 1977): 226–30.
Vital Speeches of the Day 46 (September 15, 1980): 706–10.
Vital Speeches of the Day 47 (March 15, 1981): 323.
"The Wants of the People," Labor Day address in Detroit, Michigan, on September 7, 1964 in *Vital Speeches of the Day* 30 (October 1, 1964): 742.*Washington Herald*, May 28, 1936.
Washington Herald, May 28, 1936.
We Support Health Benefits for the Aged through Social Security (New York: National Association of Social Workers, 1961).
"What Is the Job to Be Done?" Address to a Lexington, Kentucky, rally on October 1, 1956, in *Vital Speeches of the Day* 22 (October 15, 1956): 3.
Winn, Stephen. "Despite the 'Surplus,' Our National Debt Still Grows," *Kansas City Star*, October 4, 1998, 12.
Zvesper, John. "The Liberal Rhetoric of Franklin Roosevelt," in *Rhetoric and American Statesmanship*, ed. Glen Thurow and Jeffry Wallin (Durham, NC: Academic Press and Claremont Institute for the Study of Statesmanship and Philosophy, 1984).

Index